I0127799

Why Communist China Isn't Collapsing

Why Communist China Isn't Collapsing

The CCP's Battle for Survival and State-Society Dynamics in the Post-Reform Era

Feng Sun and Wanfa Zhang

LEXINGTON BOOKS
Lanham • Boulder • New York • London

Published by Lexington Books
An imprint of The Rowman & Littlefield Publishing Group, Inc.
4501 Forbes Boulevard, Suite 200, Lanham, Maryland 20706
www.rowman.com

6 Tinworth Street, London SE11 5AL

Copyright © 2020 by The Rowman & Littlefield Publishing Group, Inc.

All rights reserved. No part of this book may be reproduced in any form or by any electronic or mechanical means, including information storage and retrieval systems, without written permission from the publisher, except by a reviewer who may quote passages in a review.

British Library Cataloguing in Publication Information Available

Library of Congress Cataloging-in-Publication Data

ISBN 978-1-4985-6715-2 (cloth : alk. paper)
ISBN 978-1-4985-6717-6 (pbk : alk. paper)
ISBN 978-1-4985-6716-9 (electronic)

Contents

List of Tables

List of Figures

Acknowledgments

We would like to thank the *Journal of Comparative Asian Development* for allowing us to use part of our previously published article "Resurrection through Adaptation: The Dynamics of China's 'Comcapitalism' Model" (Copyright © 2012 City University of Hong Kong, reprinted by permission of Taylor & Francis Ltd, www.tandfonline.com on behalf of City University of Hong Kong) in chapter 2 of the book.

We also appreciate *Asian Perspectives* for granting the reprint permission to use some content in Wanfa Zhang's article "Has Beijing Started to Bare Its Teeth? China's Tapping of Soft Power Revisited" (Copyright © 2012 Lynne Rienner Publishers. This article was first published in *Asian Perspective* 36. 4 (2012), 615–39. Reprinted with permission by Johns Hopkins University Press) in chapter 8.

We are profoundly indebted to our professors in the Political Science Department at the University of Alabama during our graduate years, especially Drs. John Oneal, Karl R. DeRouen, Douglas Gibler, David Lanoue, Carol Cassel, Stephen Borrelli, Barbara Chotiner, Terry Royed and Donald Snow. Their erudition and superb teaching sowed the intellectual seeds of this book.

Our deep gratitude goes to Pete Vroom for his always generous help with commenting on, editing and proofreading our works, not only this manuscript but also our prior works. His incisive comments, thought-provoking suggestions and frank criticisms, each time, helped greatly with the quality of our publications.

We remain deeply grateful to Joseph Parry, Senior Acquisitions Editor at Lexington Books, for signing the book, and for his enthusiastic support and patience from our earliest discussion of the project to the completion of it.

We also acknowledge the anonymous reviewers for providing constructive comments and suggestions for revision.

We are especially grateful to our respective College Deans and Department Chairs, Mary Beth Kenkel and Robert Taylor at Florida Institute of Technology and Steven Taylor and Michael Slobodchikoff at Troy University, for their unchanging support and their in-time approval of our sabbaticals which gave us the much-needed time to focus exclusively on this project.

Feng Sun is incredibly grateful to her parents Yiping Fang and Hanhe Sun for their endless love, encouragement and support.

Wanfa Zhang wants to thank his former college classmates at Guithar University, Zhang Mei, Deng Wanglu, Li (Hannah) Huifang and Qiu Zhudong, for their inspiring discussions on and analyses into China's political development over the past few years. He is also obliged to his mom Liu Suchao and older sister Zhang Wanqin for their selfless support when he was working on the project during his sabbatical in China.

Finally, and above all, we would like to thank our respective spouses and child. This long journey wouldn't arrive at the end without their constant support and sacrifice. Thanks Fei and Adam! Thanks Wang Ke!

List of Abbreviations

ACFTU	All-China Federation of Trade Union
AIIB	Asian Infrastructure Investment Bank
BBS	bulletin board system
CCP	Chinese Communist Party
CLB	China Labor Bulletin
CNNIC	China Internet Network Information Center
EU	European Union
FDI	foreign direct investment
GOP	Government Online Project
IMF	International Monetary Fund
ISP	internet service providers
NBS	National Bureau of Statistics of the PRC
NCCPC	National Congress of the Communist Party of China
NGO	non-governmental organization
NPC	National People's Congress
OBOR	One Belt One Road
PAP	People's Armed Police Force
PC	people's congress (all levels)
PLA	People's Liberation Army
PPCC	People's Political Consultative Conference

PRC	People's Republic of China
PSC	Politburo Standing Committee
SCIO	Information Office of the State Council
SCMP	South China Morning Post
SEZ	Special Economic Zone
SME	small- and medium-sized enterprise
SOE	state-owned enterprise
VOA	Voice of America
VPN	virtual private network
WTO	World Trade Organization
WVS	World Values Survey

Chapter One

Introduction

The prophecy of communist China's downfall has been speculated since the establishment of the communist regime in 1949, ebbing and flowing over the past decades. The driving force for the looming meltdown is variously portrayed as unsustainable economic development, crony capitalism and rampant corruption, lack of political reform, grassroots uprising, and potential social crises caused by the recent trade war with the United States.

Nevertheless, nearly seventy years have passed with little evidence that China will comply with the prognosticators. Why the trajectory of China repeatedly defies the prophets of doom deserves more profound scrutiny not only from traditional political and socioeconomic perspectives, but more importantly by inspecting new angles and bringing in neglected elements. Based on the merits of previous studies, this book not only reexamines the factors that have had vital impact upon the survival of the Chinese Communist Party (CCP) already discussed by scholars, but also scrutinizes some equally important unexplored variables. Using a modified analytical approach focusing on traditional culture, individual political perception, economic interests, and external environment, the book explores the future of the CCP regime from multiple angles.

THE CHINA COLLAPSE THESIS

Ever since China's economy began to slow down in 2012, many Western social scientists, journalists, policymakers, business leaders, and analysts have once again become invested in the China-collapse thesis. A number of dire issues constitute the chorus of doom.

Unsustainable economic development is the most frequently raised problem. It is believed that decreasing GDP growth rate, housing property bubble, staggering loads of bad bank loans and debts, industrial overcapacity, middle-income trap, and the trade war with the United States all burden Chinese society; these issues could jointly or separately paralyze the market and lead to a sudden meltdown of the economy, pushing the CCP regime to its edge. For example, Nobel economist Paul Krugman holds a pessimistic viewpoint on the health of China's economy (Leeb 2013). However, contrary to this argument, China's economy has been robust so far. It successfully managed to remain stable during and after the turbulent financial downturns in 2008. Though the economy has slowed down since 2012, argued by some as a self-induced soft landing (Perkowski 2012), its GDP growth has sustained a relatively high rate of about 6.5 percent, compared with the average 2 percent in the West. Many argue that those with dire predictions underestimate the resilience of the China's world second largest economy as well as the CCP regime's determination and capability to maintain economic prosperity and stability. A series of economic policies have been successfully executed over the past four decades in an effort to tackle or forestall the aforementioned economic problems. Many signs of positive progress in the transition from manufacturing and investment-based to consumption-driven economy have been observed (Huang 2016; Lee 2017). Thus, whether an economic catastrophe is upcoming in China is still an ongoing debate, hardly a mature conclusion or prediction.

Furthermore, scholars believe that rampant corruption and crony capitalism will eventually wear down the ruling base of the Party. Minxin Pei (2016) makes a bleak conclusion about the future of China by providing an extensive analysis of endemic corruption plaguing the country and how crony capitalism erodes the rule of the regime. Nevertheless, corruption is not a problem confined to China; according to the 2016 crony-capitalism index,[1] of 22 countries surveyed, China ranked 11, even lower than several democratic or semi-democratic economies in the developing world. Then one must ask why other economies such as Singapore (#4), Ukraine (#5), India (#9) or Taiwan (#10) can survive crony capitalism while China can't. In addition, the degree of the severity of corruption and its resultant destructive effect in China may be overestimated. The Pew Research Center (2014a) conducted a survey in 2014 and reported that 54 percent of the respondents in China viewed corrupt officials as a big concern, well below the median value of 76 percent of the 34 developing countries surveyed. This is not to say that corruption is not corrosive, urgent or concerning. To the contrary, Xi's large-scale campaign to crack down on corrupt officials at every level of government across the country has boosted his personal popularity. However, when one tries to establish a causal link between corruption and collapse of the CCP regime, one should cautiously take into account the impact of the deeply rooted unique cultural principle "*guanxi*" (personal connection) on the individual Chinese's perception of corruption in a society; here, the majority believe that giving bribes is just a normal fact that gets them ahead in life (Pew Research Center 2014b).

Third, it is argued that lack of corresponding political liberalization will eventually deplete the energy of the economy and cause major economic downturns, putting the Party-state on the brink of collapse. David Shambaugh (2016) in his book *China's Future* predicts that without further political liberalization, the economy in China will fall into prolonged stagnation; consequentially its political and social system will crumple. However, the result of empirical studies on the relationship between regime type and economic growth is mixed (Barro 1996; Acemoglu 2014; Burkhart and Lewis-Beck 1994). Scholars find that autocracies can go to either extreme; they are more likely to be either the best or the worst performers in terms of GDP growth rate (Almeida and Ferreira 2002), indicating good economic performance is not impossible in autocracies.

Fourth, China has witnessed growing social uprising and unrest, making some observers to believe that ordinary people in China are fed up with the Party-state, so the regime has lost its popularity. Though, other studies, best exemplified by O'Brien and Li's (2006) research of "rightful resistance," posit an alternative explanation of grassroots protests: that the mass public in China use this contentious method to voice dissatisfaction and redress their grievances within the system (Lorentzen 2013; Froissart 2014; Tang 2016). Thus, such popular protests in China imply the opposite; they indicate a solid legitimacy of the CCP regime because the public is willing to resort to the government for problem solving.

Finally, conventional wisdom at the center of political commentary on China postulates that economic development or modernization may foster democratization. Decades of rapid economic growth has improved the living standards of the ordinary Chinese, brought more education opportunities, and enlarged and empowered the middle class, which in turn expanded "receptivity to democratic political tolerance" (Lipset 1959, 83). The theme of China's democratic prospect is shared and developed by many scholars in the field (e.g., Wang 2016; Liu and Chen 2012; Li 2010). They have expected the Chinese people, particularly the emerging middle class, to exert increasing pressure on the Party-state for political reform. But in China, the middle class was literarily created and is sponsored by the state and therefore they align their interests with the regime rather than overthrowing it. Nathan (2016, 8) points out that the middle class in China is fostered in a *sui generis* Chinese context that they are "not the middle class we are looking for, the one that should be prodemocracy according to Lipset's theory."

POLITICAL PARADOX AND
COUNTERINTUITIVE EXPLANATIONS

The pessimists' arguments on China's future cover political, economic, and social aspects. Typically missing from these accounts is how individual Chinese themselves envisage their government and the country's development trajectory. The collapse prophecy is untested and therefore questionable without analyzing what most Chinese people think and want. After all, social actors represent the ultimate force with the potential and ability to overthrow the regime.

Perplexingly, the various related public opinion polling and survey data contrast sharply with the dim forecasts on China's future. According to the Edelman Trust Barometer (Figure 1.1), overall public trust in government has been consistently high since 2004. The data show that in 2017, 76 percent of Chinese respondents trust in their government, in contrast to 47 percent in the US, 44 percent in Russia, 37 percent in Japan, and 36 percent in the UK. The Pew Research Center has conducted global attitudes and trends surveys since 2002. The result indicates a similar pattern of high satisfaction with the country's current condition by the Chinese respondents (Figure 1.2). The similar results have also been reported by many other surveys and public opinion polls, such as the World Public Opinion survey, the World Values Survey (WVS), and surveys conducted by individual scholars (e.g., Dickson 2016; Lewis-Beck, Tang, and Martini 2014) as well as polls by the Chinese Academy of Social Sciences. With such a high level of public support in government, the CCP regime hardly appears on its last legs.

Some scholars question the validity and accuracy of these public opinion polls and survey data in China. They argue that the communist state penetrates every aspect of people's lives; the general population has been brainwashed and their thoughts coerced to conform to communist ideology and values. Therefore, any public opinion polling responses in non-democratic regime were either false or manipulated (Welsh 1981; Warren 2001).

This outdated argument has been criticized in that it is contrary to everyday life observations online and on the street in China nowadays. The lively online political discussions, the frequent protests, petitions, and demonstrations, and even everyday conversations on the street indicate that individual citizens in China are not afraid to criticize the government (Tang, Lewis-Beck, and Martini 2013; Shirk 2011; Lei and Lu 2017). The Internet offers the Chinese public a powerful channel to speak out (Sun 2013). It is also used by the government as a real-time polling mechanism to instantly capture the pulse of public opinion, complaints, and suggestions. Thus, the Internet serves as a safety valve to carefully allow the citizens to release their negative feelings as long as they do not develop into organized unrests on the

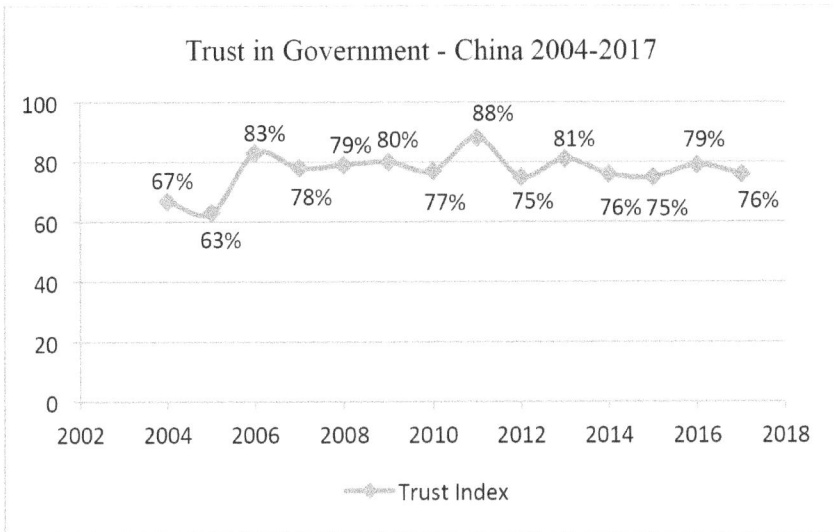

Figure 1.1. Trust in Government—China 2004–2017. Source: Author Generated. Data are from the Edelman Trust Barometer Annual Global Report from 2004 to 2017.

street. Additionally, to gain honest and insightful feedback, most surveys and polls were designed to keep respondents anonymous or conducted by third parties to help calm these worries and fears. In fact, in various public opinion surveys, the Chinese were not bashful about expressing their concerns and dissatisfaction with the state regarding issues such as corruption, inequality, social injustice, and environment degradation.

The consistent contradiction between theoretical forecasts and empirical findings has warranted great attention by China watchers, policymakers, and scholars in China studies. A large number of profound theories and arguments have been advanced to explain the persistent popularity of the authoritarian regime.

The most widely recognized theory to account for the high public confidence in the central government points out that political legitimacy in China has been primarily built around rapid economic growth since the reform. The Party-state has lifted hundreds of millions of Chinese out of poverty, resulting in an ever-growing affluent middle class. The great majority of Chinese people are happy with their personal financial conditions and attribute these greatly improved living standards to government economic policies. Survey data reveals that 77 percent of the ordinary Chinese are happy with their economic situation, believing that the country is on the right track (Pew Research Center 2015).

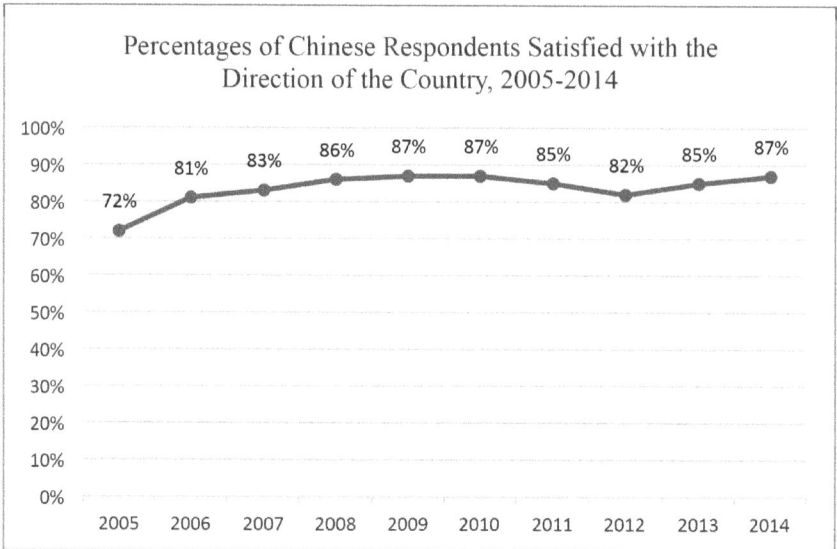

Figure 1.2.   Percentages of Chinese Respondents Satisfied with the Direction of the Country, 2005–2014. Source: Author generated. Data are from Pew Research Center Global Indicators, 2005–2014, http://www.pewglobal.org/database/indicator/3/survey/16/.

Assuming that rapid economic growth accounts for the regime's popularity, some scholars predict an imminent sharp decline of political legitimacy and consequent regime collapse if or when the economic growth in China abates (Chang 2001; Minzner 2018). However, this argument of economic performance–based legitimacy has come under growing scrutiny. Scholars point out that the economic explanation failed to account for the gap regarding political trust between China and other emerging economies with similarly high levels of economic growth, such as India and Brazil (Tang, Lewis-Beck, and Martini 2013). Others contend that slower economic growth doesn't threaten the regime legitimacy in China because economic prosperity was not the primary contributor to the popularity of the communist regime (Dickson 2016; Yang and Zhao 2015). The survey data also correspond to the findings, showing that the high level of political support has sustained even since 2008 when China's economic growth rate began to fall below double digits.

Many scholars criticize the inherent statism and empirical scarcity of the old paradigm of authoritarianism which led to its declining explanatory power. They propose an alternative approach focusing on adaptability and flexibility to explore the paradoxical longevity of modern autocracies, particularly authoritarian regimes after the Cold War. In the same line, growing research in China studies have departed from the "deterministic perspective" (Froissart 2014, 219) that often stereotypes autocracies as exclusively repressive and coercive. Scholars have been exploring the resilience and viability of the CCP authoritarian regime from various angles.

A rich body of literature ascribes the CCP's "authoritarian resilience" to its ability to institutionalize, contending that the Party-state has managed to incorporate democratic institutions such as grassroots election into its political ruling mechanism and regularize and routinize the leadership transition process as well as the embedded meritocratic system within the CCP. "Bounded institutionalization" has heightened the regime's viability and stabilize the political system (e.g., Nathan 2003; Shi 1997; Bell 2015; Edin 2003). The second strand of scholarly works defines the new feature of the regime by coining various terms such as "consultative authoritarianism" (Truex 2017), "responsive authoritarianism" (Heurlin 2016), "contentious authoritarianism" (Chen 2011), "populist authoritarianism" (Tang 2016), and "accepting authoritarianism" (Wright 2010), to capture the proactive essence of the Party-state's ruling methods. The scholars demonstrate that the regime's popularity largely attributes to its normalization of communication channels with the mass public and its capacity to be relatively responsive and tolerant (Truex 2017; Dickson 2016; Teets 2014). Focusing on the role of the media and the Internet, a third line of research highlights the Party's strategic censorship method mainly using empirical analysis. The studies reveal that the media and the Internet have been used selectively by the Party as a barometer to catch public opinions and monitor lower-tier officials (Pan and Chen 2018; Lorentzen 2013; King, Pan, and Roberts 2013). To put it succinctly, deviating from the conventional judgment and traditional authoritarian theory, these new studies imply the world's largest authoritarian regime has been taking a more sophisticated ruling strategy to improve governance and buttress its legitimacy in response to domestic and international challenges.

UNRAVEL THE PUZZLE OF REGIME VIABILITY
AND METHODS OF INQUIRY

Most of these studies try to account for the endurance of the CCP regime based on empirical evidence from various case studies, surveys, opinion polls, and field research. They make a convincing counterintuitive argument that government responsiveness solves the mystery of consistent popularity of the authoritarian government in China. However, few theoretically explore the deep-rooted source of this "authoritarian accountability." Why should or could the CCP regime be responsive, absent popular elections and free media, the important democratic mechanisms that hold the government account-able? Why are the Chinese people willing to support the Party-state, even it is characterized by heavy-handed repression and lack of freedom and individu-al rights in contrast to Western democracies? What constitutes the underlying engine that generates such a political paradox in China?

In the following chapters, we explore these questions by focusing on three themes: the CCP's sense of urgency or insecurity, traditional political cul-ture, and the international environment. The book is designed to provide an alternative examination of China's unique authoritarian ruling methods, po-litical paradox, and sustainability. It also desires to set the stage for future research and empirical studies on the subject.

Major Framework and Arguments

The Party's Constant Sense of Urgency

The CCP's unstoppable sense of urgency is the underlying source of its paradoxical responsiveness and accountability. What makes the Party-state always restless? Apparently, none of Max Weber's three basic sources of regime legitimacy—traditional, charismatic, and rational-legal applies to contemporary China (Perry 2018; Tong 2011; Weber 1984). In the Mao era, the legitimacy of the Party-state exclusively rested on its dominant ideolo-gies, Marxism and Communism. By the 1970s, serious economic stagnation forced the CCP regime to liberalize the economy and relax its ideological control over the country. The 1989 prodemocracy movement and the col-lapse of the communist camp in the early 1990s further weakened the coun-try's ideological base. With erosion of the major source of its legitimacy, the Party had to resort to the traditional Confucian concept of "*Tianming*" (the "Mandate of Heaven") and thus to rely on good performance in justifying its rule. However, as thousands of rulers have learned the hard way throughout history, performance-based legitimacy is subject to various volatile factors, and far less stable or reliable than ideological legitimacy. Moreover, it impli-citly implies a pragmatic contractual state-society relationship, requiring af-firmation frequently. The long turbulent Chinese history, including the victo-ry of the Party itself, proves that failure to deliver satisfying performance risks removal. Chinese history is full of examples of the new dynasty gaining legitimacy by toppling the ruthless emperor in the prior dynasty who no longer seemed benevolent and lost public support. As such, lack of a reliable source of legitimacy has haunted the Party incessantly and made it preoccu-pied with the task of catering to the needs of the people and building a benevolent government image.

This sense of insecurity makes the CCP very adaptive and willing to take serious measures to achieve better performance. But the Party also remains extremely conscious and ever vigilant. In the battle to maintain legitimacy on the political and economic fronts, it embarked on an unprecedented reform to revive the stagnating economy while using other active measures to ensure its political survival. Resultantly, the CCP regime has created a hybrid political-economic model "Comcapitalism," fusing communist and socialist principles with capitalist economic practices. On one hand, the Party purposely controls the pace of reform, keeping it stable and gradual to avoid dramatic social turbulence during transition; on the other hand, a firm grip on power enables it freely and effectively to tackle socioeconomic problems and correct unpopular policies, increasing its efficiency in governance. In addition, the CCP regime has strived to expand social welfare programs to enlarge its grassroots base. The implication of this political-economic model is profound. Many studies focus on how the economic reform has migrated China toward capitalism. However, few pay attention to the real effects of China's quasi-market economy with a significant state-owned sector. For example, it is no surprise that China's middle class presents very different features from the one described by Lipset (Nathan 2016), given that its evolution, composition, discourse, and political behavior have been shaped in such a unique circumstance.

Fully aware that performance-based legitimacy requires enduring effort and is inherently less stable than one derived from ideology, the Party-state has been desperate to form a new ideological base to better justify its rule despite the fact that its popularity has soared thanks to the spectacular poverty reduction and economic growth. We argue that in the fight on the ideological and cultural front, the CCP regime has successfully incorporated traditional Confucian culture into its political system and formed a new ideology "Comfucianism." The entrenched Confucian concepts of *"xiaokang"* (moderately prosperous society in all respect) and *"datong"* (great harmony and unity) perfectly interpret the two-stage goals of Marxism while using a less ideological tone. An old saying from the *Confucian Analects* "Do unto others as you would have them do unto you" (*jisuo buyu wushi yuren*) has been used by the Chinese government as an important diplomatic doctrine. Revitalizing Marxism with the coat of Confucianism not only justifies continuous reign by a communist party in China, but also redefines the regime's role as defender and reinventor of Chinese civilization.

In its struggle on the social front, the Party-state has been undertaken a strategic and cautious tactic to build a mixed "blocking, dredging, and channeling" ruling mechanism. The CCP regime is always assertive and repressive toward any threats that directly challenge its rule. But it has also sophisticatedly built relatively effective and responsive communication channels such as public hearings, opinion polling and online consultation to allow the grassroots to voice dissatisfaction and redress grievances. Many studies contend that borrowing democratic institutions to ease state-society tension would eventually backfire when the public gained confidence and experience and demanded more political rights. We claim that this democratic effect has been overly emphasized because besides quasi-democratic institutions, the Party-state has been heavily relying on traditional channeling tools such as petitioning that emphasize paternalism and guidance of the government. In addition, despite decentralization due to economic liberalization, the state never retreats. It takes all kinds of measures to penetrate society directly or indirectly. Mass mobilization, a method inherited from the Mao era, has been frequently used to ensure effective policy implementation and to establish direct linkage between the public and the state. The CCP regime has also reacted very well in terms of disaster relief which often attracts great attention, and mobilizes mass responses across the nation, bolstering its reputation and political support (Schneider and Hwang 2014; Sorace 2016).

In sum, the Party's persistent sense of urgency and insecurity seems to generate an effect similar to democratic power checking and accountability. It is this sense that makes the Party uncomfortable with itself, and to constantly seek change and improvement for optimal performance.

Influence of Traditional Political Culture

Traditional political culture is another important source of the CCP regime's durability. Scholars often tend to neglect the explanatory power of the cultural factor, dismissing it as a residual variable in China studies (Bellin 2004; Nathan 2016; Tang 2016). For example, Tang (2016) argues that the fact that Taiwan and Mainland China, both influenced by Confucian culture but yielding different political systems, proves that the cultural factor doesn't matter significantly in explaining the political orientation of the middle class.

But the effect of the political culture has been greatly underestimated. The problem lies in the way cultural effect has been explored. First, the cultural factor has usually been studied as a dichotomous variable with only two values, but it is rarely an all-or-nothing situation. The evolution of Confucian culture, the level of its application in the political system, and the degree to which it is embedded in social activities and everyday life vary considerably in every country within the "East Asian Confucian cultural sphere." Therefore, the cultural factor should be treated as a continuous variable to reflect possible variance. Second, it is important to explore the interaction effect of political culture. The effect of a specific culture often hinges on other important factors, such as international environment, regime type, ethnicity, or existence of other distinct culture and religion. For example, economically relying on or being politically allied with Western democracies would make the public more receptive to the influence of Western culture while it may simultaneously reduce the influence of its indigenous culture. Contrarily, a less secure hostile international environment will make the public patriotically cling to traditional culture and increase the effect of that same cultural factor. Third, the cultural effect in China has also been misinterpreted by some scholars. They assert that the prevalent Confucian values of hierarchy and obedience accustom the public to unconditionally favor the CCP regime (e.g., Subramaniam 2000). The definitions of values out of context simply neglects fundamental and systematic differences between Eastern and Western cultures, which often causes misunderstanding.

Liang Shuming (1921), an important Chinese philosopher in the late Qing dynasty and early Republican era, concludes that the basic spirit of Western culture and Chinese culture are different, the former emphasizing a "will" to move in a forward direction and the latter preferring going sideways to harmonize itself with the surrounding environment. The CCP regime's socioeconomic vision of "building a harmonious society" is not exclusively a top-down guideline that promotes social stability; it also largely echoes the genuine sentiment of the mass public. The disparity between Chinese and Western cultures also lies in opposite assumptions about human nature and their polar perceptions of moral stances in terms of individuals and groups. Just as Western individualism and the belief of a self-centered human nature promote democratic ideas of checks and balances and the rule of law, collectivism and the premise that human is perfectible play an important role in shaping Chinese people's political perceptions and attitudes. These must be taken into account when studying political attitudes of the Chinese people; the deeply seated systematic ideas and perceptions will not simply shift in an opposite direction along with the economic development which has been sponsored by an authoritarian regime.

The underlying message here is that Chinese traditional political culture is important and should be given credit for explaining some seemingly paradoxical findings that perplex scholars in China studies. For example, a reasonable assumption that people will fight for political rights even if it causes instability, particularly in the eyes of Westerners, is challenged by consistent survey results showing that Chinese people prefer stability over democracy (Dickson 2016; Li 2010). The statement that "Personal rule ultimately weakens a political system, no matter how effective the personal ruler" seems plausible according to Western political and cultural standards (Albert and Xu 2018). But it is less convincible in a Chinese context, given its culture that shrines "*dezhi*" (rule by virtue) and its history attests to plenty of legendary benevolent emperors. Westerners believe a democratic system is superior to an authoritarian regime because the former is "rule by the people" and people will theoretically get what they want if the government is held accountable. However, Chinese people seems focused more on the outcome, not the means. This profound difference causes perplexity on both sides. Westerners wonder how the Chinese could live under a repressive regime, even if it is effective and well performed; while the people in China are confused by the question why they should care how it rules, if the government is benevolent and caring. Along this line of reasoning, we propose a "state-society interdependent" model as an alternative to the conventional "society against state" paradigm in exploring the state-society dynamic in China. The logic of the model sits in the mutually constitutive relationship that the state relies on society for information, expertise, and support, therefore allowing bounded political space, while the public depends on the state for economic prosperity, well-being, and social stability in a complicated domestic and often disadvantaged international environment. Instead of challenging the existing political system, people are more interested in how to improve it.

Impact of the International Environment

Scholars have mainly focused their attention on various domestic factors. The effect of external factors on domestic political discourse has been largely underappreciated. We bring the variable of the international political and economic environment front and center by investigating multiple layers of external effects as important sources of regime robustness.

China's international status generates the first layer of external effect. China represents a typical example of Gerschenkron's (1962) famous late-development theory that the Party-state intervenes and sponsors the economic development to overcome the disadvantage of being a late developer in a competitive well-established global economy. This late-development position has a critical impact on state-society relations in China. It partially explains the state-dependence feature of the weak working class and "red capitalist" (Dickson 2003) in China. As the economy has grown, China's international power has mounted rapidly, exerting a positive effect on domestic society politically and economically. Besides market expansion and energy exploration, the ever-increasing soft power and capability of the Chinese government to manage overseas crises, such as evacuating citizens from warzones, have greatly boosted the regime's domestic popularity. The Party-state has also been using its hard power to fight directly or deter various perceived threatening forces and, at the same time, using soft power to gain sympathizers and cooperators. The improved diplomatic and economic relationships with neighboring and Western European countries as well as warmer relations with Russia has brought China more diplomatic opportunities and leverage, which also boost the domestic support rate. On the other hand, power escalation creates more international conflict and pressure, which has been strategically channeled by the government as fuel to increase domestic patriotism and nationalism. For example, the trade war with the United States has facilitated both government resolution of further reform and the growth of a popular loyalist response and anti-American nationalist sentiment even the government wants to hold the nationalist feelings from escalating (Li 2018).

The second layer of external effect is derived from the conditions of other countries in the world. On one hand, the CCP regime has been actively taking lessons from failing states and fallen autocracies. From the collapse of the former communist countries to the sudden meltdown of the Middle Eastern dictatorships, the fate of its counterparts has become a salient source of the CCP's sense of insecurity, pushing it to introspect frequently. On the other hand, widespread economic depressions in the West during the 2008 financial crisis, decay of liberal democracy in developed countries, as well as the poor performance of democracies in the developing world have severely discredited the legitimacy of the democratic political system in the eyes of the majority of Chinese people. The Chinese government's breathtaking economic performance and its growing international power have increased the publics' political confidence in this authoritarian regime. And the attraction of democracy has been dissipated in Chinese society.

Perceived hostile or at least critical Western attitudes toward China constitutes the third layer of external effect. The connection between Chinese society and the outside world has increased remarkably since the economic reform. Even with stringent media and Internet censorship, official propaganda is no longer the only channel for the public to gain knowledge about the world. Nevertheless, more exposure to the multiple sources of information hasn't led to a decline of regime popularity as expected. On the contrary, it not only broke the rosy image of Western countries in the mind of the ordinary Chinese people (Huang 2015a), but also rendered an increasingly shared belief that the Western media coverage on China has been hostile, arrogant, unfairly critical and negative. This huge perception gap between the Chinese public and Western media and scholars attribute to the primary identity of the CCP regime that is recognized very differently by both sides. Besides as a rising power house, China is first and foremost identified as a repressive authoritarian regime by Western media. But for Chinese people, the revolutionary victory and anti-colonialism movement have earned the CCP regime its identity as defender and inheritor of Chinese civilization, a civilization neither studied nor understood by most Westerners. The dazzling economic performance and efforts toward poverty reduction also qualify the Party-state as a benevolent government, with flaws but progressing. When the Western media tries to illuminate failure of the authoritarian regime by spotlighting every negative event that happens in China, it doesn't resonate in Chinese society. Rather than mobilizing prodemocracy sentiment, it alienates the Chinese people, induces nationalism and domestic cohesiveness and bolsters the regime legitimacy.

Conditions That May Push Communist China toward Collapse

Scholars often feel that it is profoundly challenging to forecast China's future. However, China's turbulent history has already generalized an iron-law that predicts the fate of all regimes in China, embodied by a well-known Confucian saying, "Those who win the people's hearts win the country, and those who lose the people's hearts lose the country" (*deminxinzhe detianxia, shiminxinzhe shitianxia*). In Chinese traditional political culture, winning the people's hearts requires a benevolent government that cares for the people and takes responsibility for their well-being (Tong 2011, 144).

The CCP regime has striven to win the hearts of the public in the reform era. The people-oriented ruling standard has been reiterated by all generations of leadership. It is not just a propaganda slogan but also a heart-felt sense of mission, targeting two pillars of political stability: economic prosperity and social equity. The achievement is remarkable. Since the onset of the reform, the extraordinary economic growth in China has lifted more than 800 million people out of poverty, a record by any historical metric (World Bank 2018). The number of the middle class in China is forecast to reach 700 million by 2020.[2] More importantly, communication channels are relatively effective between the state and society, so the government can successfully tackle any acute social problems. The consistently high level of political support is testimony to the fact that the Party-state, being relatively responsive, strategic, and open-minded, has won the hearts of the mass public.

So, what may push the Party-state toward collapse? The answer is straightforward: losing the hearts and minds of the people. The CCP regime will put itself in peril if the Party's major policies, programs, and campaigns no longer revolve around people's well-being, if the communication channel is closed or constrained, or the voice of the grassroots cannot be heard. Like in the Mao era the ideology-based Cultural Revolution (1966–1976) prioritized class struggle, largely neglected economic development, and put the communist regime on the brink of collapse.

Since Xi Jinping's incumbency, his pro-Mao political ideas and slogans, growing repressive censorship and cracking down on human rights lawyers, and abolishment of the presidency term limits seem to suggest that Xi is regressing ideologically back to the Maoist era. However, also in his term, China has eased its one-child policy, reformed the *Hukou* policy,[3] and abolished the infamous labor camps, policies that define the state's arbitrary power. Economic reform has been further deepened when the government decided to set up the Hainan free trade zone by 2020 and allowed more foreign investment in its financial sector at the end of 2018 (Yao 2018). Is he a nationalist leader with ambitious to revitalize Chinese civilization in his Marxist-Maoist way? Or has his power been constrained by other factions within the Party and criticism from society because there were signs of self-correction (Buckley 2018a)? Is the trade war with the United States used as leverage to force him to compromise?

The year of 2019 will be the 70th anniversary of the CCP regime's founding. In the West, there is a widespread notion that marks a little more than 70 years as the average duration of authoritarian regimes (Diamond 2013). For example, the Communist Party in the former Soviet Union had been in power for 73 years. Thus, that time limit for China is around the corner. However, it is still unclear where the country is heading under Xi. Only one thing is certain; if Xi continues to move toward an ideologically driven ruling tactic, closes the communication channels, and deprioritizes improving the perceived long-term welfare of the governed, the fate of its communist brother will loom.

THE ORGANIZATION OF THE BOOK

In the chapters to come, we seek to explore why and how the CCP takes proactive efforts to tackle challenges and threats from within and outside as well as how domestic conditions and the international environment impact state-society interaction in China.

The book is divided into three parts. The first part explores the CCP's domestic survival strategies on political, economic and social fronts. A new term "Comcapitalism" is coined in Chapter 2 to define a new hybrid political economic system developed by the CCP as a unique fusion between communist political legacies and capitalist economic practices. The chapter discusses the legitimacy crisis the CCP encountered and the urgency for reform. It assesses the challenges and difficulties facing China's economic development and how the CCP copes with these problems. The chapter demonstrates the compatibility of a non-democratic political system with capitalist economic reforms in China by examining the evolution of the "Comcapitalism" model through successive generations of CCP leadership. The nature and major characteristics of the model are examined. The last section of this chapter analyzes the achievements and problems of the model and their implications for China and the world.

Chapter 3 aims to trace the reasons, motives and courses of the CCP's actions in creating and fostering a hybrid "Comfucianism" political ideology in the reform era. Knowing that economic performance–based legitimacy can't last forever due to its intrinsic limitations, the CCP has been reviving and renovating its political ideology by incorporating traditional Confucian culture into its ideological system. The chapter examines the imperative of the CCP for a new political ideology and how traditional culture and Confucian values can be utilized for this purpose. The efforts in adopting the new ideology show how "Comfucianism" has been practiced by the successive administrations from Deng to Xi.

Chapter 4 explores China's sophisticated ruling mechanism, which combines repressive and controlling measures with channeling strategy, and its practically positive effect on social stability. It provides a detailed analysis of state's capacity to exert control on society as well as the urgent need to build and maintain communication channels with the mass public. Various repressive and channeling methods and their efficacies are examined. Based on analysis of the ruling mechanism, we propose a new "state-society interdependent" model to redefine the state-society dynamics in the post-Mao era. An updated social contract that emphasizes people's well-being and social stability has closely linked the CCP regime to Chinese society. The role of traditional culture in shaping the perception of a good legitimate government by ordinary Chinese citizens is investigated here.

Part two continues to explore the CCP regime's durability on domestic front, focusing on elites and major social forces. The purpose of this part is to answer a critical question: do any major actors of regime change in China have the incentives or strengths to topple the CCP's rule in the near future?

Chapter 5 analyzes elite politics and factionalism in general within the CCP. It addresses the political and economic interests of the Party elites. The evolution of factionalism in China and its effect on China's political and economic reform and stability are evaluated. The chapter scrutinizes the important features of China's factionalism such as collective leadership and meritocracy and their roles in fortifying regime stability. The book also tackles Xi's leadership style and its consequent influences on elite politics and China's future.

Chapter 6 reviews the unique evolution of Chinese private entrepreneurs and the middle class and discusses their consequent characteristics. It examines how the propertied class in China depends on the state for material interests and protection by analyzing the features of a developmental and patrimonial state in a late-development context as well as how the CCP regime manages the issues of the lower class. The interplay between the Party-state and the private entrepreneurs and the middle class is explored. The chapter also evaluates the value shifting of the propertied class and their political attitudes toward government and democratization in the reformist era.

Chapter 7 looks at the social class at the bottom of Chinese society: workers and peasants. It delineates the evolution of the working class and peasantry in China since the communist revolution. The chapter offers an analysis of their socioeconomic, political, cultural, and structural characteristics. It explores labor protests and rural unrest in China and provides an analysis of the strengths and weaknesses of these organized confrontations by the lower class.

The third part of this book tackles the CCP's struggle for regime durability from an international dimension. It consists of two chapters and explores the influence of the CCP's foreign policies and diplomacy on its domestic legitimacy and how the external environment impacts domestic state-society relations.

To a great extent, the CCP regime's domestic legitimacy is highly correlated to its foreign policies and their successes. China's performances on the world stage and its acceptance by the international community are also criteria for the Chinese people to judge its legitimacy at home. For this purpose, the CCP regime has been using its hard power to fight anti-CCP and anti-China forces abroad, while at the same time, it makes great efforts to win overseas sympathizers and collaborators. Chapter 8 is devoted to studying these measures of the CCP regime and evaluating their successes and failures.

Chapter 9 focuses on the critical impact of the international environment on the political perceptions and attitudes of ordinary Chinese. Bad economic and political examples in the world and their domestic effects are presented and analyzed. The chapter also explores the domestic "rally 'round the flag" effect caused by international tension, pressure, and perceived biased foreign attitudes toward China.

Chapter 10 wraps up the book by highlighting the major problem in prior works on the legitimacy issue of the CCP regime and laying out the contribution of this research to the studies of Chinese politics and authoritarian regime. It also discusses under what circumstances the CCP regime will collapse.

NOTES

1. The Index is designed by *the Economist* to measure the level of crony capitalism in various economies. It calculates billionaire wealth as a percentage of GDP, ranked by crony-sector wealth. The higher rank means higher percentage of wealth of billionaires coming from crony-sectors, indicating higher level of crony capitalism. See more details from: https://infographics.economist.com/2016/Cronyism_index/.

2. The standard used here to measure "middle class" is defined as citizen with annual individual income over 80,000 yuan. See http://news.163.com/10/0718/23/6BTN49C300014 AEE.html for more details.

3. *Hukou* is a system of household registration in China. In this system, a person's identifying information such as name, date of birth, parents, spouse and moves is recorded. The system could be traced to ancient Chinese household registration systems, but the current system is more relevant to the CCP regime's management of the economy and society in the 1950s. The registration is divided into two types: agricultural and non-agricultural residency status, which are connected to different social welfare programs.

Part I

The First Domestic Dimension

The CCP's Survival Crusade on the Home Front

Chapter Two

"Comcapitalism"

The CCP's Legitimacy Battle on the Political and Economic Front

After the collapse of communist rule in the Soviet Union and Eastern European countries in the early 1990s, China became the lone major surviving Communist regime. The entire world started anticipating the demise of Communism in China. However, 30 years later, China's political and economic system continues to reflect Mark Twain's quip that rumors of his death had been greatly exaggerated. What is more surprising and frustrating to those prognosticators is that the still self-titled Communist regime in China has not only revitalized itself successfully but has also built the country it rules stronger than ever before, as evidenced by its ever expanding political, economic, cultural, and military might.

In this chapter, we discuss how the Party-state explored, tested and experimented with new methods to retain power in an eroding situation where it was seriously threatened. In this unprecedented experiment, the Party upholds an official, if somewhat declining, quasi-Communist political ideology using Leninist-style party organization, function, and propaganda. Yet it has embraced, and increasingly relies on, a capitalist economic system to generate growth and wealth in order to justify and prolong its political legitimacy. This combination of political authoritarianism and economic liberalism has gradually evolved into a unique model that can be termed "Comcapitalism." The CCP's fight on the political and economic fronts has been highly successful, as proven by China's miraculous economic growth, the Party's continuous monopoly on political power, and popular support from Chinese society.

RELEGITIMIZATION THROUGH ADAPTATION – THE CREATION OF A NEW MODEL OF GOVERNANCE

Legitimacy Crisis and Options for Sustaining Rule

China's reform started at the end of the 1970s. The 1980s was a critical era destined to be long remembered in history. Deng's major reform policies, such as de-collectivizing farming in the countryside, allowing private businesses to flourish and permitting the bankruptcy of state-owned enterprises (SOEs), began to bear fruit during this period. By the end of the 1980s, China had already been significantly transformed; the new policies reversed those of the stagnant 60s and 70s when the country had been completely shut off from the outside world (Zheng 1997). Economic growth had brought financial benefits for many people, especially those in coastal regions, and living standards had risen substantially. Political reform also showed progressive results as the CCP's social control had gradually loosened.

From top leaders like the general Party secretaries Hu Yaobang and Zhao Ziyang to social intellectuals and students at colleges, who at this time were a relatively small educated fraction of the population, there was a strong wave of enthusiasm for deepening the new reforms, not only in the economy but also in politics. The core of political reform centered on redefining the Party's role in politics, economy and society, most notably the separation between the Party and the government, by and between the government and the enterprises. However, by the end of the 1980s, considerable tensions had emerged in the political sphere, both at home and abroad.

Inside China, societal tension had risen with growing and expanding student demonstrations against rampant corruption resulting from the Party-state's *laissez-faire* economic policies and rapidly rising inflation by the end of the decade. Politically, loosening control due to decentralization and less restrictive policies encouraged students to heighten their expectations by calling for further political reform, and participants and supporters began to come from all walks of life: workers, journalists, and small business owners. The CCP regime's decision to use military force to suppress the movement in June 1989 incurred considerable political cost both domestically and internationally. Almost all major democratic countries condemned the Communist regime and some imposed sanctions on Beijing. At home and abroad, the CCP regime was becoming increasingly unpopular and the Communist government's legitimacy was in serious doubt.

Although the iron fist of the CCP in 1989 was able to temporarily crush the anti-government movements and mute the dissidents' voices, the Party-state clearly understood that the heavy-handed approach could not suffice for long. New methods of ruling had to be found and promptly adopted to pacify and satisfy Chinese society.

The Party-state was at an inflection point where a wrong move would lead to its demise. It had basically two choices. One was to suspend the "reform and opening up" policy and reverse the relatively open society to a pre-reform state. In doing so, the Party could readopt its former methods of social control. The benefit of this policy was that readopting these familiar methods to sustain its rule was the less risky choice for the short term. Adversely, however, the Chinese society that had just begun to become dynamic would lose momentum of growth and become static again; in this scenario, society would likely regress to the situation of the Cultural Revolution era. All fruits of the reform would gradually be lost, just as the rest of the world's countries, notably Japan and even its other Asian neighbors, were witnessing modernization, economic growth and higher standards of living. Most significantly, that policy called into question whether the Party would be able to sustain its rule for long (Kuhn 2009). The other choice entailed continuous "reform and opening up," which would maintain the vitality of Chinese society and keep, even expand, the fruits of the reform. However, if not handled delicately and skillfully, this road could also lead to the downfall of the CCP regime as had happened to other communist cousins, most significantly the Soviet Union. Since further liberalization of society would create more space for dissidents and more venues for them to air their frustration and anger, it could also mean that the CCP's authority would be further challenged and weakened.

This undecided situation was concluded by the *de facto* leader of the country Deng Xiaoping who made a historical trip to Southern China in early 1992. During the trip, he made a series of famous talks that were summarized as "Speeches during inspection trip to the South" (*nanxun jianghua*), which affirmed that China would continuously adhere to the "reform and opening up" policy.

If Deng's talks were to serve as the general policy guidelines for the Communist government, then it was still unknown how the CCP would solve the irreconcilable conflict between tight political control and a capitalist market economy that would demand considerable sector liberalization in order to tap its full potential. Striking an effective balance between the two was a seemingly impossible task for the CCP. Witnessing the collapse of its Communist big brother, the Soviet Union and communist cousins in Eastern European countries, many politicians, political scientists and media workers were actually counting down the days to the demise of communist regime in China.[1]

Drawing Lessons from the Soviet Union and Exploring New Means for Survival

The collapse of the Soviet Union and other Communist regimes in the world gave the Party-state ample lessons to study. Almost immediately after the breakup of the Soviet Union, the CCP initiated and sponsored a research project aiming to directly determine the causes (Chen 2014). Over the period from 1992 to 2001, at least 600 articles and over 30 books dedicated to the subject were published in China.[2] The conclusion was straightforward: the biggest mistake other communist parties had made was their rapid liberalization of politics and society before implementation of effective economic reforms. When the political vices of communist rule over the past few decades were suddenly exposed under the sun, the various communist parties had not taken the opportunity to mend the holes and improve the economy before angered citizens overwhelmed their governments. These study results convinced the Party-state to avoid at all costs the simultaneous liberalization of politics, economy and society. Thus, the Party affirmed market reform its highest priority in order to raise general living standards, and thereby raise the public level of satisfaction with the CCP regime.

With these fundamental guidelines set in stone, economic liberalization was pushed forward relentlessly while liberalization of politics was significantly slowed if not shelved. In practice, political-social liberalization was reversed compared to earlier initiatives during the time of Hu Yaobang and Zhao Ziyang in the 1980s before their dismissals. In the following years, the new leader Jiang Zemin would hold on to the guidelines set by Deng Xiaoping (Unger 2002; Lam 1999), and these were also largely followed by his successors Hu Jintao and Xi Jinping.

Crossing the River by Feeling the Stones—Renovating New Methods of Reign

Scholars have made various arguments regarding China's path, its means of development, when discussing the country's striking success in economic development (Perry 2018; Kang 2010; Halper 2010). Some have argued that this was achieved through Chinese state capitalism; others argue that it resulted from privatization of the national economy; a third group attributes it to large overseas investment and new opportunities provided by the fourth wave of globalization after the Cold War (Dickson 2008; Halper 2010; Huang 2008; McNally 2008; Wright 2010; Yeung 2003).

Each argument is plausible and addresses certain factors that have contributed to China's success; however, hardly any underlines the dynamics of this new type of political economy—the constant friction, compromise and adjustment that have shaped this new development and governing model in a way that forced an authoritarian regime and an ever-growing capitalist economy to reach a dynamic middle ground.

China's "reform and opening-up" was initiated by Deng Xiaoping and associates in an attempt first to save the country as well as the CCP regime from collapsing at a time when the Cultural Revolution had literally devastated the country. By 1989, the Chinese government had already achieved substantial success in eliminating the radical leftist political and economic policies of Mao's time and introducing market forces into the economy to generate economic growth.

However, incompatibility between a traditional Leninist style political system and a burgeoning market force-driven economic system had caused problems of high inflation and corruption, which reached a dangerously high level by the mid- and late 1980s. Furthermore, government efforts utilizing market standards—that is, capitalism and profit seeking, to manage the economy led to the bankruptcy of large numbers of inefficient and uncompetitive SOEs and layoffs of hundreds of thousands of workers. The high inflation and omnipresent corruption practices resulting from this incompatibility, as well as the increased unemployment rate, finally led to the turbulent social uprisings in the late 1980s.

The downfall of two general secretaries of the Party in a row was thought-provoking and implicative to the CCP, providing a window on the intractable internal problems in the governance of China. Without finding remedies for solving these problems, it is questionable whether the Party itself would have been able to survive the reform it had initiated. Naturally, the Communist leadership had no intention to abdicate or even devolve political power. The profound socioeconomic transformation the Party sought to pursue in subsequent years had the primary goal of re-legitimizing itself, especially when reflecting on the unfavorable domestic and international environment of the early 1990s. By creating and maintaining a setting of relative stability and continuity, the CCP was able to revitalize both itself and the country gradually without losing control of Chinese society. This evolving process of building a new politico-economic model can be observed in the CCP's efforts as well as its determination to explore new methods of governance. It started the risky experiment with implicative historical steps that even involved amending the Constitution of the People's Republic of China (PRC).

In the first decade after the Party turned the country into a grand stage open to interested performers, the focus of Beijing was on rural reform and attracting Foreign Direct Investment (FDI). Although Beijing called for developing a private economy, its primary goal of economic reform was improving the efficiency of its SOEs. According to the Constitution of the late 1980s, private business was only considered a necessary and beneficial complement to the public economy. There was an upper limit of seven workers that private businesses were allowed to hire (Pei 1994). In 1988 the Chinese

Constitution had been amended to recognize the domestic private enterprises as a legally distinct part of the economy, but private businesses in China were not given equal legal standing with public enterprises until 1999, a decade later; economic policy implementation was gradual and cautious (Pei 1994). The Ninth National People's Congress (NPC) amended the Constitution, stressing that "Individual enterprise, private enterprise and any non-SOEs form important constituent parts of the socialist market economy."[3] Since then China's private economy has experienced dramatic development and created a new rich and middle class, demanding protection of its own property; in 2004, the Constitution was amended again to include government guarantees respecting and protecting private property.[4] For the first time in the PRC's history, private property rights—the moral, logical and economic foundation of capitalism, and, incidentally, a hallmark of democracy and the economic antithesis of pure communism—were written into a communist constitution, marking a decisive step in the official fusion of China's forms of communism and capitalism.[5]

The vital steps discussed here illustrate that China's new political economy neither evolved naturally in the course of history, nor was it the result of an abrupt and drastic change like the "shock therapy" that had occurred in the former Soviet Union. Rather, it was initiated, planned, and nurtured by a communist regime whose official political ideology still detests and rejects many corollaries of capitalism. The authoritarian nature of China's political system insists that the Party has full authority to set the scale, scope, and tempo of the capitalist experiment. However, as the "planned" experiment has progressed, second order effects have forced the CCP to continuously, though cautiously and gradually, adjust itself and its institutional settings to the profound changes in the economy and society. Now, at the end of the 2010s, the Party and the capitalist system it nurtured have become so tightly fused that they have become inseparable.

That said, the Chinese model is still evolving, with the old forces residing in its communist political system and novel forces emerging in the newly established market economy. They are all working on the same stage for coexistence and mutual benefits. This apparently contradictory and unnatural marriage between "the gravedigger"—the Proletarians' Communist Party, and "the buried"—the emerging or perhaps resurrected bourgeoisie, has worked generally well. Considering the fact that this new hybrid system is so historically unique and has been functioning robustly for nearly four decades, one may find it difficult to deny that this is an innovation of the CCP in its own method of governance. It strongly supports the conclusion China learned from the demise of other communist regimes in 1990–1991, that economic reform had to precede political reform. Furthermore, this model is not static, but dynamic, as will be elaborated in the following section.

OPTIMIZING GOVERNANCE — FINE-TUNING
THE MODEL DURING THE HU-WEN AND XI-LI ERAS

Hu-Wen Administration: Restressing the Socialistic Elements of "Comcapitalism"

The inauguration of the so-called fourth generation leadership—General Secretary Hu Jintao and Premier Wen Jiabao—in the spring of 2003, marked a new stage of "Comcapitalism." If Deng and Jiang had built a "Comcapitalist" system successfully out of Communism, the Hu-Wen administration tried to fine-tune the model by restoring more socialist democratic values and balancing development in a *de facto* capitalist environment using the Party core ideology and political values.[6] To rectify social problems that had accumulated during the reform era, especially regarding individual and regional wealth disparities that were getting increasingly serious under the relentless pressure for economic development, the CCP now emphasized that economic prosperity pursued exclusively by capitalist rationale was no longer the only priority (Fewsmith 2004). Instead, more social policies needed to be made to balance out the extremes that evolved due to policies prioritizing economic development.

As a communist regime, the Chinese Party-state was obliged to shift focus to social justice and welfare issues that had been weakened by capitalist practices and prior overemphasis on economic growth. In other words, the development strategy by the Hu-Wen administration was more social in its focus. This distinctive change derived from the CCP's concerns regarding the rising social unrest due to the widening gaps in the polity between regions, between urban and rural areas, and between different emerging social groups. Deng's "Let some people get rich first" strategy turned China from a mostly equalitarian society to an opposite one, as indicated by its alarming GINI coefficient, the commonly used measure of income inequality, of 0.474 as of 2012 compared to only 0.3 in 1980.[7] The Hu-Wen administration clearly recognized that Chinese society was on the verge of fragmenting if the government continued to focus exclusively on quantitative economic growth while ignoring the serious social and environmental problems and widespread inequality caused by decades of ruthless economic growth-oriented policies. The trend of social polarization resulting from uneven wealth distribution runs counter to the CCP's basic political ideology of socialism construction that forms the foundation of communist legitimacy, at least in propaganda. Without addressing these problems appropriately, the legitimacy of the CCP regime would have been questioned even though economic reform had already been successful. As some studies show, episodes of popular unrest in China "generally have called on ruling elites to live up to their socialist claims to legitimacy" rather than criticizing China's political system from a Western liberal perspective (Wright 2010, 8–12).

In order to solve these problems, the Hu-Wen administration adopted a "*kexue fazhan guan*" (scientific development perspective) theory, incorporating sustainable development, social welfare, increased democratic governance, and, ultimately, the creation of a harmonious environment into its policy (Fewsmith 2004). This "people-centered" socioeconomic ideology is lauded by the Party-state as an official successor and extension to earlier ideologies: Marxism-Leninism, Mao Zedong Thought, Deng Xiaoping Theory and the theory of "Three Represents" of the Jiang era. It reflects a trend within the CCP under the Hu-Wen administration to subscribe to more populist policies and guidelines in promoting coordinated development and common progress of Chinese society as a whole. This shifted policy focus highlights the communist side of "Comcapitalism"—attaining a new equilibrium between socialist theory and capitalist practice through making concessions to the left-behinds in the reform.

In 2005, the central government initiated the New Rural Co-operative Medical Care System to overhaul the health care system in favor of the rural poor (Dib, Pan, and Zhang 2008). Although the new system is tiered, and health care insurance and reimbursement depend on the location of hospitals, as of 2009, it had covered around 91.5 percent of the rural population (about 814 million people) (S. Yu 2010). In 2006, the administration abolished the millennia-old agriculture land tax on its 800 million farmers, positively affecting what was then 57 percent of the population. The central government also increased government funding to support agriculture, rural regions and farmers. It pledged to stimulate employment with an emphasis on recent college graduates, rural migrant workers, and other people experiencing employment difficulty. A critical negative result of the wave of ruthless privatization had been millions of laid-off workers who formerly worked in SOEs. Re-employment of these workers was a high priority during the Hu-Wen administration; after 2003, the central government spent hundreds of billions of yuan annually on re-employment of laid-off SOE workers.[8] Such large-scale spending also reflects the capacity of policies that can be executed by a unicameral politically centralized state in contrast to liberal democracy states where power is diffused.

New Adjustment in the Xi-Li Era—Bipolarization in Political and Economic Measures

The Xi Jinping and Li Keqiang era started in November 2012 when Xi assumed the position of General Secretary of the Party. The most striking feature during the Xi-Li era has been the bipolarization of political and economic policies—one is tightening and one liberalizing.

Politically, Xi's major policies aim at tighter political and social control with more emphasis on the people, even though he has loosened some other social policies, such as those related to the *Hukou* system and "Reform through Labor" policies. Some of his policies share similarities with those of the Maoist era. For example, he openly calls for and stresses the importance of "a closer official-public relationship" or the "mass line." The Party cadres "must ensure their professional and personal lives are led by the Party's 'strict' and 'honest' requirements" and "will continue to represent the people and serve them wholeheartedly." He similarly emphasizes that the People's Liberation Army (PLA) must maintain "absolute loyalty to the Party."[9] His other policies with regard to politics encompass tightening freedom of speech, stricter control of non-governmental organizations (NGOs) and even his termination of presidential term limits in the PRC Constitution, viewed by many as political retrogression.

Economically, Xi, at the beginning, seems to be following the policies of Mao by strengthening the role of SOEs in the economy. But soon he largely revises his policies by encouraging private business heads to join the CCP. He is especially ambitious in opening up the Chinese economy to the outside world in his second term, such as sharply expanding market access for foreign banks and securities and insurance companies in China and significantly lowering import tariffs (Yao and Patton 2019). These opening-ups are not easy since these are sensitive areas all previous administrations since Deng had closely guarded. Xi is also an ardent advocator of China's greater involvement in managing the world economy. For example, at the G20 Summit Meeting in September 2016, he openly declared that China would support the G20 establishing a Global Infrastructure Hub and helping the World Bank set up a Global Infrastructure Facility. He also promised that China would contribute its share to global infrastructure investment through such means as the building of the Silk Road Economic Belt, the 21st Century Maritime Silk Road, the Asian Infrastructure Investment Bank (AIIB) and the Silk Road Fund.[10] These examples highlight his contrarian views against the world's recent trend of reversing globalization, specifically the recent conservative policies in the United States and Europe. His speeches underline China's new role as a major active player in global development and his personal ambition of managing the world economy as a peer of other global leaders.

In other words, the communist element in "Comcapitalism" is becoming more communistic as the traditional Leninist style rule returns, while the capitalist element is becoming more capitalistic and susceptible to market forces. Under Xi, China's involvement in world affairs, especially the global economy, is reaching a much higher level.

A UNIQUE MODEL OF GOVERNANCE AND
ITS NATURE AND MAJOR CHARACTERISTICS

The Unexplainable China Case and the Paucity of Theory

From the publication of *The Communist Manifesto* in 1848 to the success of the Communist Revolution in Russia in 1918, there have always been various anti-Marxist political ideologies and scholastic arguments. Many scholars believe that if socialist policies are followed, disaster to personal liberty and society will ensue. Among them, the most famous scholar is none other than the Austrian-British economist, political philosopher, and the author of *The Road to Serfdom*, Friedrich Hayek. One of Hayek's most poignant points is his stark warning "of the danger of tyranny that inevitably results from government control of economic decision-making through central planning" (Ebeling 1999). He further expounds that abandonment of individualism and classical liberalism inevitably leads to a loss of freedom, the creation of an oppressive society, the tyranny of a dictator, and serfdom of the individual.

In retrospect, despite the fact that some Communist regimes were able to create economic miracles and prosperity in their beginning days, very few were enduring. Generally, the tragedies these regimes had caused during their reign, as described by Hayek, were so gargantuan that their achievements paled in comparison. To illustrate the common iron fist and Orwellian control of society and the extensive violation of human rights, consider examples of the tragedies that have been caused: the Big Purge in the Soviet Union in the 1930s, the Cultural Revolution in China in the 1960s and 70s or the Massacre under the Khmer Rouge in Cambodia in the 1970s. Today's North Korea provides a living example of the extremes of Communist governments in history and a present-day dystopia.

However, one needs to be aware that the form of communism practiced in China has mutated significantly from what was described in either *The Communist Manifesto* or *The Road to Serfdom*. "Comcapitalism" in China is rather a remarkably unique political and economic model that has absorbed broad elements of capitalism, whose effective operation demands certain kinds of *laissez-faire* spirit, using a market environment moderated but not directed by Party oversight. In China, a country where collectivism forms a foundational value and tradition of Chinese culture, decentralization has seen considerable development. The smooth functioning of "Comcapitalism" needs a free enterprise spirit, an adventurous attitude, and pioneering enthusiasm, which are all difficult to realize under strict collectivism. China's miraculous growth over the past four decades testifies to the existence and dynamics of this side of "Comcapitalism." The appearance of a dictator like those absolute rulers in other former Communist countries, including Stalin and China's Mao, is unlikely to happen in China today; he or she would not last long.

In opposition to Hayek, there are scholars who deny the failure of Marx's theories. For example, Phil Gasper, compiler of one of the versions of *The Communist Manifesto*, denies the failure of Marx's theories in practice. He argues instead that genuine socialism was never practiced in the Soviet Union and Eastern Europe and, according to Marx and Engels, socialism meant workers running society. However, in those countries, while the state owned the economy, it was a privileged bureaucratic elite who controlled the surplus wealth created by workers. Therefore, those regimes were nothing more than a variety of bureaucratic state capitalism rather than genuine socialism (Marx, Engels, and Gasper 2005, 27).

Is China's system an example described by Gasper? The answer is no. Although the CCP regime still controls a large number of SOEs, the share of private and foreign businesses rival those under Beijing's direct control (Li 2006). Their influences are something the CCP regime has to take seriously and reckon with carefully. Critically, the Party-state has only partial control of surplus wealth created in the Chinese society. The central government does continue to make and carry out five-year plans as it did under the old-style socialist system; nonetheless, the kind of "government control of economic decision-making through central planning" as Hayek argued is no doubt significantly weaker than ever before. The other economic sectors are well beyond the direct reach of the Party.

It needs to be pointed out that these arguments do not deny the influence of the CCP in managing the Chinese economy and society. Politically China's Leninist-style vertical social control mechanism still exists, and Party branches that have permeated deeply in all sectors of society still function strongly. Any open challenge to the Party rule or calling for building a multiparty system is unlikely to go unaddressed by the Party. Chinese society is still relatively oppressive in terms of political choice. These are the evidence of the vestiges of Chinese Communism, which demonstrates the communism side of China's "Comcapitalism." No matter whether Hayek's pessimism about Communist society is true to history or if Gasper's defense of genuine socialism holds water, socialism and communism as practiced in China today have deviated from orthodox Marxist ideology and evolved into a tremendously different form. The successful operation of capitalism under an authoritarian communist regime demonstrates the paucity of extant theories in addressing this unique model and demands more elaboration.

The Nature of the "Comcapitalism" Model

China's unique model of development and governance, featuring a combination of political authoritarianism and economic liberalism, has distinguished itself from all other models that have historically shared aspects of it. Among these, two are most relevant: the Soviet/Russian development model and the Asian capitalist model.

The Chinese model shares similarities with the Soviet/Russian model in terms of historical origin and the process of transformation. The PRC's original political and economic system was cloned from the Soviet model after the CCP led by Mao won final victory in the Chinese civil war in 1949. The political economy of both countries was characterized by a strong centrally planned economy and tight political control over politics and society. Any political leader who attempted to deviate from the main Party line would be purged as in the cases of Stalin's Great Purge in the 1930s and Mao's Cultural Revolution in the 1960s.

Yet, such political economies began to demonstrate weaknesses and unsustainability in the 1970s and 1980s, forcing the political leaders of both countries, Deng Xiaoping in China and later Mikhail Gorbachev in the Soviet Union, to contemplate changing course (Raiklin 1989). Consequently, both countries started to desert their old system and embrace capitalism as a vital step in their reforms. Their adoptions of two contrasting paths of reform eventually led, however, to very different outcomes.

The Soviet *perestroika* and *glasnost* turned out to be the strategy of liberalizing politics first, in which the director of the political and economic drama was abruptly marginalized; but the sudden loss of directorship led to catastrophic chaos in the Soviet Union. Participants from all walks of life were suddenly permitted to flock onto a stage with no director and all rules of the game eliminated. Compared to Russia, the game in China progressed in a piecemeal but far more orderly fashion. The gamers here remained the gamers, who joined in step by step, and rules for the play became the results of bargaining among all participating parties, under CCP direction. In the Chinese play, with a completely new look and novel sets of enforced rules of the game, hardly any serious scholar on China still thinks China is a "socialist" country in terms of its economic system, much less in the sense of the Maoist era.

China shared many features with its Soviet prototype in political and economic systems before the reform era; however, it has more features of Asian capitalism than Soviet-style socialism (Arnove et al. 2003; Kang 2002). A growing number of scholars, such as Dickson, Huang, McNally and Yeung, are treating China as an authoritarian "capitalist" country (Dickson 2008; Huang 2008; McNally 2008; Cao 2005; Yeung 2003). The main controversy lies in the disagreement over which popular capitalist style in modern Asia pertains to China more closely: *coordinated capitalism*, *network capitalism*, or *crony capitalism*.

McNally, who discusses and compares all the three styles in his research, provides some useful clues to the puzzle. He argues that the main feature of coordinated capitalism is the existence of a strong state that can effectively coordinate investment behavior throughout the economy by forging close cooperative relations with private business, similar in many respects to National Socialism. Network capitalism is generally associated with a generic model of Chinese capitalism that is also called *"guanxi* capitalism" (McNally 2008, 108). Coordinated capitalism is represented by Japan's *keiretsu* and South Korea's *chaebol*, while network capitalism often refers to regions where overseas Chinese businesses dominate, but with less integration vertically or horizontally than the former, including Taiwan, Hong Kong and the overseas Chinese communities of several Southeast Asian nations (McNally 2008, 108; Kang 2002). And crony capitalism is defined as a system in which capitalists build a close partnership with state officials who use their influence over government to create an anti-competitive oligopolistic or monopolistic environment in which only their firms can prosper (McNally 2008, 106; Huang 2008; Kang 2002).

Examining the Chinese model using the lens provided by McNally, one would easily find evidence supporting each style. For example, the Chinese Party-state still wields great power in making policies that influence the overall condition of the economy and it also controls the largest SOEs in the country. The state can effectively direct the investment in the country as demonstrated by the Chinese government's channeling huge funds into infrastructure building, including highways, high-speed railroad, port and airport construction, especially since and partly as a response to the start of the 2008 economic recession (Dickson 2016; Bell 2015). Examples of network capitalism also abound in China. Personal connections usually play a significant role in each section of the chain from financing through production to final sale of goods; at the extreme end, *guanxi* consists of bribes and/or other forms of influence. This last form folds into the third description: As far as crony capitalism is concerned, it is an open secret that "family members of central or local leaders and former bureaucrats" use political lineage to derive commercial prerogatives and harvest economic benefits (McNally 2005, 153; Huang 2008). A 2006 study by several Chinese research institutions showed that nearly 90 percent of China's top leaders in sectors encompassing finance, foreign trade, property development, construction, and stock trading were relatives of top government officials. About 90 percent of China's billionaires were the children of high-ranking officials (Frank 2009). It is interesting to speculate whether a more meritocratic basis for enterprise leadership would have made China's growth in recent years even greater.

Taking all factors into account, China's political economy today exhibits a combination of all the characteristics of the multifaceted Asian capitalism model. It is true that the Party-state makes preferential policies toward the large SOEs; however, the Chinese government has also been making earnest efforts to facilitate the growth of small- and medium-sized businesses. In reality, economic development at the local level is largely out of the reach of central control; local entrepreneurs are relatively free, except from local officialdom, to make their own policies concerning investment, production, capital movement, and international trade (Hsu, Wu, and Zhao 2011; Cao 2005; Chang 2001). Under typical circumstances, they rely on their *guanxi* to network and conduct business and help with their capital accumulation and growth. When discussing the effect of crony capitalism, McNally himself also concludes that "there are other factors at work that make China's political economy much more dynamic and multifaceted than pure crony capitalism," downplaying explicitly the significance of crony capitalism upon its economy (McNally 2005, 106). That is to say, elements of crony capitalism do exist in Chinese society, but it is inaccurate to simplistically define China's development model as crony capitalism. Considering the size of the Chinese economy, regional disparities, and the complex situation of the country at different levels of development, any argument for the dominant role of one single capitalism model might be hasty.

These facts lead to the logical but complicated conclusion that China is no longer a replica of the Soviet-style socialist economy, nor has it evolved into an Asian style coordinated capitalism, network capitalism or crony capitalism. It is a new, hybrid political economy that has retained largely the political legacy of a Leninist state in social control. In this system, a communist party blends all its functions in ideology domination, tight organization and strong propaganda of a survived Leninist-style political party linked to a relatively more liberal capitalist economic system that has incorporated, or more accurately assimilated all the major elements of Asian capitalisms. This special political economy or innovative method of governance is definitely unique (Dickson 2016; Bell 2015; Jacques 2009; Cao 2005).

Major Features of the Model

To summarize, there are five critical features that distinguish China's "Comcapitalism" from other models of development. These features are not only end products of interactions between the various social forces in the reform era, but also key factors that prevented the CCP from repeating the fate of the Communist Party of the Soviet Union and its Eastern European communist satellites. They are the remedies that have helped the survival and revitalization of the Chinese communist regime from its impending doom since the early 1990s. Similarly, they facilitated the strengthening of the CCP and its rule by building and expanding the country's economy successfully.

Internal Drive for Re-legitimization

The original legitimacy of the CCP was built on the mission of helping a wartorn and poverty-trodden China stand on its feet at the end of the 1940s.

The initial adoption of the Soviet model and the resultant economic stagnation of the 1960s and the 1970s forced the CCP to seek a new sustainable legitimacy basis by launching political-economic reforms at the end of the 1970s. The sudden collapse of the Communist Party in the Soviet Union and concurrent domestic economic and social chaos greatly deepened the sense of crisis within the CCP in the early to mid-1990s, motivating a great effort to re-legitimatize itself through raising the standard of living of its citizens by various means and creating national prestige for itself and the people. Its subsequent success in achieving these goals has weakened voices challenging the legitimacy of the Party-state. Unlike any other communist party in the world, the CCP enjoys widespread and apparently enduring support of the majority of its citizens (Wright 2010, 13–17).[11] China's change, to a great extent, was driven by the intrinsic need and motivation of the CCP for re-legitimization and its willingness to use incrementalism in policy adjustment (Bo 2007, 2010).

Policy Execution of Testing and Diffusing

Due to the vast size and complexity of the country, the Party-state always tests a new vital policy on a small scale in limited regions before it is gradually applied nationwide. This pilot method gives the central government ample room and opportunity to evaluate, adjust, or abandon a policy depending on feedback and test results. An early trial example was China's creation of its first Special Economic Zone (SEZ) in Shenzhen, where various market experiments were conducted. Subsequent establishment of four more SEZs along the southeast coast happened only after the success of Shenzhen; thereafter the special policies allowed only in SEZs were diffused to the whole country after further successes. More recent cases of such experiments include the gradual loosening of the One-Child policy and *Hukou* control from a limited number of cities to the whole country. At present, the highly controversial property taxation is under test in several cities. This trial and diffusion method, though seemingly slow on the surface, effectively prevents the CCP regime from making a vital mistake that is disastrous but incorrigible. The "shock therapy" policy of the Soviet Union would not happen in China.

Efficiency in Governance

Though usually regarded as negative, the hierarchical organizational structure of the CCP gives its governance high efficiency. Vital policies regarding economic development are made by the Party oligarchy and passed quickly down from the top. Local Party organizations take orders and jump into action promptly. This authoritarian governance enables the CCP to both respond to emergent situations swiftly and to implement policies effectively. China's fast pace in surpassing all other major economies of the world except for the United States in a relatively short period of time provides empirical evidence of "Comcapitalism's" effectiveness. China's strong performance during the global economic recession that began in 2008 lends further credibility to its development model (Bell 2015). Today, the dictatorship of the Party in political as well as economic and social affairs remains unchallenged.

Great Assimilability and Adaptability

Throughout the whole process of reform, the CCP regime has been under considerable pressures at home and from abroad (Chang 2001). Rather than reversing its experiment by terminating capitalist practices and closing its door again, or by giving up on confronting these pressures as happened with many of its former communist cousins, the Party-state has shown great assimilability and adaptability. It has been able to experiment on its own terms and at its own pace. When it sees apparently beneficial methods, the CCP borrows quickly from the outside world and assimilates them into practice customized to China's realities and the Party's needs. Conversely, it will not hesitate to either block or discard methods the Party considers harmful. Where needed, the Party-state voluntarily makes widespread concessions through system innovation—with the precondition that its monopoly on power is not threatened. The Party's amendments to the Constitution guaranteeing the protection of private ownership and encouraging domestic capitalists to join the Party are strong footnotes.

Political Incrementalism

China's pace of liberalization in both politics and economy is gradual. Thus, its economic transformation never experienced the shocks, economic degradation and ultimate oligarchy of the former Soviet Union. Privatization of failed SOEs and the laying off employees have been managed cautiously and incrementally throughout the reform era. Political change is even slower, always lagging behind in economic reform.[12] Political concessions, such as making various laws to accommodate economic and social changes, and meeting the diversified needs of various social sectors, have proceeded step by step. Overall, hardly any abrupt changes in political, economic and social policy have occurred.[13] "Comcapitalism" of China is increasingly displaying characteristics of social democracy similar to those in European countries.

In summary, these features, which started to take shape with the inception of the reform, have been consistently accompanying China's changes. Each administration since the Deng era has been adding new contents within its framework and testing new ways to reconcile contradictory forces in society based on the actual situations and social needs at the time.

THE CCP'S SUCCESSES ON THIS FRONT
AND IMPLICATIONS FOR THE WORLD

If one evaluates the level of success of the CCP in the reform era, it is factually evident that most of its goals have been realized, which can be seen in the following ledger of achievements.

The Ledger of Achievements

Success in the Innovation of Governance and Continuous Monopoly on Power

Among all the measures taken during the reforms, the most noteworthy is the CCP's innovation regarding its system of governance. This innovation lies in its successful creation of a hybrid politico-economic system, in which the CCP made use of its privileged status in the country's political system to forcefully impose a seemingly contradictory capitalist economic system. Now the political and economic elements are intertwined with each other to such an extent that the failure of either one of the two would lead to the collapse of the other, subsequently leading the entire system toward complete collapse. This hybrid model has worked well in China and has withstood the test of time for almost four decades. It's also why the CCP continues to enjoy its monopoly on power.

Success in the Economic Reform and Raising the Standard of Living of Its People

China has been able to maintain overall political and social stability and to raise people's living standards at the same time (Perry 2018; Yang and Zhao 2015). Its GDP per capita has risen from $156 in 1978 to $8,827 in 2017, a nearly 57-fold increase, and adjusted net national income per capita has grown from $141 in 1978 to $6,309 in 2016, a nearly 45-fold increase over this period.[14] Once luxurious consumer goods unimaginable for previous generations such as private villas or apartments, cars, motorcycles, large-screen TVs, etc., have become ordinary family staples. Many families are even able to afford the expensive tuition fees of European and American universities; Chinese students have firmly become the largest international student body on many American campuses.

Success in Raising China's International Prestige and Influences

China's rapid ascent in the rankings of various socioeconomic indicators has won China media attention and praise from around the world. For example, the Indian economist Jayanta Roy commented after his trip to China that: "I was happy to see that there is a hope for a developing country to outstrip the giants, in a reasonably short period of time" (Ramo 2004, 5). In two of Beijing's ambitious initiatives that are globally influential but strongly opposed by Washington, Beijing was able to win both: AIIB and One Belt One Road (OBOR) Initiatives. In the former, Great Britain took the lead while in the latter, Italy became the first among G7 member states to join hands with Beijing. Both long-term American allies ignored Washington's warnings and embraced Beijing, demonstrating China's growing influence in the world.

Implications for China and the World

Having traced and analyzed the dynamics and effectiveness of the "Comcapitalism" model for the CCP's fight for legitimacy, two important questions remain. First, what kinds of inferences can draw from this model? Is it a unique model applicable and effective only in a Chinese scenario or it can be a universal model that could be applied to other developing countries? China's success in economic development under an authoritarian regime is a serious fact with global implications, making such a discussion necessary, especially given the liberal democratic premise that with generalized wealth democracy emerges. Second, although this model is vibrant, is it sustainable?[15] If so, how? As time goes on, issues in the Chinese model, such as suppressing human rights in the name of development and the "social credit" program have started to materialize. Facing these moral weaknesses and other negative implications, one may wonder if this development model should be replicated and extended more widely (Bell 2015, 195). Moreover, even assuming willingness to assume the whole model, what stage of it should another country adopt?

One could be pessimistic. First, power monopoly by the CCP prevents the emergence of any substantial opposition forces. Politically, corruption is still rampant among government officials, businessmen, and other people who hold power. Rent seeking is still a common phenomenon in China. Socially, rapid urbanization and changes in society have been causing the disintegration of traditional society and deterioration of moral values and standards. Environmental degradation has led to serious health issues and widespread complaints. These political and social maladies could erode the basis of support for the CCP regime and pose threats to the CCP's legitimacy and its effective rule of the vast country (Chang 2001; Zheng 1997). A buildup of resentment could reach a dangerous breaking point if not solved.

Second, the CCP's fear of mortality excludes any possibility of political liberalization in the near future (Pei 2006, 1994; Chang 2001).[16] The Party remains legitimate at present thanks to the nearly double-digit growth over most of a four-decade-long period and the beneficial social policies that have led to the overall satisfaction of its citizens. The relatively good situation at present has veiled many problems that are worsening quickly. Furthermore, a scenario in which China falls into the middle-income trap and that society stagnates as happened to many other developing countries always looms (Cai 2015); also, the social policies could no longer be effective or inappropriate or too late to satisfy society. What would the Party utilize then in order to justify its legitimacy? Various historical cases have shown that democracy and extensive public participation can provide important legitimacy for a regime even if it is not that capable. Introducing these measures into China's politics is a potentially viable solution to prevent future legitimacy crises and subsequent chaos if and when the economy stagnates and growth no longer covers up or justifies accumulated social problems.

Third, China's prior GDP obsession relied on excessive exploitation of natural resources, energy imports, and degradation of the natural environment. The gap between the rich and poor has been widening, corruption has always been a threat which seems aggravated occasionally, and secessionist movements in Tibet and Xinjiang are still strong. Taiwan's prevalent mood toward secession is almost set in stone barring a formal declaration of independence; the prospect of a peaceful reunification is becoming increasingly dim. Anti-China forces are widespread in Western countries and even in OBOR developing countries where China's FDI loan terms seem onerous or where local politicians are seen by the public as corruptly gaining most or all of the benefits. Both the United States and the European Union (EU) are undergoing a new wave of China rise fear and are starting to take actions to counter China's growth. The Trump administration's policies toward China's telecommunication giant Huawei and the generally compliant attitude of European countries are the most recent evidence.

Nevertheless, one also has reasons for optimism. First, most of these challenges, such as corruption, are nothing new. They have been accompanying and plaguing the CCP ever since the founding of the PRC and the Party had also launched various anti-corruption campaigns from Mao to Xi to curb it. Xi's campaign is unprecedented, however, in its range; it has caused the downfall, imprisonment, even suicides of high-level officials that are commonly called "tigers" and low-level functionaries called "flies." He has effectively curbed the abuse of public funds by officials, such as luxurious international and domestic travels and meals. Though corruption is never eradicated, the CCP has been dealing with it consistently.

Second, the special but strong role of the CCP in executing policies allows it to possess great authority and strong determination, along with abundant measures and vehicles to handle them. Its capacities can be most often observed in its economic policies. The most notable of these is the consistent making and executing all the five-year plans since 1949.[17] Since the mid-2010s, for the purpose of avoiding the middle-income trap and lifting China's economy to the next level, the CCP regime has started to shift its development focus from quantitative into qualitative growth by eliminating small-scale and inefficient enterprises. To achieve these ends, it has adopted strategies that emphasize originality and creativity, encourage research and development, and expand investment in education.[18] A wide slogan that permeates society is to change "Made in China" into "Created in China." In Guangdong Province, then–party chief Wang Yang started his ambitious "*tenglong huanniao*" (Empty the Cage and Change the Birds) policy even as early as 2007 (Li 2012). This is a policy aiming at restructuring the economy of China's export hub by substituting cleaner and high-end manufacturing and services for labor-intensive and polluting industries. At the national level, the central government started to conceive and promote the "Made in China 2025" plan, aiming to boost China's capability in technology-sophisticated manufacturing. The policies that nurture related private enterprises have borne fruit and some highly salient and internationally competitive hi-tech conglomerates, such as Alibaba, Baidu, Tencent, Huawei, have been born in China. These are the most important foundations for the CCP regime's goal of avoiding the middle-income trap and moving up the value chain in industrial production and technology.

Third, since the reforms, the CCP has been very flexible, pragmatic, and less constrained by any dogmatic political ideology in its policies (Leonard 2008). It even took such extreme actions as amending the Constitution a number of times to foster and accelerate the growth of capitalism. Such resilience has enabled the CCP to cope with new circumstances accordingly and thus pliant enough to tide over various difficult, even dangerous, situations.

Fourth, the CCP has now amassed great financial capital and other solid hard power to tackle problems and accomplish policy goals. For example, when the whole world was bogged down in the 2008 financial crisis, the Party-state was able to introduce a huge 4 trillion Yuan stimulus package to alleviate itself, which was both effective and successful (Yu 2010). Socially, Beijing has launched various poverty reduction programs, such as the countryside development plan. Environmentally, the Beijing regime has passed more and stricter laws about protecting the environment and the trend of environment degradation has been halted generally. Some degradation has even been reversed, such as the greening of the Kubuqi Desert.[19] Factually, most of these policies predate the Xi-Li era; they existed throughout most of the reform era, but some of these have been greatly strengthened over the past decade. One thing is constant—great funds are needed to realize these policy goals and the CCP regime possesses the needed capital to invest in addressing these social or environmental issues.

Additionally, China's growth in overall capability also emboldens Beijing to tread in areas and regions such as Africa, Latin America, and the Southern Pacific that were once dominated by Western powers. The OBOR Initiative, launched in 2013, is bringing more countries and regions into Beijing's financial and economic empire. Authoritarian regimes facing collapse or stagnation under Western pressure now find not only new *raison-d'état* and ways to survive but also direct support from a putative role model. China's example, along with investment and financial and moral support, injects new vitality into these regimes.

China's new political economy and method of governance are not only challenging all current political theories that favor democratization and democratic rule, but also the balance of power in a post–Cold War world previously dominated by the West (Bell 2015; Lum 2000, 2009; Sutter 2009; Peerenboom 2007; Thompson 1996). With the growth of Chinese power and a likely power transition between China and the United States in the coming decades as predicted, it is well worth efforts to study and demystify "Comcapitalism" and understand the dynamics inherent in this model. Capturing its essence and mechanisms and acknowledging its strengths and weaknesses are an important start.

NOTES

1. For a detailed description and analysis of the global geopolitical currents and the political and social changes in China in the early 1990s, see Roy and Kraus (2016). J. Stapleton Roy was the former U.S. Ambassador to China who received his assignment during the crises. See also Fukuyama (1992) for the implications of the failure of the international communist movement for the post–Cold War world politics and economy.

2. The data come from Liu Guohua and Xue Xiaorong, *"Sulian Jieti Yuanyin Shinian Yanjiu Zongshu* (A Comprehensive Study of the Ten-Year Research of the Causes for the Disintegration of the Soviet Union)." *Research on Russia, Central Asia and Eastern Europe*, no. 6, 2002 as quoted from China Social Sciences Net, February 2, 2011. http://www.cssn.cn/gj/gj_gjwtyj/gj_elsdozy/201311/t20131101_821149.shtml.

3. See the Constitution of the PRC, Chapter 1, Article 11. An English translation of the Constitution is available at: http://english.peopledaily.com.cn/constitution/constitution.html and http://www.npc.gov.cn/englishnpc/Constitution/node_2825.htm.

4. See the Constitution of the PRC, Chapter 1, Article 13.

5. Yu (2005) provides a summary of China's stages of opening-up.

6. For a detailed discussion, see Cheng (2012).

7. The data are from "GINI Coefficients of China, 2003–2016" (*Zhongguo Jini Xishu*). China National Bureau of Statistics (NBS). According to the data, the most recent number is 0.465 in 2016, which has dropped from its peak value of 0.491 in 2008. These data are available at https://www.ceicdata.com/zh-hans/china/resident-income-distribution/gini-coefficient.

8. See *Report on the Work of the Government of the PRC* in various years from 2003 to 2018. Chapter 7 also has a detailed discussion on the CCP's polices to pacify and contain the lower class.

9. For a discussion of Xi's governance style and characteristics in his first term, see the article "Xi Jinping: Governance Thought in Shape." *Xinhuanet*, June 19, 2017. http://www.xinhuanet.com/zgjx/2017-06/19/c_136365058_2.htm.

10. For details, see *"Xi Jinping de Dianjing Zhiyu—Pandian Xi Jinping G20 Jianghua* (Summarizing Key Phrases of Xi Jinping's Speeches at G20 Meetings)." *CCTV*, 2016 http://news.cctv.com/special/xjptG20/.

11. This argument is also supported by the survey results of the Pew Research Center's Global Attitudes Project released in different years such as "Obama More Popular Abroad Than at Home, Global Image of U.S. Continues to Benefit" on June 17, 2010. The Chinese

government and its policies enjoy especially high rate of support among its citizens. http://pewglobal.org/2010/06/17/obama-more-popular-abroad-than-at-home/4.

12. There are many cases showing that such lags could cause very negative consequences that threaten social stability. For example, Lampton (2008) observes that "China has moved more quickly toward market than it has constructed institutions appropriate to regulate and cushion it" when he discusses the institutional deficiencies in China's political and social systems.

13. Shambaugh (2009) also argues that the CCP's political reform in the future will take the same incremental path, which is likely to be a new kind of political hybrid with a variety of foreign and indigenous practices grafted together.

14. The data come from World Development Indicator of the World Bank, available at https://data.worldbank.org/.

15. Some scholars doubt about the sustainability of China's model of development. Huang (2008) argues that a crisis may happen during the Hu-Wen administration that ended in 2012. And the best way to prevent this from happening is reforming Chinese political governance: empowering the people to fight the social vices. More than 10 years have already passed since then but the "Comcapitalism" model still works strong.

16. Although there have always been Western scholars predicting China's democratization with the liberalization of its economy, this situation has started to change over the past few years. There are more scholars calling for accepting the fact of a third way for China. For example, James Mann (2007, 101–12) argues that people outside of China should give up the fantasy of China's political liberalization soon and accept the fact that "trade and investment with China are helping to perpetuate the one-party system." Halper (2010, 6) also argues that the "inevitable democratization" predicted by many scholars may not happen soon.

17. For a summary and background of China's Five-Year plans, see "*Beijing: Zhongguo Jingji Fazhan de 'Wunian Jihua'* (Background: China's Economic Development and 'Five Year Plans')." *BBC*, October 7, 2010. https://www.bbc.com/zhongwen/simp/china/2010/10/101004_timeline_fiveyearplan.

18. See "*Zhongguo You Nengli Maiguo 'Zhongdeng Shouru Xianjing'* (China Has the Capability to Avoid 'the Middle-Income Trap')." *Xinhuanet*, January 29, 2018. http://www.xinhuanet.com/politics/2018-01/29/c_1122330259.htm.

19. See the following sources for China's recent achievements in greening the land and reversing desertification: NASA's news release "Human Activity in China and India Dominates the Greening of Earth, NASA Study Shows" on February 12, 2019, and "NASA Recognizes China's 'Outsized Contribution' to Global Greening Trend, as Kubuqi Alone Reclaims Over 6,000 km² of Desert." *Digital Journal*, February 12, 2019. http://www.digitaljournal.com/pr/4160980.

Chapter Three

"Comfucianism"

The CCP's Fight on the Ideological and Cultural Front

The failure of the international communist movement and the CCP's *de facto* abandonment of orthodox Marxist ideology left a huge ideological vacuum in China in the 1990s. This vacuum left Chinese society wide open to various thoughts and ideas: from materialism, consumerism, and hedonism to religious cults; and politically from Western democratic values to extreme nationalism. This spiritual crisis and concurrent moral malaise pervaded and plagued Chinese society. The loosening control of society and public communication also exposed the excessive and egregious acts of damage to historical relics and cultural traditions under communist rule. The result was growing public blame on the CCP. These doubts and challenges posed perceived and perhaps real threats to the authority and legitimacy of the CCP.

Facing these relentless inroads of new ideologies and doubts about its legitimacy, the Party became eager, sometimes desperate, to find measures to address the concerns of Chinese society. It understood that it had to take concrete actions in restructuring its ideology, mending the severed cultural traditions and reclaiming people's hearts and minds. The CCP strategically reverted to China's traditional culture, hallmarked by Confucianism, to achieve this end. On the one hand, the CCP continued to hold onto its Marxist ideology, its original foundation of legitimacy (Sundqvist 2016). On the other hand, it made earnest efforts to conflate the fundamental principles of Marxism with traditional Chinese culture and Confucian values. In this process of new ideology building and reconciliation, a new hybrid ideology "Comfucianism" emerged. This new ideology has become the guiding motto in the CCP's political propaganda and cultural recalibrating that would facilitate the Party's rule.

LEGITIMACY CHALLENGED ON ANOTHER FRONT

While the CCP's fight on the economic front was highly successful, it was confronting growing uncertainties and challenges on the ideological and cultural fronts in the 1980s as the reform effects became more salient. The Party leadership had largely underestimated the negative effects of reform in many sectors and regions, and the incontrollable social power that it had unleashed through political decentralization and devolution. The repercussions of the Soviet implosion and loosening communist ideology in China culminated in the student democratic movement in 1989 that openly called for the termination of one party rule in the country. With the suppression of the movement by the CCP with force in June 1989, the Party lost credibility both at home and abroad. Domestically, latent forces were already working hard to accelerate the collapse of the CCP rule. Internationally a number of Western economies immediately imposed strict sanctions on the Beijing regime. As all these subversive forces converged, the threat to regime legitimacy became real and substantial. A series of threats to the Party's rule had never been so formidable and imminent.

Declining Communist Ideology and Subsequent Ideological Chaos

The dramatic decline in the influence and luster of Communist ideology following the domino-like collapse of the communist regimes at the beginning of the 1990s began to bear on China quickly. Although China became the *de facto* sole major country with a communist regime in the world, widespread public cynicism regarding Marxism was posing significant challenges to the fundamental core of the Party's ideology. Communism *per se* could no longer be understood as playing a leading role as the inevitable universal ideology envisioned by Marx; this perceived reality resulted in ideological chaos in China. The state ideology was abandoned by the public and replaced with a new worship of money, along with occasional extreme nationalism, various religious sects, etc. The CCP lost the power of its state apparatus of mind control. What concerned it most was that some of these movements and new beliefs, such as the religious cult *Falun Gong* and radical nationalist movements, directly threatened the Party's rule and regime stability (Reynolds 2009; Cabestan 2005, 59).

Spiritual Crisis That Arose from Deepening Market Economy Volatility

The market economic reform and consequential privatization spearheaded the nation's shift toward capitalism, corroding the fundamental ideological basis of Marxism. Deng's famous statement "To get rich is glorious" encouraged and honored any activity in pursuit of profits, predictably creating an atmosphere of money madness and a Social Darwin struggle in Chinese society. Traditional moral virtues, especially collectivism, were regarded as outdated and useless and were abandoned. Pragmatism, materialism and consumerism became the dominant social values, especially among the young. This spiritual crisis and moral malaise sparked rising public discontent and harsh criticism against the CCP government.

Threat of Western Liberal Democratic Values

China's new openness gave its citizens more access to the outside world. The populace was increasingly exposed to Western values like universal suffrage and freedom of expression. They began to know and understand more about how democratic countries were governed and how ordinary people exerted effective control over their publicly elected officials. Compared to their own powerlessness *vis-à-vis* the CCP, public discontent increased. Such sentiments were reinforced as they saw that kindred Asian societies, such as South Korea and Taiwan, had been moving on the track of democratization and that these were also much better off than the CCP ruled Chinese economy. People admired democracy and expected that it could be realized in China.

Rising Social Unrest Due to Worsening Corruption and An Increasing Wealth Gap

Visible rampant corruption, rent seeking, and power abuse by party officials largely undermined the public trust and support for the CCP government which had purportedly vowed to devote itself to the public welfare since the beginning of its establishment. The phenomenal economic growth in China had been accompanied by increasing income inequality and a widening social divide, ironic for a communist regime, sowing the seeds of social upheaval. The Party realized that in order to maintain its legitimacy it had to tackle growing social problems accumulated over the reform-era before sporadic incidents developed into large scale revolutionary upheavals reminiscent of Tiananmen. One of the strategies was to repeatedly invoke the importance of the Confucian idea of "*hexie shehui*" (harmonious society), implicitly suggesting the wrong nature of such incidents.

Increasing Blame on the CCP as a Destroyer of Chinese Culture

With the growing exposure of the vices of the Culture Revolution, intellectuals were made aware of how many of the historical relics and cultural traditions which had even survived the repeated foreign invasions during the previous century had been destroyed during the CCP rule. Blame on the CCP and demands for explanation and repentance were mounting. Even though subsequent Chinese leaders managed to divert the blame to the Cultural Revolution launched by Mao, it was impossible for the contemporaneous Party to shirk its responsibility completely.

Retrospectively, new policies introduced in China in the mid- and late 1980s largely underscored the famous observation of the French political thinker and historian Alexis de Tocqueville, "The most dangerous moment for a bad government is when it begins to reform." True enough, the outright public outcry for ending the CCP rule happened at a time when the CCP leadership was attempting to carry out radical political, economic, and social reforms.

THE CCP'S URGENT NEED FOR A NEW
IDEOLOGY AND RELEVANCE OF CONFUCIANISM

The Need for a New Political Ideology

Under pressure from within and without, the Party had an urgent need to address them in order to avoid repeating the fate of other communist regimes. All the following factors provided the CCP with sound rationale and motivation for the creation of a new political ideology to substitute for an outdated and shelved Marxism. It also needed to clarify and redefine its role with regard to traditional culture that had been badly emasculated by its rule.

Need for a New Political Ideology That Supports Its Authoritarian Rule

For the CCP, the critical consideration of every policy was whether it perpetuated the Party's authoritarian rule. Hence, any alternative ideology had to meet these conditions: be politically compatible with authoritarian rule, possess the traditional appeal of historical governance to the public, but not contradict the continued use of Socialism by the CCP as appropriate for political and social development. Finally, this new ideological basis had to be able to justify and reinforce the importance of social order and stability. Confucianism, due to its inherent characteristics being consistent with these requirements (Bell 2010), presented itself to the authorities as a logical and natural substitute.

Need for Alternative Political Discourse as an Antidote to Western Democracy

Due to the change of China's and the world's situations, the CCP could no longer simply emphasize class struggle, hatred of the rich, and opposition to capitalism. Instead, post-reform China had to domestically confront growing regional inequality, deepening economic disparity, and enlargement of the social hierarchy. Given the global situation of the era, the social and econom- ic ideologies of Western liberal democracies had gained widespread support and even became dominant in the 1990s, to the point that an American scholar prematurely asserted that history had come to its end (Fukuyama 1992). As the Western liberal democratic concept conflicted squarely with the CCP's desire and self-interest in perpetuating its authoritarian rule, it was highly likely that people would question and eventually challenge the legiti- macy of the communist regime in China. An ideology that was able to coun- ter Western thoughts but be compatible with the CCP's need to sustain con- trol was essential.

Need for an Attractive Blueprint of a Society for the Chinese People

In the reform era, it was imperative for the CCP to provide the Chinese populace with a new direction. Furthermore, due to great damage to tradi- tional culture resulting from the Cultural Revolution, the Party needed to clarify its attitude and rebuild its role with regard to its historical legacy. The Party took this into consideration when conceptualizing and forging its new ideology. Confucianism's focus on order, harmony, hierarchy, obedience, and family/social obligations would be rebuilt into a blueprint that would comfort the general public, address the social problems, and fill the moral void in Chinese society.

Need for a Benevolent International Image as China Rises into a Quasi-Superpower

Along with the rise of China, speculation has grown that a strong authoritar- ian Chinese regime may pose a threat to its neighbors and even the world. Historically and regionally, imperial China had subdued its neighbors before. This kind of speculation is not only prevalent among China's smaller histori- cal neighbors, but also, given the global reach afforded by modern technolo- gies, strong in the great powers, especially the United States. They worry about intent as well as actions of this rising authoritarian power. Alarmed by the potential damage this aggressive reputation might cause to the country's international environment as a growing powerhouse, the Beijing authorities have made earnest and great efforts to cultivate and wield soft power, though with mixed results (Zhang 2007, 2012). In its overseas propaganda cam- paigns aimed to establish a benevolent and appealing image, Beijing needs to find an icon that is both positive and well known in the world.

All these needs point to the fact that the Party-state has had to take prompt action to find a substitute for its outdated political orthodoxy. As it happens, the traditional Chinese culture, represented by Confucianism, provides the most fertile soil from which the CCP can grow and nurture its new ideology. Its applicability to foreign affairs remains to be seen.

Utilities of Confucianism and Traditional Chinese Culture to CCP Rule

In ideology building, the CCP has two priorities in consideration. First, the CCP must retain its communist legacy because negation of that would be self-denial of its established political legitimacy since 1949. Any move toward a complete breakup with its past would be political suicide. Second, the new ideology must be acceptable to the Chinese people. Pluralization of Chinese society and the formation of more and increasingly diverse interest groups make finding something that can be accepted universally by all major constituencies in modern China a challenging task. The CCP optimizes its goals by digging into the traditional Chinese political culture that usually favors authoritarian rule.

Indeed, turning to traditional culture and Confucian values is not a novel tactic, given China's history. The ebb and flow of Confucianism through two and a half millennia of Chinese history has proven its resilience. Each era has reinterpreted the ancient worldview to fit contemporary sociopolitical conditions and deal with relevant issues in the extant sociopolitical culture. In the 1920s, the utopian resemblance between Marxism and Confucianism was emphasized by some Chinese intellectuals when they introduced Communist philosophy to a Chinese society already deeply influenced and cultivated by the traditional cultural system based on Confucian ideas and values (Jiang 2016; Bell 2006). As American China expert Vera Schwarcz observed, "In traditional China, history took the place of religion." Therefore reviving the past became a "sacred commitment" (Schwarcz 1991, 76–77). This observation applies to contemporary Chinese culture, even when associated with the revered sage Confucius. Confucianism and China's traditional political culture became the raw material for the CCP's ideology construction.

Among all the Confucian values, respect for authority and a hierarchical social structure have been the most significant, because they precisely provide a conceptual and ideological justification for a ruling class. In addition, Confucius' emphasis on benign rule and the creation of a harmonious society facilitate actions by the CCP, which are perceived as promoting the peace and stability of a society; they can be portrayed as beneficial to society itself. Given the legitimacy needs of the ruling class, they extol and at the same time emphasize the importance of Confucianism. Over the long course of Chinese history, a special political culture has gradually taken shape, which culminate in the concept of the "Mandate of Heaven." This is the legitimacy basis of Chinese rulers equivalent to the "the divine right to rule" in the West before the modern age. In both cases, as with so many other empires and kingdoms, especially prior to the industrial revolution, feudal hierarchy rests on this source of legitimacy, a conflation of political and religious power.

This Confucian political culture embodies a mutual exchange relationship in which Chinese society operates in a hierarchical way such that the subjects respect and obey the authority, while the authority rules following strict moral standards and provides protection and public goods to the subjects. The more straightforward reflection of this relationship in Confucius's teaching is "*Jun-Chen-Fu-Zi*" (monarch-minister-father-son). The implication is that none should violate this basic principle and hierarchy. If the ruler is not benign, thus having forfeited the "Mandate of Heaven," the subjects have the right to overthrow him. Conversely, if one of the ruled does not obey, he should be punished accordingly (Billioud 2007, 2015).

Notably, traditional feudal values and Confucian virtues are still very relevant to Chinese society. It has influenced and dominated almost every aspect of Chinese people's life for more than two and half millennia. Despite Mao and the CCP's earlier attempts to dispel them as evil symbols of the noxious oppressive past and imperial regimes, these deeply rooted indigenous cultural and Confucian values were never really erased from the hearts and minds of the general population. They have continuously provided the moral foundation for the conduct of life in China (Jiang 2016). Ordinary Chinese see their ethical behavior, self-discipline and cultivation, social and family relations, and habitual ways of life overwhelmingly in a context calibrated according to traditional cultural and Confucian values. Filial piety, for example, is still widely endorsed, expected and practiced. Therefore, it is not surprising to see the enthusiasm the general public shows in its new incarnation. One evident example was the continuing popularity of "*Yu Dan's Reflections on 'The Analects'*"[1] by a professor of media studies at Beijing Normal University. Her book has become a best-seller in China, with a selling record reaching 10.2 million copies within a year (Melvin 2007).[2]

With ownership of an authoritarian political system, the CCP naturally welcomes elements in Chinese political culture that favor strong central control. In the post-Mao era, all leaders, from Deng to Jiang to Hu to Xi, have adopted a wide range of policies, first reviving Confucianism and then distilling from its essence elements that can be concocted into policies and programs to promote and strengthen the rule of the CCP and stability of the society (Dotson 2011; Chan 1993).

SEEKING LEGITIMACY AND NEW ROLE IN TRADITIONAL CULTURE

Efforts in the Deng, Jiang, and Hu Eras

Ironically the CCP's original legitimacy was partially built on negation of almost everything about old China in an earnest attempt to build a new country. Tragically this concept, revolution rather than evolution, became the guiding principle of the CCP in its first three decades of rule. Hence in all the political movements, "destroying the old" became a necessity. The direct results of these policies were the disappearance of numerous historical treasures, especially material relics, and suppressing intangible things, such as traditional customs, while the Great Leap Forward and the Cultural Revolution also produced massive human suffering and death.

These extreme acts had not stopped until after Mao's death in 1976 and the reform that was launched. After the end of the Cultural Revolution period, the CCP started to take concrete actions to reverse the self-negation and self-destroying movement. Terminating criticism of traditional culture and recreating respect for it, as exemplified by visible actions such as reconstruction of damaged temples and historical relics, were some of the earliest efforts (Billioud and Thoraval 2015). With the fading of the impact of the Cultural Revolution and normalization of the judgment of historical figures and events, China's traditional culture started to be treated as honorable and normal. Since Deng's time, state-sponsored rehabilitation of imperial China's Confucianism has been undertaken to justify the CCP's socioeconomic activities as well as its countrywide rebuilding and renovation of dismantled or damaged historical relics.

Confucian revival during the Deng administration was relatively slow. Deng questioned the utility of orthodox Communist ideology when he liberalized the public mind by his famous maxim "It doesn't matter if a cat is black or white so long as it catches mice." The statement and his reform theories have dramatically transformed the dogmatic CCP from strictly following Marxist and Maoist doctrines into a pragmatic communist party. The leading core of the CCP recognized that its legitimacy had to be performance-based and anything that promoted modernization and economic growth while preserving CCP rule in China was welcome (Bell 2015; Dotson 2011). This phenomenal change in party principles made rehabilitation of traditional culture and Confucian ideas both necessary and expedient in the modern environment.

Confucius's rehabilitation by the Party-state was confirmed at a 1984 symposium in Qufu, where he was again accepted as "one of the glorious figures of China."[3] This event itself was highly symbolic since it was the first time Confucius's status was recognized in the post–Cultural Revolution China. Contrasted with the movement "*pilin pikong*" (Criticizing Lin Biao and Confucius) launched by Mao, this was a seminal moment in reestablishing Confucianism officially in the CCP's political dogma.

During the Jiang Zemin administration, large scale privatization began. The consequent public dissatisfaction and social instability due to unpopular job cuts and massive layoffs during the economic transition called for an urgent search for a new social philosophy to comfort and pacify the public until increasing general prosperity could ameliorate the sense of insecurity.

Traditionalist themes resurfaced in both intellectual discourse and party rhetoric. At the beginning of Jiang's term as General Secretary of the CCP in 1989, he stated that Confucius was one of China's greatest philosophers and the Party should study his ideas to select the essential ideas which should be used to educate the people (Chan 1993). There was a wave of construction of Confucian-studies institutions, sponsored by the government (Billioud and Thoraval 2015). In the 1990s, the CCP also experimented with using traditional values and Confucian political ideas to define the substance of communism with "Chinese characteristics" (Delury 2008).

In the subsequent Hu Jintao era, the use of Confucianism for practical purposes became more widespread. Not only did the study of Confucianism become fashionable, but it was even used officially as guiding principles in conducting domestic politics and foreign affairs. There have been dozens of official events endorsed by the CCP government that signify Confucianism's "re-entering" the public space in China during the post-reform era (Billioud and Thoraval 2015). In response to increasing social and regional inequality, Hu promoted a succession of official slogans, including "*hexie shehui*" (harmonious society) and "*xiaokang shehui*" (a moderately prosperous society), implying patience and tolerance, which have very strong Confucian undertones. These Confucian concepts cultivate an attractive image of an ideal society by assuring the public regarding the CCP's commitment to social welfare and justice. The concept of such a harmonious society has extensive facets, including the benign rule of an authoritarian government, reduction of income inequality, high levels of cultural development, etc. Thereby, it provides an alternative secular faith and political ideology that the CCP could use to guide the general public through life in a country with dramatic changes. By emphasizing a harmonious society, the CCP justified the increasing socioeconomic inequality and reiterated the crucial importance of a stable social political environment. In 2007, the CCP government officially sponsored the worship of Confucius on his birthday and broadcasted the event nationwide through CCTV. Since then, Confucianism has also been employed extensively by the Chinese state propaganda apparatus: in the opening ceremonies for the 2008 Beijing Olympic Games; in a historical epic film about Confucius produced by a state-owned film company in 2009; and in a large statue of Confucius erected on the edge of Beijing's Tiananmen Square in early 2011 (Dotson 2011).[4] Confucian study programs have mushroomed throughout the educational system of China, from kindergarten to college. In kindergartens, school kids recite the classics; while at universities, Confucian programs appear in philosophy departments and Confucian-themed executive-education programs have even started to offer sage guidance for business people (Billioud and Thoraval 2015; The Economist 2007).

"Xideology"—"Comfucianism" in the Xi Era

Among all the Chinese leaders since Deng, Xi has been the one who extolls Confucianism and Chinese culture most ardently. His strong attitude favoring Confucian and traditional culture extensively permeates his speeches.[5] Xi commends Confucius so highly that he attended a seemingly unimportant event in person—the International Conference in Commemorating the 2,565th Anniversary of Confucius' birth and the fifth Congress of the International Confucian Association—held on September 24, 2014 (China Today 2014). He becomes the first state leader of China to attend an event commemorating the birth of the Chinese philosopher and educational "saint." It is also the third time in a year during which he openly interacted with Confucian scholars and showed his supportive attitude (He 2014; Li 2014; Bol 2018, 251).[6] On different occasions, Xi regularly voices his respect for Confucius and other Chinese intellectual saints such as Wang Yangming[7] and touts the importance of traditional culture to the Chinese nation by directly quoting their words and ideas. During one visit in Shanghai, for example, he openly expressed his disapproval of removing classical poems and prose from text books, saying that classics should be ingrained in students' minds and become the "genes" of Chinese culture (China Today 2014). While on another, Xi showed warm concern about the Confucius Academy (*kongxuetang*) located in the faraway city of Guiyang, Guizhou Province when he met with delegates from the province at a meeting in Beijing in March 2014.[8]

Even though Xi has continued the path of developing and improving "Comfucianism" like his predecessors, his ruling style is increasingly characterized by his own vision of present and future China and how his vision is to be turned into actual policies. These visions and policies are increasingly being forged into a new ideology with their own characteristics: "Xideology." This ideology is remarkably distinguished in the bipolarization between his tightening political and social control while liberalizing economic policies.

Xi's political and social policies bear such strong resemblance to those of Mao's time that some observers have even likened him to Mao. For instance, he makes considerable efforts to alleviate poverty, especially in the countryside, and institutes preferential policies for economic and social underdogs. He has also enforced strict policies to control the Party, such as launching large scale campaigns to curb and fight corruption and practice modesty and austerity (An 2013). However, he also shows signs of returning to the Mao era by dropping presidential term limits, creating the opportunity for him to perpetuate his rule. Similarly, evidence of personal worship is not rare. He has also instituted policies that have reduced freedom of speech, notably using modern technologies, to prevent people from criticizing the Party and government. Also, mandatory political studies, prevalent during Mao's time, have been reinstituted. All these measures are reminiscent of communist China before the reform.

Concurrently, Xi's other practical measures bear strong marks of traditional Chinese culture. For example, as he tackles the corruption problem, he deals with it using a more Confucian concept of *"dezhi"* (rule of virtue) rather than the way of *"fazhi"* (rule of law) by attaching great importance to the personal virtue of public officials. "To govern in virtue" is one of the important themes of Confucianism, which emphasizes individual morality and ethics. Confucius believed that in order to govern others one must first govern himself. Vowing to crack down on both "tigers" and "flies"—powerful leaders and lowly bureaucrats in his campaign against corruption, Xi has shown the public his determination to build a virtuous Confucian *"dezhi"* political mechanism.

Internationally, Xi lauds the *"mingyun gongtongti"* (community of common destiny) and *"liyi gongtongti"* (community of shared interests), and advocates *"goujian renlei mingyun gongtongti"* (building a community with a shared future for mankind). All these concepts are strongly earmarked by Confucian and traditional Chinese perceptions of the human, the community and the world—*"sihai yijia"* (all in the four seas belong to the same family) and *"tianxia datong"* (unity of all lands bring great harmony).

Even so, Xi's policies and thoughts have not deviated from the path cultivated by the three preceding generations of leaders. His slogans, doctrines, and styles all center on the core idea of governing China using a combination of both Confucian values and CCP authoritarian rule. As Xi expressed explicitly in his speech at the ceremony commemorating the birthday of Confucius: "The CCP members are always the faithful inheritors and advocators of China's excellent traditional culture. From Confucius to Sun Yat-sen, all of us are keen in absorbing nutrients from it."[9] Obviously, Xi is also trying to promote the new image of the CCP as an intrinsic part and inevitable natural product of Chinese culture and history.

In summary, "Xideology" is an evolving form of "Comfucianism" ideology, thus with a similar dynamic to Comcapitalism, discussed earlier. It is more heavily accented by his simultaneous emphasis on both Confucianism and traditional culture and by the legacies of Chinese Communism. As an extension and expansion of this synthesis, it stresses both tenets of the ideology. As acutely observed by both domestic and international observers and analysts, the combination of the sinification of Marxism with traditional Chinese culture is being developed to a significantly higher level during Xi's administration and its Chinese characteristics will be greatly strengthened. The increasingly distinct "Xideology" is evidence of these observations.

"COMFUCIANISM": NATURE AND FEATURES

After the efforts of four generations of leaders in the reform era, a hybrid ideology utilized by the CCP to replace the original orthodox Marxism and reaffirm its leading position in Chinese cultural revival has taken shape. "Comfucianism" is actually a new political ideology created by a communist party attempting to rejuvenate its ideological appeal and reestablish its political legitimacy after the *de facto* failure and abandonment of its experiment with original orthodox Marxism. Over the years, this ideology has demonstrated a number of salient features which have permeated the CCP's domestic and foreign policies extensively.

Political Authoritarianism That Extols Benevolence

The Chinese government has always emphasized the building of a "*hexie shehui*." The concept of such a society originated in Confucianism, stressing a hierarchical social order characterized by *Zhong* (loyalty to the monarch and state)*, Xiao* (obedience and serving to the parents), and *Ren* (benevolence). In China today, the Party-state has replaced the traditional monarch and state. Loyalty is expected to go to the state controlled by the Party. Moreover, the Party has constantly presented itself as the parents, as evidenced by a large number of propaganda stories and "red songs."[10] The Party and state leaders always display an image that they are benevolent family heads like a father and have been practicing *Ren* all the time. By doing these, they hope that they can garner loyalty from the people. Obviously, both *Zhong* and *Xiao* are features of a hierarchical society, where in contemporary China, the Party is the one that sits at the very top of the hierarchy. The Party also reiterates that a harmonious society and prosperity can only be achieved through a powerful and effective unitary government. On the contrary, China's suffering and misery in history are fairly linked to a weak and fragmented country with a decentralized, factional government.

Elitism that Highly Values Outstanding Performance

This is a meritocracy system that is extraordinarily imprinted with the mark of "Comfucianism"; that is, the country must only be ruled by the best of the educated elites rather than the ignorant masses. In the Communist system in China, bureaucracies are not staffed by elected officials but by cadres, mostly party members evaluated and selected by their superiors. Their career advancement is highly dependent on their work performance and achievements, a very typical feature of historical Confucian merit system (Puett 2018, 233–235). Furthermore, one has to pass the civil service examination to even be admitted to the government system or the SOEs. This exam is not new but a modern adapted version of China's two thousand year old *"keju"* (imperial civil service examination) system. Both meritocracy and civil service exam practices exactly replicate the legacies of Confucian governance, now embedded into a Leninist-style authoritarian system.

Economic Capitalism that Emphasizes State Control and Regulation

The CCP is also skillful in utilizing another important feature of traditional Chinese culture: collectivism. Not only a salient traditional value, collectivism is the cornerstone of all China's social activities and social organization. A derivative of this feature in the Party policy is its repeated jargoning *"jizhong liliang ban dashi"* (centralizing powers so as to accomplish big schemes), indirectly emphasizing the benefits of political authoritarianism and economic planning and state control. An extension of this ideology is the CCP's justifying the *raison d'etre* of large SOEs. Although China's private business sector has experienced dramatic growth since the start of reform, its SOEs have always played an important role in the modern national economy. It is also the vehicle through which the Beijing regime carries out various regulations in economic and social life despite extensive criticism of their privileges, low efficiency, red tape, waste, and corruptions. Although certain statements by the Beijing regime that keeping the strategically important businesses in the hand of the government benefits the national economy might be true, it is self-evident that controlling such businesses also facilitates and benefits the continuous rule of society by the CCP. As Hayek (2007) argues, once government controls the economy, it also controls society (Hayek 2007). This is one of the numerous ways that the CCP maintains its reign.

Societal Liberalism That Promotes "Rule of Virtue"

In terms of social management, the CCP promotes the rule of virtue, one of the most prominent features of Confucian political thinking, rather than the rule of law as emphasized in the West; the distinction is profound. Compared to the pre-reform era, the CCP regime has granted considerable freedom to Chinese society. Except for political freedom, freedom in other areas such as the economy, limited religious beliefs, and literature and artistic expression are permitted and even encouraged so long as they are not perceived to expressly challenge the authority of the CCP. However, in building what the Party calls a "harmonious society," the Party usually resorts to moral rather than legal justifications to play its controlling role. The Party always emphasizes in its propaganda the urgency and significance of building an effective legal system, and indeed has done much toward that goal; however, China is still far from completely achieving the rule of law. By granting relatively more freedom in society, the CCP demonstrates social progress that makes most segments of society more satisfied with its rule. By encouraging moral rather than legal control, the Party can maintain an unchallengeable position in solving problems in society while retaining great flexibility. If the rule of law were strictly enforced, the Party itself would have to abide by the same laws, thus eroding its own power and privileges.

Cultural Nationalism That Emphasizes the Glorious Past

Apart from the utility of applying Confucianism to politics and economy, reviving China's traditional culture, especially under the directorship of the CCP, helps fill the gap left by the diminished and receding Marxist ideology. It will also strengthen Chinese nationalism, as an important adhesive force, under the control of the Party, which in turn helps rally the Chinese people around the Party flag. On the mainland, the government subsidizes heavily various "cultural projects" that galvanize China's history, such as the rediscovery and re-presentation of historical figures and events, archaeological excavations, construction of statues of prominent historical figures, recovery and reconstruction of damaged historical relics, and even restoration of ancient ceremonies (Billioud and Thoraval 2015). By using slogans like "Reinvigorate China" and "National Revival," the Party presents itself as a preserver of China's tradition and culture and as the leader of the Chinese people striving toward those goals. By stressing nationalism through various cultural activities, the CCP tries to convince the Chinese people that it is the only political force in China that can achieve all the deserved glory of the Chinese nation as expressed in Xi's "China Dream" (The Economist 2013).

Military Pacifism That Calibrates Peaceful Rising and Opposes Any Use of Military Force

With regard to national security and military, the Beijing regime also adheres to Confucius's and Mencius's teachings of *jisuo buyu, wushi yuren* (treat others the way you want to be treated) and "*yide furen*" (persuade others with virtue) rather than with "*wu li*" (force), at least at the level of rhetoric. Indeed, among all the great powers in the world, China is the one that has used its military least in the post–Cold War era. Guided by this principle with strong Confucian and Mencian influences, China very seldom gets involved in the domestic strife or civil wars of other countries. Compared to the more active interventionist policies of other great powers, particularly the United States,[11] China's "non-interference" policies present a contrastive example. When dealing with conflicts, Beijing normally calls for a stronger role of the United Nations in helping solve problems of the world rather than unilateral action that involves the use of military forces.

Diplomatic Neutralism That Develops Balanced International Relations

Furthermore, Beijing has been following a "maintaining a golden mean and never go extreme*" (zhongyong zhidao)* policy in foreign affairs. Beijing has always emphasized that all states, big or small, should be equal. In dealing with international crises or conflicts of other countries, China very rarely shows a strong attitude toward a particular party—if the vital Taiwan issue or domestic human rights is not involved. It constantly reiterates that it will always remain neutral among the involved parties and always tries to cultivate a middle road. As a logical step, Beijing has also been following the guiding principles of non-alliance, generally opposing military alliances of any kind.

These features combined have clearly defined a new ideology distinct from others. In politics, economy, social organization, culture, propaganda and foreign policy, the influences of traditional Chinese culture are evident, emphasized and dominant. The CCP has successfully embedded traditional Chinese culture into a rule characterized by communist legacies. Today it is not shy to tout its role as the inheritor as well as promoter of traditional Chinese culture.

With the Xi-Li administration entering their second term, efforts in fine-tuning the "Comfucianism" ideology have neither dissipated nor slowed. Xi's evolving policies have continued the path of the three earlier administrations in their pursuit of this new ideology to continue CCP rule of China.

As a matter of fact, the CCP's efforts have been rewarded immensely; it has not only retained its Communist political legacy and continued monopoly on political power, but also has been given credit for developing China's economy and significantly raising the general living standards of its people. Even though the Chinese government is criticized often for human rights issues in the West, it downplays these issues domestically and is still very popular among the various sectors of Chinese society. This similarly suggests that the CCP's new political ideology has been well accepted and its political legitimacy remains sound.

Unsurprisingly nowadays, as belief in pure Marxism dies, layering Party principles and goals with the traditional "sacred" Confucian scripts, and promoting patriotism appear to be the best way to evolve a new party ideology without changing the core course of "communism" or whatever term best describes this new system. The CCP has accomplished these successfully. It is expected that the Party-state will continue to utilize, develop, and adjust this ideology according to the new circumstances, as it has done in the past.

In short, as one scholar points out: "The 'Theory of Three Represents' proposed by former President Jiang Zemin, the 'Scientific Outlook on Development' offered by former President Hu Jintao, and the 'Chinese Dream' introduced by President Xi Jinping are the latest efforts by the Party to address its concerns over the ideological crisis of its legitimacy" (Ruan 2015). These official discourses have rarely referred to the CCP's revolutionary past; instead all of them emphasize the current leading role and aspirations of the CCP in adapting to the ever-changing social environment and to reform itself from within (Ruan 2015). So far, the CCP has adapted well to the new circumstances. It has also won the battle on the ideological and cultural fronts.

NOTES

1. *The Analects* is a collection of words and ideas of the Chinese philosopher and educator Confucius (551 B.C.–479 B.C.) and his contemporaries. They are traditionally believed to have been compiled and written by his students and followers.

2. Yu Dan's book was published in December 2006.

3. See "*Ruxue Zouxiang Fuxing Zhilu* (Confucianism Is on the Way to Revival)." *China Confucius Foundation*, May 20, 2007. http://www.chinakongzi.org/rjwh/lzxd/200705/t2007 0520_2165097.htm.

4. The statue was later removed from the square due to controversy on April 20, 2011.

5. Examples include speeches at the first session of the 13th NPC on March 20, 2018, the 19th National Congress of the CCP (NCCPC) on October 18, 2017, and the rally marking the 95th anniversary of the founding of the CCP on July 1, 2016. More can be found in "*Xi Jinping Wei Chuantong Wenhua Daiyan* (Xi Jinping Speaks for Traditional Chinese Culture)." *Chinese Youth Online News* (*Zhongqing Zaixian Xinwen*), June 19, 2018. http://news.cyol.com/content/ 2018-06/19/content_17302514.htm.

6. The other two events are his visit to Qufu, Shandong Province, the hometown of Confucius, in November 2013 and his visit to the famous Confucian scholar Tang Yijie in May 2013.

7. Wang Yangming (1472–1529) is a Chinese idealist neo-Confucian philosopher, official, educator during the Ming dynasty (1368–1644). He is regarded as one of the four greatest masters of Confucianism in history along with Confucius, Mencius, and Zhu Xi. His works and thoughts were frequently quoted by Xi in his speeches. For a discussion of the relationship between this ancient philosopher and Xi's political thinking, see Johnson (2017).

8. Deng Dongmei (pseudonym), interview with the author. Personal Interview. Guiyang, March 5, 2019. According to Deng, a scholar at Guiyang Confucius Academy, this academy is a new institution dedicated to the study, proliferation and education of traditional Chinese culture. Its establishment is partially an answer to the call of top Chinese leaders, including Hu and Xi, for respecting, protecting and reviving Chinese culture. Its construction was completed in 2013. The Academy is located close to the province's two flagship higher education institutions Guizhou University and Guizhou Minzu University.

9. See the article "*Xi Jinping Chaochanggui Jinjian Kongzi Youhe Huawaiyin?* (Xi Jinping Commemorates Confucius on a Super High Profile. What Are the Implications?)" *Youth.cn*, September 25, 2014. http://pinglun.youth.cn/wywy/shsz/201409/t20140925_5776907.htm.

10. Red Songs usually refer to a group of patriotic songs composed from the 1930s to the 1970s to eulogize the Chinese revolutionary courses led by the CCP and the subsequent socialist construction after the founding of the PRC. They were composed for inspiring people's respect and love for the CCP and the Communist regime it created.

11. See the conversation between former President Jimmy Carter and current President Trump on U.S.-China relationship.

Chapter Four

"Blocking, Dredging, and Channeling"

The CCP's Struggle on the Social Front

It is widely acknowledged that coercion and repression constitute a major part of the CCP's political ruling strategy. Despite decades of profound economic liberalization and human development, the CCP regime has been constantly criticized by China watchers and specialists for its heavy-handed control over the media, the Internet, financial and business markets, religious groups, and social organizations as well as its ruthless crackdown on human rights protests and dissidents. The repressive nature of the communist regime seems to correspond with the conventionally presumed authoritarian imperative that illiberal regimes rule rigidly on coercion and over-centralization. By this logic, non-democratic regimes suffer weak legitimacy and strong opposition, therefore are inherently fragile. In China this proposition seems to be echoed by increasingly widespread mass public demonstrations and protests occurring in a daily basis, making some scholars and observers conclude that the Chinese people are fed up with the Party and the communist regime is on its last legs. However, various survey and polling data stand strongly against this theory and predication. Not only does the CCP regime enjoy high level of political support from its people, but the public also shows strong confidence and trust in the important institutions such as courts, police, media, NGOs, and businesses.[1] This apparent contradiction indicates there is something critical missing in the traditional paradigm of autocracy and authoritarianism.

Since the end of the Cold War, a new line of research has surged to account for the viability of non-democratic regimes. The new approach highlights the importance of institutions, legislatures, and cooptation mechanisms in autocratic ruling tactics. The autocracies are capable of adapting to the changing global and domestic political, social and economic environment by incorporating ostensibly democratic institutions into its authoritarian governance (e.g., Gandhi and Lust-Okar 2009; Acemoglu and Robinson 2005; Nathan 2003). To prolong their rule, autocratic rulers opt for optimal ruling and repressive measures: they loosen control over the media and the Internet (Nathan 2003; Pan and Chen 2018), coopt business groups and social organizations (Wintrobe 1998; Nathan 2003), and even selectively tolerate, if not encourage, social uprising. Some scholars point out that these new tactics that contemporary autocracies have embarked on to grip onto power may blur the traditional lines between autocracy and democracy, broadening the popular basis for their rule.

Following this line of enquiry, we postulate that it is oversimplified to assume that the CCP's ruling solely relies on the extensive repression mechanism. The China-collapse prophecy based on the similar assumption is an illusion. In fact, the CCP regime has inherited and adopted an ancient management strategy "blocking, dredging, and channeling" used by Yu the Great thousands of years ago in combatting the recurrent flooding of the Yellow River.[2] Analogizing social awareness to water and social contentions and discontents to flood, the Party has responded to the "social flooding" with sophisticated compound tactics of repression and division in conjunction with responsiveness, persuasion, and cooption. The CCP regime has formed its unique ruling mechanism by both absorbing tactics from the ancient Chinese imperial political history as well as acquiring selective Western democratic institutional methods. Based on this hybrid ruling mechanism, the authoritarian regime has intentionally granted certain political space to the mass public to monitor lower-level government performance and keep in touch with public sentiment. In order to balance out the risks of rising demands fostered by the quasi-democratic institutional arrangements, the CCP has also exerted extensive repression to block any potential or ongoing organized contentions or collective actions that perceptively undermine the regime's rule. We further argue that it is important to recognize and understand how the "dredging and channeling" part of the CCP's ruling mechanism has practically affected social stability and the state-society relations in China. The political strategic settings, together with remarkable economic performance, has greatly impacted the political perception and attitude of the Chinese people toward the authoritarian regime: they have reshaped the relations between the ruler and the ruled from a conventional "society against state" model to a discourse more featured voluntary compliance and self-discipline.

BLOCKING THE SOCIAL FLOODING

State's Strong Will of Blocking

In search of an understanding of the roots of repression and coercion of the CCP regime, we must begin with a review of the long and contentious political history of China. Elizabeth J. Perry (2001, 163) once stated that "No country boasts a more enduring or more colorful history of rebellion and revolution than China." One of the myths about Chinese political culture is the assertion that Confucian values such as hierarchy and obedience have greatly shaped the public attitudes in favor of authoritarian regimes. In fact, the value of obedience the Great Sage aspired is never unconditional. It is contingent on whether the ruler observes his duty to be benevolent and caring. If he fails to fulfill the duty, grassroots unrest and even revolutions are encouraged and justified by the very fundamental principle of the Confucian "Mandate of Heaven." The establishment of the CCP regime itself is an evident proof of the efficacy of this rule of thumb. Fully aware of the turbulent contemporary history of China and the power of the people, the Party has constantly remained vigilant, sometimes even paranoid toward any discontents or contentions from the grassroots. Therefore, the Party's exerting coercive power to keep people in awe, not simply subjugation, is mandated by its very survival instinct to hold on to power.

For the rulers of the CCP regime, no historical lesson has been more vivid and intensive than the prodemocratic movement in 1989. The decade since the onset of the reform was the most liberalized period in the post-Mao era. Economic liberalization forced the government to decentralize and delegate, loosen media control, allow various Western democratic ideas to penetrate society, and permit the public enthusiastic political participation. The experience of nearly being overthrown made the CCP regime come to a very clear conclusion that the price of loosening control over society is too high to bear. Even though heavy suppression of social uprisings proves to be politically and economically costly, if the party elites believe the regime's survival is under threat, they will not be deterred by the high costs associated with mass repression. The Tiananmen Square movement marks a remarkable watershed in the CCP's ruling strategy. The Party tightened up its control and has stayed on high alert ever since.

Four decades of economic development have brought unprecedented material progress and financial advancement to China, but at the price of increasing income inequality and regional disparity, as well as serious environmental degradation. The deep structural transition and privatization has generated heavy cost, incurred enormous social problems and injustice, and heightened mass grievances. As a result, the CCP regime has encountered a great number of protests, demonstrations, and petitions over issues such as pollution, land acquisition and forced demolition, labor disputes, and corruption, etc. In 2010 alone, "mass incidents" occurred at an average rate of about 500 every day in China (King, Pan, and Roberts 2013). Although the definition and accuracy of these data have been questioned, the number does reflect an ascending trend of social unrest and instability and has enhanced the will of the regime to take repressive actions, particularly toward those organized contentions that challenge the Party-state and pose potential or clearly direct threats to its rule.

The Party's will to resort to coercion has also been heightened by the pervasive Internet penetration in China. Outperforming traditional media, information technology has greatly undermined the very foundation of authoritarian rule by enabling the masses to express, communicate, and mobilize. Unrestricted information flow shatters the media monopoly by the state, exposing the public to the true level of social discontents and empowering them with effective tools of organization as well as knowledge to evaluate feasibility of revolt (Lorentzen 2013; Sun 2013). The Arab Spring, a wave of Internet-driven democratic uprisings, swept the Arab world, toppling two authoritarian regimes, and setting off alarm bells for the CCP regime. The Party's will to tighten control over the Internet is determined and pragmatic: it must prevent an "Arab Spring" from happening in China.

State Capacity of Control

The absence of state capacity to monopolize legitimate means of violence, raise revenues, and formulate and implement its security policies largely compromises its will to crush any social rebellions and revolutionary uprisings. Theda Skocpol (1985) emphasizes the importance of the state's strength and capacity for an authoritarian regime to maintain its coercive rule over a discontent and turbulent society. The democratic transition in most Sub-Sahara African countries stands as a prominent example of how lack of state power facilitates regime change in developing countries (Herbst 2001). The Arab Spring demonstrated a catastrophic end for some authoritarian regimes in the Middle East when state coercive power failed to keep up with empowerment of the public via information technology.

In the context of China, the CCP regime not only possesses the will for harsh repression, but also has developed a strong capacity to ward off any organized contention. Decades of economic growth have brought sufficient revenue to provide a strong financial foundation for an extensive and powerful coercive state apparatus. China's domestic security expenditure accounted for 6.1 percent of total government spending in 2017, implying a threefold increase since 2007, from 348 billion yuan to 1.24 trillion yuan ($196 billion) (Zenz 2018). The portion of spending allocated to maintaining domestic security and stability has exceeded its military defense expenditure for eight consecutive years since 2010, and this gap continues to grow.

The primary security-related government department and agencies include, but are not limited to, the Ministry of State Security and its agencies in the provincial and municipal level, the Ministry of Public Security and all its agencies from provincial to street level, that is, the regular police force and the People's Armed Police Force (PAP), which is a semi-military institution under the dual jurisdiction of the State Council and the Central Military Affairs Commission of the Party. But the day-to-day working-level frontiers of the state security apparatus rest upon local security establishments and administrative extensions such as police stations, street offices, urban residents' committees, and rural villagers' committees.

China now has about 1.5 million citizens in the PAP; among them about 330,000 are deployed specifically for internal security (Yang 2018). The number of nationwide police personnel has grown from 600,000 in 1986 to about 1.9 million in 2014.[3] Although the ratio of police to the population is relatively low compared to many other countries, the regime has hired, trained, and incorporated substantial number of joint prevention team members and auxiliary police into its public security system, reaching between 100,000 to 200,000 in 2004 (Li and Li 2004). In addition, there are 31,639 rural township offices and 8,266 urban street offices in 2018 in China, which means there are at least 39,905 local police stations nationwide,[4] almost double the number of total police agencies including college campus patrols and federal agencies in the United States. The numbers of the villagers' committees and urban residents' committees have reached 553,000 and 107,000, respectively, by 2018.[5] More importantly, the penetration of Party influence in everyday life has long been a fact in China, where over 4.57 million grassroots party organizations exist in government agencies, public institutions, urban and rural residents' committees, state-owned and private enterprises, and various social groups.[6]

The rural villagers' and urban residents' committees are household-based self-governing grassroots organizations designed and created by the CCP regime to exert its direct control over the mass population, deal with policy and livelihood issues, deliver basic community services, and maintain social order and stability. The concept of the political settings of local control can be traced back to the *baojia* since the early Song dynasty, approximately 1,000 years ago.[7] The organization laws of the villagers' and urban residents' committees define both as mass autonomous organizations that are elected, constitute of, and run by the villagers or urban residents.[8] In practice villagers' and residents' committees maintain a close tie to the base level authorities—township government or street offices, and are dependent on the latter for financial resources, personnel matters, activity direction, and performance assessment (Read 2000). In the rural area, direct election at the village level has been practiced for three decades, though under supervision and intervention by the township level authorities and the local Party (Nathan 2003). Direct elections of urban residents' committees weren't actively promoted until 2000 (Gui, Cheng, and Ma 2006). In most cases, members of the residents' committees were recruited and paid by the street-level government (Nathan 2003; Read 2000). In this sense, both villagers' and residents' committees are far from a form of direct grassroots democracy that operates autonomously. The Constitution of the Party stipulates that the CCP branches should reach to the village and urban neighborhood level.[9] Therefore the pseudo-election procedures and direct supervision by the Party cramp any possible contribution by those mass associations to democratic changes. On the other hand, neither villagers' nor residents' committees are qualified to serve or have legal standing as a real part of the local government. The fact that the committee members live in the same village and neighborhood, delivering basic services and being acquainted with most of the residents, makes them more trustworthy than the local government officials, thus more effectively implement the Party policies and perform surveillance.

Compared with the villagers' committees in the rural area, the urban residents' committees have warranted more attention from the CCP regime in terms of socioeconomic functions and social order maintenance, since the cities are where industrialization activities concentrate, and most protests and demonstrations occur. According to the law, the residents' committee comprises of five to nine members and covers a residential area of 100 to 700 households. In the pre-reform era, the CCP regime's omnipresent control over the urban mass public primarily relied on the state-owned work units, which provided salary, housing, benefits, and even basic community services to the employees (Read 2000). The residents' committees then served a complementary role to cover people such as the retired and housewives who were usually left out of the work-unit system. Reform has incurred structural changes in both economic and social dimensions. Reforms of the SOEs and later privatizations in the 1990s have liberated the work units from most of the political and social functions. Some of the functions have been shifted to the local government, increasing its burden. Administrative decentralization has become imperative. Privatization of the public and work-unit housing has created governance vacuums in these neighborhoods. Since the reforms, China has witnessed an influx of laid-off workers, rural migrants, and self-employees who fall out of the traditional work-unit system the CCP previously relied on to control the urban masses. In response to these challenges, the Party-state has embarked a nationwide campaign of "Community Construction" since the late 1990s in an effort to rebuild its control over society through thousands of urban residents' committees. Since then, the residents' committee has evolved into a semi-administrative organization. Some residents' committees in big cities have formed a collaborating interagency network including property management companies, homeowner committees, and local police within the neighborhood. The major functions of the residents' committee are threefold: first, maintaining social stability by organizing voluntary security patrols, watching for crimes, and reporting possible protests and discontents; second, implementing policies and performing administrative duties such as helping with government surveys, mediating disputes, or enforcing family planning; and third, delivering welfare subsidies and other community services.

In addition to building organizational footholds in society through villagers' and residents' committees, the CCP regime has woven a visual security network to fortify its censorship over the media and Internet. In China, there are around two million "Internet public opinion analysts," commonly called "Internet police," working for the government, major Chinese news websites, and commercial corporations to monitor and analyze online opinion, fabricate social media posts, and censor contents on the Internet. It is believed that Internet public opinion analysts emerged in the early 2000s. In 2013, the government officially recognized "Internet public opinion analyst" as a legitimate occupation and began to provide vocational training and official certification.[10] The CCP regime also relies on cutting-edge information technology to tighten its control over the visual world. The Great Firewall project was launched in 1998, only four years after the Internet arrived in China. Over the past two decades, the Firewall has effectively limited domestic access to foreign information sources, keeping foreign Internet social media tools and mobile apps out of the country, and filtering sensitive contents by identifying keywords. Moreover, the government has started to crack down on virtual private networks (VPNs) that allow the netizens in China to circumvent the Firewall since 2015. In 2018, the Party-state began to officially ban any non-state sanctioned VPNs (Griffiths 2018).

The CCP's ambition isn't limited to claiming its cyber sovereignty: the government is taking systematic steps to build an "omnipresent, completely connected, always on and fully controllable" nationwide video surveillance network fitted with facial recognition technology. The number of cameras in China reached 176 million by 2017, and another 450 million will be installed within the next three years (Mitchell and Diamond 2018). While this is supposedly meant to identify and catch fugitives and terrorists and deter criminals, it can also make the task easier to target individuals who defy the government. The government has also launched an ambitious "social credit" program to rank all 1.4 billion citizens based on their political, economic, and social behaviors. It is said the program is being piloted among millions of people already and expected of fully operation nationwide by 2020 (Ma 2018).

Apparently, economic liberalization and decentralization doesn't lead to retreat of the state in China. To the contrary, relying on grassroots organizations and advanced information technology, the CCP regime has managed to increase penetration in all aspects of life. The determined will and overwhelming state capacity of coercion and repression send a clear warning message to the mass public, making many social forces and anti-government groups reluctant to mobilize politically due to high costs and low efficacy.

Tactics of Controlling and Repression

Despite the harsh repression will and power, controlling a society with a population of 1.4 billion is an extremely time-consuming and resource-expensive operation. The CCP regime has taken painstaking efforts to increase the effectiveness of repression and to maintain social stability. Instead of a full overview of the repressive history of the Post-Mao China, this section examines the most important social control and repressive strategies and patterns that appear to have evolved over the years.

Stringent Internet Censorship

China's Internet population has exploded since broad Internet access started in the 1990s, from 620,000 in 1997 to over 772 million by the end of 2017 (China Internet Network Information Center (CNNIC) 2018). The exponential growth of digital activism has increased the Party's concerns over the Internet's potential subversive effects to empower the public with free information and mobilization ability. In order to effectively control online public opinion, limit the dissemination of critical and discontent contents and block foreign democratic ideas, various censoring strategies have been developed and implemented, backed by dozens of restrictive Internet regulations and laws.

The CCP regime has fostered the growth of an "internal Internet" by simply blocking sensitive foreign websites and mobile apps via its pervasive censoring system since 1997. Nearly all the foreign commercial social media, search engines, and video-sharing online services have been denied entry to the country. The benefits of an isolated internal network are profound, at least for the short term. The competition-free environment has greatly facilitated the development of domestic Internet industries. The country's rapidly growing online economy has been dominated by the Chinese domestic companies such as Tencent, Alibaba, and Baidu. Almost every foreign commercial Internet service can find its counterpart in China's internal network: Baidu for Google, Weixin for Facebook, Zhihu for Quora, Sina Weibo and Wechat for Twitter, Meipai for Instagram, Youku and Douyin for YouTube, to name only a few. Due to language barriers and technical restrictions, most people in China prefer to use domestic Internet services than the blocked foreign sites even sometimes the VPNs could help bypass the block (MacKinnon 2011). The well-functioning "internal Internet" has not only satisfied the increasing demand of the public, but also effectively reduced Western influence.

The CCP regime has also ramped up its effort to build an Internet real name registration system. In 2012, the China's Legislature postulated that internet service providers (ISPs) must require real name identity authentication when providing Internet access or information related services to the users. The decision to develop the real name registration system was reinforced by the Cyber Security Law in 2016. A year later, China announced a set of regulations of Internet real name registration meant to eliminate online anonymous posts and comments by users. Thus, individuals who want to post or follow comments online, communicate via social media service, or use websites and apps that feature information dissemination are required to verify their accounts with cellphone numbers. The government could identify the real person via the phone number because citizens are required to use their real names and resident identity numbers to register SIM card for their mobile phones.

To lower the cost of implementing the real name registration system and other restrictive regulations, the CCP regime has delegated censoring responsibility to the ISPs and emphasized their role in self-censorship. The prosperity of these domestic industries largely depends on the CCP regime's Internet isolation policy and sponsorship. Moreover, the Party has incorporated the Internet business elites into its political system. Several influential technology entrepreneurs such as Robin Li of Baidu, William Ding of NetEase, Lei Jun of Xiaomi, and Pony Ma of Tencent, all hold political positions. All of this makes it easier for the authorities to apply their delegating tactics.

Facing skyrocketed online activism, one of the effective tactics the CCP regime adopts is selective censoring. The government has begun to specifically target online activists with large social media followings. Those so-called Internet leaders who are usually writers, journalists, lawyers, and scholars are among the earliest to post news or social events, deliver follow-up information, and even conduct offline independent investigations. The influential bloggers' enormous broadcasting and rally power to reach out to ordinary people and mobilize the like-minded has hit the government's nerve. Restrictions have been applied to contain the most prominent web influencers. In 2013 the Supreme People's Count ruled that Internet users who deliberately spread false information that is defamatory or harms the national interests could face up to three years in jail if their posts were either viewed 5,000 times or shared more than 500 times (An and Cao 2013). These laws and regulations on online expression have imposed enormous pressure on critical bloggers and journalists toward conformity. For example, an influential blogger with about 150,000 followers has been fired by the Beijing Normal University where he worked in the real world as an associate professor for his online negative and critical comments (Hong 2017). Studies also

confirm that the government's censorship efforts have been primarily orient-
ed toward any online activities that may represent or contribute to ongoing or
potential organized contentions (King, Pan, and Roberts 2013; Gallagher and
Miller 2017).

Last but not least, in light of the growing significance of the Internet as an
unexplored political battleground, the CCP government has shown its determination to increase online government presence and master the art of guiding and shaping online public opinions. One strategy is to turn the Internet
into a principal supplement of propaganda by flooding it with the government's own contents. In 1999, the State Council launched the Government
Online Project (GOP), aiming at establishing websites for all levels of
government departments and agencies. Since then, the number of "dot-
gov.cn" domain has increased dramatically, from fewer than 500 in 1999 to
about 50,000 in 2017 (CNNIC 2018). Government sponsored online news
providers have also increased coverage of political scandals, social unrest,
and crimes of the foreign, particularly Western countries. More invasively,
tens of thousands of Internet police have been recruited to manipulate the
available online information either by posting positive comments, manually
deleting critical and sensitive contents, or flooding the comment section and
pushing down the critical comments (Gallagher and Miller 2017). The number of estimated fabricated posts and comments has reached 448 million a
year—that is, one in every six contains fake or propaganda information
(King, Pan, and Roberts 2013; Gallagher and Miller 2017).

Control the Youth

Students' political engagement and mobilization has long been a prominent
feature of movements of regime change in the developing world. They are
intellectually engaged, sensitive to social inequalities and injustice, and have
a largely ideational basis and capacity for self-mobilizing and undertaking
political actions. Their perceived innocence and idealist nature can enable
them to attract more attention and sympathy of the populace and the mass
media. Moreover, historically the emergence of student movements often
echoes a more general rise of political contention in society (Tarrow 1995),
igniting the fire of deeper and broader social and political reform and upheavals. Chinese students have been politically engaged, with a rich history of
activism and radicalism dating back more than two thousand years ago. In
modern China, students were deeply engaged in the anti-colonial nationalist
struggles from the very beginning of the state, which has conferred historical
legitimacy on them. From the May Fourth Movement to the Tiananmen
Square protests, Chinese students have demonstrated their ability to challenge state legitimacy as a dynamic social force.

In the wake of powerful student activism in the 1980s, the CCP regime has exerted increasingly stringent control over students. Mandatory patriotic military training has been imposed on all college freshmen ever since 1989 in a bid to indoctrinate the future elites with regime-sponsored values. To shape the mindsets of the youth through education, more political courses or contents emphasizing Marxism as well as the CCP's representative position and revolutionary history have been added to the curriculum of schools and universities in China. Political knowledge including theory of Marxism and socialism, important state policies and traditional political culture are required contents being tested in the national higher education entrance examination as well as in the graduate level entrance examination. Since Xi's incumbency, the government has embarked on a campaign to further strengthen ideological study and propaganda against Western values at universities (Martina 2016). Some university professors have been suspended or fired due to "false or negative" speeches (Hong 2017).

In order to control university students' online activities and forestall any forms of political mobilization, in 2004, the Party-state banned outside users to access university Bulletin Board Systems (BBSs) and required all users within each campus to register with their real identity, almost 10 years earlier than the nationwide enforcement of the real name registration system.[11] Since then, some of the most influential university BBSs such as the one of Tsinghua University (smth.org) and Nanjing University (lilybbs.org) have been restricted to university users only. Students have been cut off from communication with and influence by visitors outside the university who might otherwise be important contributors to the comments and conversations of these BBSs. At the same time, the CCP regime has called for the university to absorb students as Internet commentators in a bid to guide online narrative and to report critical and negative comments. Huang (2015b) finds that the heightened propaganda and control make the university youth believe that the regime is strong in maintaining social order and less willing to participate in political dissent.

Chinese students have been actively involved in articulating nationalist sentiment since the early 20th century. Taking advantage of the youth's susceptibility to extreme political beliefs and thoughts, the CCP regime has re-instilled nationalism and patriotism in university students to divert their focus from domestic affairs. Student activism in the recent decades has featured a lack of direct mobilization against the CCP regime, but with increasing nationalism and an anti-Western tone. In some cases, such as the 1999 protest over the bombing of China's Belgrade embassy, the CCP regime has encouraged the students' nationalist demonstrations by publicly endorsing them on national television and providing transportation and slogans for protesters (Perry 2001). Xi's "China Dream" has further stirred nationalist sentiment among the students.

China has started a large-scale expansion and commercialization of higher education since the early 1990s. The number of the college graduates has jumped from 1.14 million in 2001 to 8.2 million in 2018.[12] Although it maybe not the intent of the CCP, this change does lead to quick diminishing of university students' elite status, which once made them feel responsible as representatives of the broader public and more politically engaged in a society bereft of educational resources. Increasing competition in job market in conjunction with pervasive commercial values further depoliticize many university students, making them prioritize economic concern over political motivation. In addition, the Party-state is fully aware of the danger of a large population of unemployed educated young people and has focused on improving the employment rate of the college graduates. The employment rate for new college graduates has increased from 85.5 percent in 2008 to about 92 percent in 2017.[13]

Mass Mobilization

Mass mobilization and political campaigns profoundly fueled the communist revolutionary change and political dynamics in the pre-reform era (Perry 2001). There is mounting evidence that the legacy of *Mass Line* politics and popular involvement strategy has continued to exert a powerful influence over the political practices of state authorities and the social engagement of ordinary people alike. For instance, the aforementioned recruitment of Internet police and commentators from ordinary Internet users serves as a typical example of how the CCP regime attempts to reconfigure mass mobilization tradition with a view to address its new challenges in a high-technology environment.

In addition, the CCP regime has launched a "Mass Mobilization and Prevention" (*qunfang qunzhi*) campaign to enlist mass participation in community crime prevention and social order maintenance as supplement force to local bureaucratic administration and law enforcement. In each urban residents' committee, the "backbones" are selected (who are often retired party members) and voluntary residents are recruited, led by local police and street cadres, to carry out specific tasks such as regular community patrol, neighborhood watch, family visit, information collection, or Party propaganda. In Beijing, about 1.4 million people have been mobilized to participate in "Mass Mobilization and Prevention" to maintain stability. In 2017, the number of "public security volunteers" registered with real names reached 850,000 (Guo and Pei 2017). Besides regular tasks, these public security volunteers in big cities have also played an important role as thousands of lookouts during special events such as the annual meeting of the Party Congress to report any unusual situations and suspicious strangers including foreign journalists, petitioners, or ethnic minorities from Tibet or Xinjiang

(Levin and Wong 2013). The majority of the mass constituency upon which the CCP regime based its mobilization effort to maintain public security and social order are mainly senior retirees. But recruitment of many younger volunteers has reduced the average age of the public security volunteers in Beijing to 50 years old (Guo and Pei 2017).

Mobilized by a common fear of social instability, the public security volunteers along with the base level cadres have committed themselves to the cause of social order maintenance. They operate within the neighborhoods and address security needs of residents. They are trusted and welcomed by the rest of the residents. Public security volunteers' actions and beliefs influence their families and friends. Mass mobilization not only serves as a powerful strategy to improve governance effectiveness, but also helps the CCP regime successfully rebuild its bases and footholds in Chinese society, suppress dissent to prevent social uprising, and consolidate its power.

Delegation and Division between Central and Local Governments

Since the start of the reform, the CCP regime has proceeded to decentralize and delegate power to local governments through the financial responsibility system (started in the 1980s) (Yang and Zhao 2015) and the cadre responsibility system (started in the 1990s) (Edin 2003). Through decentralized, the unitary political arrangement ensures that the central authority is overwhelmingly powerful over the localities. Local authorities, particularly the heads of the local Party and governments, are held accountable to the CCP regime by signing various performance contracts which play a critical role in annual administrative assessment and evaluation. The performance targets given to the local governments are substantial and incontestably prioritize social order and economic growth. Nevertheless, the wording of implementation is very general and vague (Edin 2003). The discretionary power and revenue stimulus greatly encourage local governments to achieve their targets by all possible means. Some means used by local governments were self-serving and abusive, evoking widespread dissatisfaction and grievances among the targeted mass public. For instance, reducing number of complaint letters and petitioning was a critical criterion in local administrative evaluation until 2014 (Edin 2003). Some affected petitioners, who then went to Beijing to seek attention of higher-level officials, were often intercepted, detained and retrieved forcefully by local officers and cadres. Sometimes, however, complaints and petitions have succeeded: in the last decade, a series of protests has swept the country against massive industrial projects with negative externality by the economically driven local governments. In most cases, the angry environmentally conscious public successfully induced authorities to suspend or to stop the projects. In responding to the strong wave of rising environmental activism, the central government intervened and began to take actions to tackle environmental problems, adding environmental targeting to its subsequent Five-Year Plan and amending Environmental law in 2014 (Corne and Browaeys 2017).

Thus, the Party-state strategically takes advantage of this division between central and local governments: if state policy was well implemented by the localities or the goal was attained, the central government eventually reaped the credits of economic growth and social stability. Had it not gone well like the aforementioned cases, where the mass public suffered and protested due to bureaucratic malfeasance and power abuse of local governments, the central government would hold a moral high ground, step in and take actions, either correct the unpopular policy or punish the corrupt or abusive local officials. This delegation strategy has not only enhanced the central authority's control over the lower-level governments, but also made the localities directly liable for the unpopular policies and subsequent social problems. It helps the CCP regime divert mass public discontent toward local governments. This separation of grand policy decision moving on the top and policy implementation on the bottom explains why widely reported protests and demonstrations in China have mainly been directed at lower-level authorities while the central government enjoys higher level of satisfaction and strong support.

DREDGING AND CHANNELING THE SOCIAL FLOODING

Purpose of Dredging and Channeling

The strong will and powerful state coercive apparatus of the Party-state to suppress social uprisings have nipped regime change impulses in the bud, at least for the short term. But no autocracy can solely rely on repression and coercion for its longevity: the costs are too high, especially in a modern industrial and technological environment. Contemporary authoritarian regimes seem to strive to boost legitimacy by accommodation and adaption, that is to say, increasing governance and responsiveness. However, unlike in democracies, where government is held accountable through various institutions such as elections, independent legislature and free media, authoritarian regimes lack transparency and meaningful check and balance political settings. Even though arguably more and more autocracies begin to incorporate democratic institutions into their political system, they have no intention of enforcing democratic principles and values for political liberalization purposes (Nathan 2003; Gandhi and Lust-Okar 2009; Froissart 2014). So, how does an authoritarian government like China manage to enforce accountability when it is endeavoring to improve the performance and governance? To address this question, we explore the incentives of the CCP regime and mechanisms it adopts to apply its dredging and channeling ruling strategy.

Monitoring Lower-Level Officials

For the Party-state effective governance rests on the ability to monitor and strengthen its political control over the lower-level officialdom. Failing to gather precise and reliable information about the actions of the local governments significantly weakens the regime's capacity to make decisions, implement policies, and respond to emergencies and social crisis. Since the economic reform, the Party has taken steps to decentralize and delegate power to stimulate lower-level governments to actively engage in local socioeconomic development (Yang and Zhao 2015). Decentralization and marketization have conferred great discretion and resources on lower-level authorities. Some areas, particularly the eastern coastal provinces with more advanced economic development, have become considerably autonomous and powerful vis-à-vis the central government (Edin 2003). A series of official hierarchical evaluation and communication systems have been developed and applied to monitor and control the lower-level officials. However, the fact that the local offices of monitoring bureaus are part of the same level government discredits the integrity and validity of evaluations of their localities (Huang 1995). Pan and Chen (2018) find that some public complaints of corruption and wrongdoings through official channels have been intercepted and concealed from the upper-level authorities in China. The logic behind this lies in a typical principal-agent dilemma, in which median level officials act to their own best interests and choose not to pass information of negative performance and consequential public dissatisfaction to the upper-level because their own political careers might be jeopardized by the wrongdoings of the subordinates and the social unrest they provoke (Pan and Chen 2018, 3). Succinctly put, the official monitoring system has loopholes that prevent the central authority from gaining accurate information on the localities. It is imperative that the CCP regime open an informal channel of monitoring and communication with the local community by loosening the media censorship and social control, for example, by allowing a certain amount of social media freedom to inquire valuable information regarding local corruption and malfeasance. Moreover, this informal grassroots monitoring mechanism has served as incentives for the local officials to improve their effectiveness and efficiency (Chung 2015; Chen, Pan, and Xu 2016).

Probing Public Sentiment and Opinion

Conventional authoritarian model states that the authoritarian rule doesn't rely on popular support. Rather, nondemocratic regimes resort to repression to maintain control over the masses as well as cooptation to seek political endorsement from small but influential groups of elites (Bueno de Mesquita et al. 2003). In this vein, for authoritarian rulers, public opinion is meaningless and negligible. Contrary to this argument, the statecraft wisdom of imperial China has emphasized the critical role of manipulating public mood and sentiment in strengthening its rule. From the famous saying of Mencius "Whoever wins the hearts and minds of the people rules the world" (*ying minxin zhe detianxia*) to Xunzi's proverb which was appreciated and underlined by the revered Emperor *Taizong* of the Tang dynasty (618–907) "The water that bears the boat is the same that can sink it (Xunzi analogizes water to the people and the boat to the emperor)" (*shuineng zhaizhou yinengfuzhou*),[14] China seems to have an imperative legacy to build legitimacy based on performance which could satisfy and mollify the populace (Yang and Zhao 2015). The *Mass Line* adopted in the Mao era and the continued "mass mobilization" strategy carried out in the post-Mao period reflect the fact that the Party fully understood the power of the mass as well as the importance to constantly master public perception, moods, and preferences.

However, authoritarian regimes lack the functioning institutional settings to help collect reliable and accurate information regarding public opinion, for example, free and fair election which directly reveals genuine public preference and sentiment in democracies. Official information acquisition through state security surveillance, police monitoring, and government and party internal reports often suffer skewness and inadequacy because the officials try to conceal information due to the principal-agent dilemma (Xiao and Womack 2014). Thus, the Party is desperate to create informal channels to monitor what the public really thinks and feels. Given its powerful and sophisticated repressive capacity, the CCP regime is less concerned about the risk brought by the bottom-up communication compared with other authoritarian states.

Understanding the true climate of public opinion and sentiment could help the Party-state evaluate policy implementation, gauge the quality of governance, and measure the level of social tension. Based on bottom-up information and analysis, the CCP regime could take corresponding actions such as correcting or removing unpopular policies, tackling the most prevailing social problems to satisfy and appease the populace, or channeling mass discontent into constructive activities to prevent them from escalating into large scale social uprisings. Moreover, the Party could adjust the degree of repression and censorship based on perceived social atmosphere. The government could tighten its control if dissatisfaction and contention prevail and loosen up for other political purposes when the discontent pressure eases.

Easing Tension by Allowing Anger Venting

History shows that public discontent and anger is a powerful tool that can be used to force regime change. Negative feelings accumulate into popular consensus if there is no outlet. The public will feel being abandoned with no hope. When their anger builds to the boiling point, there is high possibility that aggrieved citizens will take their fury directly to the street. Regime is on the edge of collapse "when its people stop bringing grievances to the state since it is an indicator that the state is no longer regarded as legitimate" (King, Pan, and Roberts 2013, 14). The CCP regime realizes that it is critical to create channels for anger and dissatisfaction venting as a means to regulate public emotion and sentiment. King, Pan, and Roberts (2013) suggest that the Party-state seems to recognize that being embarrassed by harsh verbal criticisms is much safer than being threatened by real world unrest. Moreover, along with the rise of China as a global power, the regime has perceived that public anger venting could be used as an instrument to ease the tension between government and society by channeling the anger into nationalism and patriotism. The Party thus purposely allows the Internet to become a place to vent grievances and dissatisfactions as long as it is under control.

Promoting Economic Development

Deng's famous saying "crossing river by touching the stone" has inspired the establishment of a potent policymaking and improvement process, in which local initiatives and experiences have been fed back into national policy formulation and correction. A series of prominent policies critical to the reform such as household responsibility system and opening to foreign investment have been shaped through this point-to-surface policymaking mechanism (Heilmann 2008). Yang and Zhao (2015) posit that the key to the successful development doesn't reside with specific good government policies, but attributes to the societal demand for good performance as well as the regime's imperative to adjust and implement new policies in response to feedbacks under this pressure. Therefore, this hallmarked policy formulation strategy, which is consider critical to economic prosperity in China, requires large-scale and long-term state-society interaction and bottom-up communication. For example, the project to reform land and property tax system with various interest-orientations began in 2006 and is still under experiment and feedback consultation up to the present. In this sense, without a guarantee of a basic vertical channeling mechanism, policymakers could go blind and leap in the dark; the economic reform could run off the rails.

Furthermore, the prosperity of the newly emerged digital industry is closely associated with the level of censorship. China has a huge market of Internet business, among every two people there is a user with an average 3.8 hours per day on the Internet. Its online shopping market hit 7.18 trillion yuan in 2017. The total market value of the cyber business also reached 8.97 trillion yuan by the end of 2017 (CNNIC 2018). Moreover, some leading Internet companies with top market value in China such as Tencent, Baidu, NetEase, and Sina Weibo provide news services, search engines, social media, and microblogging. Cyber activism, ranging from blogging, discussions, comments, and even online protests addressing sensitive issues like corruption, social injustice, homeowner rights, and pollution have generated high hits and large web traffic attracting more users; all of this is crucial for these profit-seeking digital giants (Sun 2013).[15] For the CCP government a supportive and relatively free digital environment stands crucial for its domestic economy.

Strategies of Dredging and Channeling

Media and Internet as Channeling Tools

China's rating on the Freedom House index of media and Internet freedom rose from 80 in 2002 to 87 in 2017, indicating a harsher online environment.[16] Though stringently censored and restricted, in the past two decades China has witnessed a mushrooming growth of digital activism in both number and visibility. Compared with the traditional media, the Internet features real-time news broadcasting, speedy dissemination capacity, easy and free access, and flexible grouping and assembly functions (Sun 2013). Empowered by the new media technology, the masses in China have strived to voice their grievances and views on a wide range of issues from corruption to social justice, the environment, health care, and inequality. Often described as a double-bladed sword, the Internet challenges the Party by strengthening the public's ability of horizontal communication and mobilization, while at the same time ushering in opportunities for the CCP to probe genuine public mood and sentiment and to monitor officials and spot social problems. To unravel the dilemma, a variety of tactics have been undertaken by the government to channel the public through the Internet for its regime survival without risking overthrown.

A Harvard empirical research has confirmed that the CCP regime intentionally allows and tolerates individual online criticism of the authorities but focuses its repressive effort on online activities associated with organized contentions (King, Pan, and Roberts 2013). That is to say, any cyber contents attempting to organize street protests or stir up mass sentiment against the authorities are almost certain to be filtered and removed, while individual grievance, anger venting, or complains are less likely to be censored when the government doesn't feel there are serious threats of mass mobilization. This selective censorship tactic enables the Party to harness public opinion for its own use while "clipping social ties whenever any collective movements are in evidence or expected" (King, Pan, and Roberts 2013, 1).

Beyond eliminating ongoing or potential online collective actions, the CCP also constantly balances flourishing online public expression with tightening cyclical censorship. Some scholars argue that oscillating between restricting and channeling online expression reflects the government's incompetence to solve the dilemma (e.g., Qiang 2011). However, Lorentzen (2014) posits that the state skillfully adjusts the level of censorship contingent on the underlying social tensions it perceives, based on the information collected from the online public expression. Regardless of these two propositions from opposite angles, the censorship pattern exists for both media and online public discourse. The period from 2007, the "Year One of Public Events," to 2012 featured unprecedented potency of online activities in setting the agenda of public discourse (Qiang 2011, 47). Local incidents go viral online, being discussed and circulated exponentially, attracting so much attention and interest across the country, and force the traditional media to cover the story as well. Scholars even believe that "'politically liberal voices' have dominated the Internet in China" (Denyer 2013). Thanks to Sina Weibo and Tencent Wechat, China's equivalents of Twitter, which were launched in 2009 and 2011, respectively, the online reports and debates have been disseminated in a larger scale and at a greater speed, with the number of followers' comments often exceeded millions. In 2013, concerning the "politically liberal voice" that has purportedly dominated the Internet, the CCP began to take steps to crackdown on online activism, targeting the cyber opinion leaders. Some influential Weibo accounts with over 10 million followers have been forcibly closed. Online censorship was eased relatively from 2014 to 2017 and in 2018 the CCP again began to constrain online activism by striking VPNs, thereby denying Internet users access to foreign information by circumventing the Great Firewall. The enthusiasm of online public debate and participation rises and falls along with periodical censorship tightening.

Apart from the tactics used to constrain the subversive effect of online activism, the CCP regime has built various channels for public opinion solicitation. Relying on official media outlets for opinion channeling was a primary traditional method until the Internet rose as a mainstream force for public opinion collection. In the 1980s and 1990s, almost all the official media outlets established special departments to process letters of complaints and suggestions from the public. The investigative reporting has grown rapidly since the early 1990s and reached peak in the following decade (Stockmann 2013). Some influential and shocking stories and incidents have been investigated and exposed by the flagships of Chinese media outlets such as the *Southern Weekend*, the *Economic Observer*, and *China Economic Times*, and even prime-time investigative news shows by the official Central Television (Guan, Xia, and Cheng 2017; Li 2002). But most investigative reports remain classified and are only circulated within the upper-level officialdom (Lorentzen 2014; Qin, Stromberg, and Wu 2017; Denyer 2013).

As a result of increasing Internet penetration and growing media restriction, Chinese investigative reporting has declined in the new century. The Party has increasingly placed reliance on the Internet for online public opinion monitoring and solicitation. Besides the government agencies devoted to online public opinion summarization and analysis at the central and provincial level, some major cyber media outlets such as people.com (dubbed as "People's Daily online") as well as academic institutions and universities, all formed online public opinion monitoring centers or units. Billions of posts and comments have been sorted and analyzed by cyber information analysts, and the processed information regarding public sentiment and moods has been funneled to party leaders. Moreover, the CCP regime has also incorporated social media into its propaganda and channeling mechanism. By 2013 Sina Weibo had hosted over 100,151 government accounts (Meng 2014). In 2012, the estimated number of government-affiliated accounts amounted to 600,000 (Qin, Stromberg, and Wu 2017).

Furthermore, the government has been skillful and sophisticated in its response to online crises with relatively high and quick response rates, particularly regarding those major incidents being greatly circulated and triggering massive nationwide reactions (Chen, Pan, and Xu 2016). Scholars find that many local officials with their names and corruption details exposed through Sina Weibo have been charged by the central regime later (Qin, Stromberg, and Wu 2017). Several government construction projects such as Dalian PX chemical factory plan and Shanghai maglev rail extension project have been canceled or postponed by the authorities in light of strong opposition online and in the street. Some incidents, which stirred up fierce online debate, have become milestones of important policy shifts. For example, the Sun Zhigang incident[17] in 2003 led to the abolishment of the regulation on "the custody and repatriation of vagrants and beggars in cities," which had been in effective for decades. In 2016, the government issued an order requiring all related agencies to respond to major online events or crises within 24 hours and to other less severe cyber incidents within 48 hours.[18] It doesn't mean that the Party-state determined to be held accountable as in democracies and to respond to all the complaints and criticism from the public. But this selective responsiveness tactic helps increase public political efficacy, rebuild the CCP regime's reputation, and consolidate its authoritarian rule.

Public Consultation and Deliberation Mechanism

Starting in the late 1980s, the central government began to resort to polls conducted by universities and other academic institutions for public opinion solicitation. Since the State Council launched the GOP in 1999, a plethora of government websites and blogs have been opened to build channels of bilateral interaction and solicit public feedback on policies and services. Recently the governments at various levels turn to private polling companies for public opinions on a wide range of subjects, including market reform policies, environmental protection, religious belief, attitudes toward most senior leaders and even prodemocracy protests in Hong Kong (The Economist 2015).

Public opinion polling and solicitation has assumed increasing importance in drafting laws and regulations and making major policies in China. The drafts of new laws and regulations will be posted on the website of the NPC for a month to solicit public opinions and comments. Since the early 2000s, some local governments have been holding public hearings to catch public opinion, suggestions, and complaints about administrative and legislative issues (Ergenc 2014; Fishkin et al. 2010).

Another important public consulting mechanism rests in the NPC and the Chinese People's Political Consultative Conference (PPCC). The role of both the national legislative and consultative institutions in China has widely been dismissed as "rubber stamp" with little practical effect. However, studies find that there might be a "bounded representation" existing in an authoritarian environment (Truex 2017; Manion 2015). Though the candidates assigned by the government in local congresses reflect Party ideology and loyalty, more candidates nominated by the ordinary people have been elected because they can represent their constituents to address people's priorities and problems (Manion 2015). The Party-state has intentionally regarded the various levels of congresses and consultative conferences as a channeling platform to allow depoliticalized proposals addressing various social grievance and concerns. The representatives' opinions mainly serve as references; but their ideas and suggestions are derived from the masses, particularly the growing propertied class, and thereby send warning signals to the higher level of authorities and provide critical information on public sentiment as well as major social problems.

Cooptation and Corporatism

State cooptation and corporatism have played a significant role in channeling the elite group interests and needs in China. To prevent the rapid-growing capitalists from challenging the regime rule, the Party-state has built a cozy coalition relation with private entrepreneurs by offering them enough stake in the status quo. In addition to cooptation with the socioeconomic force for regime survival, the CCP regime has also made efforts to channel the diversified public interests through instruments like grassroots associations and nonprofit social service agencies. In the last two decades, China has witnessed the proliferation of various social groups, including nonprofit organizations, private foundations, and civic associations in the business, professional, and academic fields (Han 2016; Guo and Xia 2016; Xia and Guan 2014). By 2018 the number of NGOs in China had risen to 767,434.[19] Though required to register with the state and under supervision of relevant government agencies, the newly emerged NGOs in China enjoy relative freedom in terms of leadership appointment, financial operation, and agenda orientation (Han 2016). The proliferation and growing independence of social organizations in China conflicts with the argument of traditional state corporatism, which emphasizes a patron-client relation between the state and NGOs in authoritarian states. NGOs in China are not able to engage in full political participation like their counterparts in democracies. However, more discretion has been granted by the Party to encourage the NGOs to better provide social services and channel grassroots collective interests, as long as their agenda is apolitical. The bottom-up and self-organized features make the NGOs an increasingly important channel by which the masses' interests and needs could be aired and heard by the government. Some NGOs such as environmental organizations, community service associations, or even labor organizations have been an integral part of the government social policy decision-making process (Xia and Guan 2014; Zhu 2016).

Petition System

The Chinese petition system, which draws its historical roots from ancient imperial bureaucratic settings, has been established since the 1950s by the CCP regime in a bid to assist the citizens to appeal and challenge government decisions that negatively affect their lives and to resolve specific grievances and injustices. The petition system constitutes thousands of "letters and visits" (*xinfang*) offices residing in various levels of the Party agencies, governments, courts, and people's congresses (PCs). It is estimated that the whole system receives over 10 million petitions annually (Minzner 2009). The petitions often cover the most acute and intensive social problems. The real effect of the petition system is far less ideal than expected. The system is flawed due to several factors, including the principal-agent problem and lack of resources and independence. Moreover, human rights concerns arise when the petitioners, who try to seek help from the provincial or national petition bureaus, are forcibly intercepted, retrieved and detained by the cadres or thugs hired by the local officials against whom petitions are being filed (Lin 2015).

That being said, the Chinese petition system is much more important for the Party than a mere democratic formality. In 2014, the government suspended ranking abnormal petition as evaluation criteria for local officialdom and began to focus more on the effectiveness of problem solving (Gao and Long 2015). The CCP regime has undertaken a strategy to selectively address the petition cases. Over half of the petitions are referred to the relevant government departments and agencies for action. The most resources and attention have been focused on the petitions that reveal prevailing social problems and may generate social disorder and uprising. In extreme circumstances, the core local Party or government leaders may intervene to preempt mass protest attempts (Minzner 2009). The petition cases referred from the higher petition bureaus to lower-tier governments have also taken priority over others. In addition, the petitions provide crucial information on local government corruption and misconducts. According to Bernstein and Lu (2009), 80 percent of the clues about the official malfeasance could be traced from the complaint letters filed by the petitioner. Thus, by granting the public limited political participation, the Party-state has skillfully taken advantage of the ancient petition system to collect critical social information, monitor lower government, improve its image, and most importantly, forestall any potential organized contentions.

Grassroots Elections

A hallmark of democracy, election is also widely considered as an institutional tool adopted by the authoritarian regimes to collect information on level of political support and dissent (Gandhi and Lust-Okar 2009), to coopt potential opposition political forces (Wright 2008), and therefore helps prolong their rule. Featuring a single-party communist political system, the CCP regime has also incorporated elections into its channeling mechanism, but in a manner of constrained competition, transparency, and scope. Grassroots elections have been installed and carried out nationwide since the early 1980s. The related laws postulate that villagers' and urban residents' committees hold free elections on a regular three-year cycle by all villagers and urban residents. Since the first election took place in Hezhai village of Guangxi Zhuang autonomous region in 1980 (Wang 2018), the rural grassroots elections have spread across the country and become a crucial platform of political participation by hundreds of millions of peasants. While the urban neighborhood elections weren't actively promoted until 2000 and have so far only been fully implemented in big cities such as Shanghai, Beijing, Shenyang, and Nanjing, hence they are less influential (Read 2000; Gui, Cheng, and Ma 2006).

Like all elections in authoritarian political systems, the Chinese grassroots elections also have been restricted by the authorities to ensure the democratic institutional setting won't energize the public in challenging the government. In some cases, the candidates have been sponsored by the local authorities, the voting procedures have been tailored to favor government nominees, or the electoral results have been changed and tampered with (Su et al. 2011). Nevertheless, growing evidence indicates that grassroots elections in China are not just window dressing, always interfered in by the state. In the majority of cases the elections are fairly free and competitive, as long as the government is not under direct challenge or threat (Sun 2014).

Grassroots elections in China have established a channel of vertical communication between the government and the mass public for decades. For the CCP regime, the base-level mass election provides vital information regarding the perceived competence and loyalty of the local officialdom. Relatively free and clean elections help the state accurately probe mass public attitudes and policy preferences and gauge regime political popularity. Empirical analyses assert that grassroots elections enhance public service effectiveness, reduce village leader corruption, and warm the relationship between the villagers and local authorities (Kennedy, Rozelle, and Shi 2004; Manion 1996). Moreover, grassroots elections also open a space, though limited, for political participation and self-governance. Being able to hold the village and neighborhood leaders accountable and influence local policy decision making, or at least being able to express grievances through voting, has largely increased the political support of the masses and reduced contention and potential conflicts. Manion (1996) finds that the constituents' interests influence policy preferences of local leaders who gain such positions through competitive village elections.

Protest and Demonstration

China has encountered a great number of popular protests and demonstrations on a near-daily basis in the post-Mao era along with the economic development. The number of "mass incidents" has jumped from around 9,000 in 1994 to over 74,000 in 2004, 87,000 in 2005, 90,000 in 2006, and 180,000 in 2010 (Chan, Backstrom, and Mason 2014; King, Pan, and Roberts 2013). A wide range of social groups has participated in these grassroots political collective actions, including farmers, workers, teachers, veterans, environmental activists, homeowners, students, intellectuals, and ethnic minorities, etc. However, most frequent social unrest in China are concentrated on several common themes related to socioeconomic issues. Peasant collective contentions are usually motivated by exorbitant agricultural surcharges and taxes or by land seizure and confiscation without proper compensation by the local governments. Labor protests often arise in the context of large-scale privatization of SOEs, unequal treatment between different cohorts of workers (local vs. migrant or private vs. SOEs) and deteriorating working conditions in private businesses, delayed payment of wages, or layoffs with unpaid wages. Mass unrest by urban residents are by and large driven by concerns and grievances over issues such as pollution, homeowners' rights, forced evictions and housing demolition by local authorities for infrastructure or business projects. The rest of the popular protests generally involve random anger-venting mass incidents targeting social injustice or local malfeasance, nationalist activism, and ethnic uprisings.

A trend of mushrooming popular protests in China is often interpreted as a signal of weakening state capacity to control the society. But an analysis of the patterns and features of these mass protests, as well as how the CCP regime responds to various protests, implies that this form of public political participation has often been tailored by the government for its own purposes.

A new strand of research has highlighted the unusual role of mass protests and demonstrations as an important integral part of authoritarian governance for grassroots information collection and lower-tier government surveillance (O'Brien and Li 2006; Lorentzen 2013). For the CCP regime, relying on popular protests to bestow political legitimacy bears the imprint of its imperial past and the *Mass Line* practice of the Mao era as well.

Predominant mass protests in the post-Mao era, particularly after the 1989 Tiananmen Square movement, are small and localized, always seeking redress of grievances over specific socioeconomic issues or remedies of local governmental wrongdoings. These nibbling collective contentions have no political agenda, rarely attacking the CCP regime or the political system at large. This type of grassroots protest may be suppressed by local governments but is usually tolerated and even encouraged by the central authority. The CCP regime often takes a relatively moderate approach in dealing with such mass protests. On one hand, the news of the unrest will be strictly censored and related posts on social media will be quickly removed to forestall public awareness of the popularity of the dissident and prevent localized incidents from coalescing with others and escalating into nationwide social uprisings. On the other hand, either the provincial or central government will step in, requiring local authorities to rectify wrongdoings and issuing new policies and laws to redress specific grievances depending on the level of grassroots pressures. For example, in order to mollify the growing discontent of veterans regarding inadequate benefits and poor job prospects, the central government set up a Ministry of Veterans Affairs in 2018 and gradually improved veterans' care and benefits.

Compared to the sympathized attitude and moderate approach to go easy on economic-focused and identity-based grassroots protests, the CCP regime has undertaken decisive and ruthless tactics to crack down on any protests targeting the CCP regime or the political system in general, including human rights unrest by the human rights lawyers and activists, prodemocracy protests and demonstrations such as the Charter 08 movement led by Liu Xiaobo, religious protests like Falun Gong demonstrations, and ethnic protests in Tibet and Xinjiang. The only large-scale mass protests led by the students and young intellectuals that have been tolerated and sometimes even encouraged in China are nationalist movements. The central authority has been skillful to divert general dissent and anger into nationalist upheaval against the West and/or its Asian rivals. On the other hand, the government has been cautious to preempt any potential coalition that might turn a student nationalist protest into a brewing anti-government social movement.

In contrast to other forms of channeling tactics like petitioning or grassroots elections, protests may bring risks of insurrection or instability. But mass protests usually directly and acutely shed light on the most serious social contentions, official malfeasance, and policy failures. The Party-state has absorbed protest and demonstration as an indispensable element of its channeling mechanism on which it relies to keep in touch with the public mood and sentiment, monitor local officialdom, and enforce national policy implementation.

STATE SOCIETY RELATIONS

The CCP regime's repression and channeling methods present seemingly contradiction. It prevents the citizenry from protesting and tries to reduce the cost of repression, yet meanwhile relies on grassroots collective contentions to gain critical information and monitor its officialdom. The Party obviates any trajectory toward democracy. However, it is also the Party itself that ushers in democratic institutions to accommodate the discontents and lessen the risk of being overthrown. Scholars have noticed this intrinsic contradiction of the Chinese political landscape (Lorentzen 2014; Dickson 2016; Heurlin 2016; Tang 2016; Truex 2017; MacKinnon 2011). It seems that the CCP regime has encountered a great dilemma once acknowledged by Mikhail Gorbachev when he initiated political reform *glasnost* in the former Soviet Union. Some scholars warn that the deepening dilemma may constrain the viability of the CCP regime (e.g., Dickson 2016). Others believe that "soft authoritarianism," which is coined by David Shambaugh (2016, 2) to refer to political liberalization and loosening from 1998 to 2008 in China, is the key of regime durability and prosperity. If the authority changes its path to constrain civic life and hold back political liberalization, as happened particularly after Xi Jinping's incumbency, the regime will become stagnant and rigid and may eventually collapse (Shambaugh 2016; Pei 2016; Minzner 2018).

Absorbing democratic institutional settings in its political system is no doubt an important factor to prolong the CCP regime's authoritarian rule. But will this "political liberalization" deepen the government's dilemma and eventually result in the demise of the Party-state? Or will political retrenchment restrain socioeconomic development and unleash the dissatisfied societal forces for regime change? What is the nature of and where is the balance between the paradoxical political ruling strategies? How does the coexistence of repression and channeling impact on the state-society relations in China?

Based on the detailed analysis of multifarious blocking, dredging, and channeling tactics of the CCP regime in the above two sections, here we present an alternative explanation to illustrate the state-society relations in China. The repressive and channeling tools adopted by the Party-state have interwoven and evolved into a sophisticated ruling mechanism. In China, more political space and channeling venues, though bounded, soften the state-society relations, which contributes to the persistence of the regime.

However, it is important to recognize that this bounded public space doesn't necessarily imply successful democratic penetration in China's authoritarian system. More political space for public engagement is not just concessions made by the state under the increasing pressure from society; it is more of an imperative tactic of the state to deal with information deficiency, policy misinterpretation, and principal-agent problem in a conscious effort to manage its massive bureaucratic system. Moreover, the channeling methods adopted by the pragmatic state are not exclusively democratic institutional settings that were borrowed from the West. Some of the methods are inherited from the imperial past or the Mao era, emphasizing paternalistic role of the state and at odds with the democratic rule of law. The intriguing fact is that, despite the growing number of petitions and organized contentions, public support of the government constantly remains high. Thus, we propose that the paradoxical ruling mechanism entails a unique state-society relation which has reached a quasi-equilibrium via a constantly updated social contract. Furthermore, political liberalization is never among the fundamental consensus reached by the state and society to form their social contract. Therefore, prediction of regime collapse due to lack of further liberalization miscalculates the essential elements that maintain the stable, sometimes even collaborative, state-society relation and how this relation impacts the regime durability.

An Updated Social Contract

The social contract thesis, developed by Enlightenment Age theorists Thomas Hobbes, John Locke, and Jean-Jacques Rousseau, theorizes the relation between state and individuals and sheds light on the origin and formation of government legitimacy, obligation, and social order. This theoretical framework of a contractual state-society relation has been tailored by scholars in the 1970s and 1980s to account for stability in the post–Stalin era communist autocracies (Cook 1993). They ascribe the social quiescence and conformity to a calculated agreement between the communist rulers and the ruled to exchange material benefits for regime support. This social contract thesis also explains the dissolution of the former communist countries in the Soviet Union and Eastern Europe, partially as a consequence of failure to fulfill the socioeconomic commitment due to stagnant planned economies (Cook and Dimitrov 2017).

The Chinese equivalent of the social contract concept can be harkened back to the Shang Dynasty (1600 B.C.–1046 B.C.), when the overthrow of the last emperor of Xia was interpreted as losing the Mandate from Heaven due to his immoral behavior and failure to care for and protect the people. Later, this idea was adopted by Confucius and Mencius to form a mature political doctrine justifying imperial rule in China. Developed based on the paradigm of perfectible human nature, the Confucian concept of "Mandate of Heaven" emphasizes the morality of the ruler and his benevolent reign as the fundamental source of regime legitimacy. The contractual nature lies in the pragmatic precept that instantly legitimizes successful power takeover by the rebel leaders, if the previous ruler loses his morality and benevolence and therefore can no longer be supported by the people and is worthless for the Heaven.

This "feudal superstition" social compact has bonded state and society for thousands of years, guiding ebbs and flows of over a dozen of dynasties in China. This Mandate of Heaven social contract concept is still very much relevant in the 20th century and even the new millennium, though Confucianism was largely discredited and declined after the Qing dynasty was toppled (Perry 2001; Tong 2011; Zhu 2016). It was Sun Yat-Sen's "Three Principles of the People" that helped evoke the Chinese people to break the social contract with the decaying Qing dynasty. Mao's *Mass Line* and land reform successfully mobilized the populace in the power struggle with the corrupt Nationalist government. In the Mao era, the underlying social contract was not dissolved. To the contrary, it was reinforced by incorporating a second dimension which highlighted the guardian role of the monolithic communist state in wealth accumulation and public good provision. But soon this simple implicit exchanging material well-beings for regime support was stalled by the crippled planned economy, just as happened in the former Soviet Union and the Eastern European countries.

When the socialist pact confronted a dead end, the pragmatism of the Confucian dimension of the Chinese social contract saved the fate of the CCP regime. The social contract was renewed when the communist party decided to resort to economic capitalism for regime survival. During the early phase of the reform, the liberalization and openness have resulted in an influx of Western democratic ideas and dramatic political loosening of the government. In the first time of contemporary Chinese history, the relatively relaxed political environment in the late 1980s tipped the state-society balance in favor of the latter. Chinese society grew more autonomous and discontent, in contrast to a decentralizing state with fledging economy, declining ideology, old-fashioned repressive ruling methods, and prevailing corruption and inflation. The consequent tragic Tiananmen Square Massacre has marked a watershed in terms of state-society relations in China. Both the Party-state and Chinese well being society have become more practical and strategic ever since the tempestuous 1989.

Since Deng's Southern Tour, the Chinese social contract has been recalibrated. The pact is no longer a simple deal of trading economic advancement for political rights and civil liberty. It features guardianship, mutual compromise, and collaboration. The Party-state enjoys continuous political monopoly on the condition of social stability, economic prosperity, and benevolent governance. In other words, the ruled, that is the various socioeconomic forces, acknowledges and supports the privileges of the CCP in its complete reign of political power; conversely, the CCP vows to boost the economy by all means including privatization, even though at odds with its official ideology, and guarantees to make the rules of the game as fair as possible to ensure ample chances for all participants to fulfill their benefits and interests. The CCP regime continues to assume the responsibility as the guardian of Chinese society, sponsoring economic reform and development, building infrastructure, promoting modernity, and providing public goods and welfare. What is distinguished from the old simple version of social contract is that the Party not only strives to stay attentive to social needs and grievances, but also takes steps to accommodate diverse demands and enlarge its supporting constituencies using various cooptation and channeling methods. For example, the Party-state has exerted an effort to institutionalize a consultative and deliberative system by initiating public hearings, holding opinion polls, taking online suggestions and providing feedbacks (Kornreich, Vertinsky, and Potter 2012; He 2014).

In exchange for better livelihood and social stability, the public has become cooperative and collaborative rather than opposite and challenging. That being said, it doesn't mean the Chinese people are obedient and quiescent and the regime is free of political contentions. To the contrary, the public continues to demand political space and to reap concession from the government, but in a bid to push the CCP regime to fulfill the contract, assist the government to better implement state policies, provide public goods, and achieve socioeconomic goals, not to overthrow it. Take mass protest for instance: it represents one of the most radical forms of public political confrontation with the state; nevertheless, most protesters in China believe they are the defenders of the grand policies, values, and laws of the Party-state (O'Brien and Li 2006; O'Brien 2013). Taking advantage of the division within the government, the Party-state has dealt with the collective contentions effectively and skillfully, diverting public dissatisfaction and grievances toward the localities and establishing a responsive image of the central government. Moreover, the CCP regime endeavors to stress the necessity of social stability, the benefits of political continuation and the urgency of economic development, which can only be provided by the Party itself.

Two fundamental pillars underlie the persistence of the social contract in China. Consensus has been reached between the Party-state and the mass public over two priorities, the primacy of people's well-being and social stability. The economic reform initiated by the Party in the late 1970s is an imperative remedy to the stagnant planned economy. Subsequent astounding economic growth has largely boosted the government's popularity, since the Party tightly associates regime survival with its economic performance. Centuries of poverty and underdevelopment has enhanced the desperation of the populace for economic growth and material progress. Being a late developer, China was forced to start up its economy in an established competitive global economic environment. The disadvantaged development position has further convinced the Chinese people that a strong and determined state is the only choice to help achieve their dream. All these has led many observers to believe that the popularity of the authoritarian regime rests entirely on the rapid economic growth. However, this intuitive conclusion is at odds with the continuing high support rate of the regime even as its GDP growth rate has fallen since 2012. Shi (2000, 553) finds that economic income is only weakly associated with people's confidence to engage in politics and has no effect on their political attitudes toward government. It is important to note that a deeply rooted understanding of good governance in Chinese society— *minben*—is not exclusively correlated with economic prosperity. A bad economy surely erodes regime legitimacy. But when the average living standard has reached a certain point, the public interest is diverted, and will demand the government to tackle other critical socioeconomic problems, being responsive and taking care of their livelihood as a whole. Whyte (2015) finds in several national surveys that the public angers are less driven by economic issues but more by bad governance. Apparently, the Party-state is fully aware of this. The CCP regime, particularly during the Hu and Xi administrations, has embarked on a series of populist policies to address various challenges such as rising income inequality, environmental degradation, and rampant corruption, even though some of the policies may conflict with short-term economic goals. More studies posit that the Party-state somehow has managed to be relatively accountable even absent a democratic system (Heurlin 2016; Tang 2016; Wright 2010; Teets 2013).

Second, the turbulent imperial past, the long-lasting internal conflict through the contemporary history, and the disastrous mass campaigns of the Cultural Revolution and the Great Leap Forward all have left deep imprint on Chinese society. The resultant economic recession and social mayhem after the collapse of the Soviet Union and Eastern European communist countries, as well as the chaotic aftermath and deteriorate economic situation of the North African and the Middle Eastern countries after the Arab Spring have reminded the Chinese people of the dangerous consequence of losing a powerful and stable political central authority. No other political force in China is strong enough to provide economic sponsorship and social order that is essential for continuing growth, opportunity and prosperity. As Halper (2010, 207–208) points out "It is the fear of chaos, of losing political and social control, that runs like an iron spine through the entire Chinese body politic." A history of mass poverty and starvation tend to sharply focus the mind. According to a survey in 2003, when asked where stability ranked as a social value, the Chinese respondents ranked it number two. The average position of stability among citizens in other countries was 23rd (Ramo 2004, 23). The

CCP regime has successfully managed such fear to its advantage as a typical autocracy. It wins the support from majority of its citizens by promising social order and political stability. To put it briefly, since the majority of Chinese people have a stake and bet in the game and many are winning, the incentive to change the status quo is tenuous. The fear of social disorder and concern of losing material gains have persuaded the masses to tolerate, sometimes even justify, the CCP regime's repressive control. The goals of general economic advancement and social stability have bonded state and society together, which largely underscore the central regime's longevity.

Taken all together, it appears that the relation between the state and Chinese society is molded by a dynamic social contract based on common goals and mutual obligations and benefits. To better understand the paradoxical phenomenon of political popularity of the CCP authoritarian regime and its self-conflictual ruling mechanism, we may need to depart from a "society against state" paradigm.

"Society against State" Model versus "State-Society Interdependent" Model

Civil society is widely regarded as an important instrumental indicator of state-society relations. During the past two decades, the phenomenal growth of diverse social groups has evoked heated scholarly debate on whether a civil society has emerged and promoted democratization in authoritarian China. Some scholars embrace the notion of a causal sequence between economic liberalization and political democratization, arguing that market mobility has released the mass public from the constraints of the state and promoted a nascent civil society in a transitional China. Others reject the optimistic proposition by revealing the state-dependent and cooperative nature of the emerging Chinese civic associations. Although these two lines of literature present opposite arguments, they both draw conclusions based on a common analytic framework, assuming that there is a confrontational relation between the state and society in China. Those who believe China has civil society demonstrate that eventually Chinese society will become autonomous and powerful and challenge the communist regime for full political rights and liberty. Those who hold a pessimistic view posit that the social groups in China are controlled, coopted, and sponsored by the state, thus are meaningless in representing the true sprint of the citizenship.

The civil society literature sheds lights on the development and some important features of the Chinese civil groups. But the arguments are exclusively based on the theoretical framework that derives from Western values and experience. Being overwhelmingly preoccupied by democratic criteria has led to neglect of the indigenous nuances of the state-populace interaction as well as the genuine effect of the citizenry activism on state-society relations and regime stability. No surprise, failure to explore Chinese state-society relations from its historical and cultural roots has also led to perplexing conclusion at odds with the empirical evidences.

The history of the emergence and transformation of European capitalism and democracy has largely contributed to the formation and preoccupation of the "society against state" paradigm in studying state-society relations. Both liberals and Marxists have historically highlighted the independent and protagonist role of the capital and labor as historical agents in the power struggle with the hegemonic agrarian state who represents the feudal interests and therefore largely constrains the political and socioeconomic opportunities of the newly emerged capitalist forces. The self-mobilization of the bourgeois "civil society" against the state authority lies in the heart of the evolution of the capitalist economy and Western democratization. Thus, the hegemonic state is inherently viewed by the individuals in the West with suspicion and hostility and often regarded as intruder carrying out its own interests and goals. And the intrinsic Western individualism adds another shade to the "society against state" mentality.

However, the historical roots and condition from which the Chinese state-society relation derives is very different from the one in the West. The presumed development process of capitalism which has strained state-society relations in the nineteenth century Western industrializers never took hold in the context of China as a late developer in a competitive world economy. Capitalism here emerges from a state-planned socialist economy. But this time the state plays a leading role in sponsoring economic liberalization and development, catering the interests and benefits of the emerging socioeconomic groups. From the perspective of political calculus, the key social forces have little incentive to act against the reformist state.

Go beyond aforementioned rational weighting, in China this political discourse has been heavily influenced and shaped by the traditional Confucian political culture as well as communist and socialist legacy. First, unlike in the West, where the paradigmatic assumption (and culture) holds that the human nature is imperfect and self-centered, the premise that man is inherently good and virtuous rests in the heart of the dominant political culture and philosophy in China. *The Trimetric Classic (sanzijing)*, which is a classic Confucian reading as one of the required texts for the young students in the imperial past and often used by the parents as a text for early readers now, starts with a well-known introductory verse, "People at birth, are naturally good" (*renzhichu xinbenshan*). The two opposite assumptions of humanity pave the foundation for the contrary views of the Westerners and the Chinese toward their respective state authority. In the West, it is widely acknowledged that the power of state and leaders need to be checked by various institutions and hold accountable by the people. While the Confucian culture emphasizes introspection and self-discipline as a means for the rulers to stay as role model with morality and virtue. The inner-Party "criticism and self-criti-cism" campaign in the Mao era is a typical reflection of this Confucian principle. The method has also been revived by Xi as a powerful weapon to rally the Party and the Chinese people and boost the government image and regime legitimacy.

Rule by virtue, not rule of law, has been widely acknowledged and wor-shiped throughout the Chinese history. Of course, the divined ideal virtuous ruling is materialized into "rule by wise man" in the real world. Lucian Pye (1992, xi) points out that "Awe of the magic of personal leadership rather than reverence for the majesty of law still governs Chinese feelings about power and authority." The traditional concepts of "*Qinchai*" (state-assigned special inspector) is continuously active and deeply entrenched in Chinese people's mindset. The Central Leading Group for Inspection Work, which is a coordination body established by the Party to manage disciplinary inspec-tions nationwide, has played a critical role in Xi's anti-corruption campaign. The specially assigned inspectors acted just like *Qinchai* in the imperial past. The discourse of "being mistreated by the corrupt local officials, suffering, petitioning, and finally being saved by the upright officials sent by the central authority" has frequently popped up in the popular films, TV series, and news stories. While people are inspired and cheered by how the righteous side defeats the bad and corrupted, few question the lack of effective institu-tions to check the abuse of power in the first place. The surge in the number of petitions contrasting with the relatively low increase in litigation and mediation (Chen 2011) suggests that Chinese people are more likely to use informal or non-institutional means for problem solving and grievance re-dress. All of the above reveal that in China the public's perception and attitudes toward power and authority are very different from their counter-part's in the West, which in deed characterizes the most earnest expectation for the state and deep trust with the regime.

Second, the Confucian concept of the "Mandate of Heaven," which is deeply rooted in Chinese society, postulates a paternal role of the state to care for the well-being of the populace. The moral and competent leaders repre-sent "Heaven" in their respective mandates to rule the state, serving as guar-dians of the people. Chinese society holds high expectation of the state and respects the authority as head of the family. The built-in sense of community and collectivism further enhances this positive view about the state authority. The traditional term of "*Fumuguan*" (parent official), though being criticized as outmoded, has persistently appeared in people's day-to-day vocabulary, reflecting an enduring paternalistic and Confucian image of the government in the societal subconscious (Tong 2011, 152). The founding father of West-ern capitalism Adam Smith limits the government obligations to three major functions: national defense, law and order, and the provision of public goods. Quite the contrary, traditionally the Chinese people expect a strong and big government to take care of every problem (Pye 1992). The modern lifestyle has made the ordinary Chinese even more dependent on the state for all kinds of problem solving and public goods provision. For example, the public frequently craves the state for protection of their financial interests, such as to intervene in the stock market to reverse the downturn, or to bail out the hundreds of collapse P2P companies in the lending crisis in 2018 (Zhang and Glenn 2018). Hence, as long as the CCP regime keeps perceptively catering to the needs of the public, the state enjoys the support from society.

Martin Jacques (2009) in his book *When China Rules the World* identifies China as a "civilization-state" instead of commonly known "nation-state." He argues that the glorious history, diverse culture, religion, and ethnicity, and ways of thinking are all integral part of China as a state. His innovative notion has profound implication to the state-society relations in China. Great potency of assimilation and accommodation make it possible for the Chinese civilization to survive repeated wars, foreign aggression, division and integration, and changes of dynasty throughout thousands of years. For the ordinary Chinese people, their sense of belonging and national identity has been primarily shaped by this strong and continuous civilization. Thus, one important source of state legitimacy in China comes from the mass public's instinctive desire for the extant authority to revitalize and prolong the civilization. While the Westerners may discern a clear line between the young communist regime and old imperial China, the people in China are more likely to see the Party-state as the embodiment and defender of the Chinese civilization. After all, it is widely perceived that the communist party has played a critical role in anti-colonialism movement and led the anti-Japanese war, saving China from "a century of humiliation" by foreign invaders.

In addition, the political attitudes and perception toward state authority in China has also been calibrated by Marxism and Communism legacy. The decline of Marxism and prevailing of pragmatism created a false sense that the communist ideology is obsolete, with its fading impact on the Chinese people. However, the ideology was never uprooted in China. In their book *Communism's Shadow*, Pop-Eleches and Tucker (2017) find that people with more living experience in a communist country, especially as adults, are less supportive of democracy and more in favor of public welfare provision. Though practicing capitalism economically, China is still officially ruled by a single communist party. The mass public has been exposed in a communist regime for a lifetime. Although it has officially broken away from the planned economy doctrine, the CCP regime has never ceased to educate the young generation with Marxist ideas and knowledge. Of course, in an environment of growing consumerism and pragmatism, the communist ideology is no longer dominant. However, the mandatory education and daily propaganda has equipped the Chinese public with an alternative way of thinking. For example, when looking at China through a Western prism, the focus is more on its non-democratic authoritarian nature. But in the eyes of Chinese people, China is first a peripheral developing country. The 2008 financial crisis, the election scandals in the West, even the escalating trade war has kept reminding the Chinese people that Karl Marx might be right about many things, such as flaws of the capitalist system, economic cycles, and how economics determines politics. Scholars even find that the Chinese people are generally supportive of state propaganda (Esarey, Stockmann, and Zhang 2017).

Public perception and attitude toward the central authority is a crucial instrumental barometer of society-state relations. The earlier analysis suggests that rational calculation, Confucian political culture, and communist legacy all play important roles in shaping the Chinese public's attitudes and perception toward the CCP regime. The society-state dynamics in China is not necessarily bounded by a zero-sum "society against state" paradigm. Moreover, transcending a contractual relationship, there are signs of ecological interdependence and partnership between the CCP state and society. The mass public relies on the government for industrial development, material benefits and welfare provision in a late-developing economy. In return, the public's demand and support for economic development help the reformists justify and promote further market liberalization policies. The state depends on grassroots organizations such as residents' committees to expand service provision and administrative capacity in response to the budgetary deficiency and growing needs of the public due to improvement of the living standard and modern lifestyle. Various social groups anticipate that the state will fulfill their interests and policy preferences. To improve governance, the state has resorted to growing NGOs and social associations for their professionality, expertise, and resources. The CCP regime has to count on the public through various communication channels to keep an eye on lower-level governments, get feedback on policy implementation and outcome, and identify severe social problems so as to contain them before escalating into large scale social uprising. Exploiting the state-supervised political space and the division within the government, the public finds legitimate avenues to redress grievances, vent anger, and participate in policy decision making. Though controlled by the government, this bounded political participation has increased the public efficacy and political support, smoothing the authoritarian rule. Furthermore, the indifference of majority of the populace toward organized contentions make it easier for the government to crack down on dissident movement with political agenda.

At this point, we need to reassess the nature of the repressive and channeling ruling mechanism in China from this "society-state interdependent" angle. Using the Western standard of "civil society" to dismiss the quality and sphere of the public space generated by the channeling methods leaves out a huge part of public activism that is meaningful and significant to account for the dynamic interaction between the CCP regime and Chinese society. Based on our analysis of channeling methods of the Party-state, we roughly divide various forms of state-society interaction into three categories.

First, there are state-society interplays through institutional arrangements that have been borrowed from the Western democracies such as election, public hearing, NGOs, and consultation and deliberation. These institutional settings promote democratic values by allowing the public certain political rights practices and accumulating democratic participation experiences. It is this type of interaction that catches most attention from scholars thanks to its democratic propensity to trigger the public's growing demand for further empowerment. However, analysis based on "state-society interdependent" model may yield different prospects. Although the Party-state has adopted these democratic institutions, it has no intention to use them for the democratic purpose; rather, it has co-opted or adapted them. All the Party desires is to improve governance and boost its image as a benevolent government. Therefore, these institutions have been redevised to fit the Chinese authoritarian context and reduce their subversive features. For example, election has been limited to the sub-national level and voting procedures have been constrained (Read 2000; Sun 2014). Nevertheless, these institutions are far more than mere façade. The Party shows quite a degree of sincerity to channeling the mass public, indicating its dependence on society. The state has taken steps to build communication infrastructure and bureaucratic capacity to mobilize and facilitate public participation (Huang and Yang 2002). For example, in the village elections, people enjoy relatively freedom to vote for the candidates they genuinely support, and the candidates sponsored by the Party are allowed to lose (Schubert and Ahlers 2012). Most villagers' committees are elected rather than appointed by local governments (Sun 2014).

When scholars focus on the effects of institutionalization on the stability and democratic prospect of the regime, few pay attention to the fact that some important institutional settings draw their roots from the imperial past or the Mao era such as petitioning, government special inspection, or residents' committees. This second type of interaction through non-democratic institutions along with the third type of informal direct interplay such as protesting and online mass incidents share features that highlight the guardian role of the authoritarian state. The motivation for the mass public to petition rests on their belief that the local government may be abusive, and some cadres may be corrupted, but that the central authority is still responsive and caring and there are always upright and conscious officials that could help redress their grievances. The findings of "rightful resistance," that the protestors may use laws, state policies and values to attract attention and intervention of the higher levels authorities, clearly illustrates the significant role of the guardian state concept in shaping contentious strategy and behavior. Besides, traditional channeling institutions and informal direct state-populace interaction foster a populist way of citizenry participation. The Party-state has a tradition of promoting mass mobilization to achieve policy or political goals. For instance, the state has recruited Internet police from college students and ordinary citizens. Trusted retirees have been organized through residents' committees as neighborhood patrols to watch for any signs of unrest and irregularity (Levin and Wong 2013). Tang (2016) argues that *Mass line* strategy encourages direct communication between state and the public, fostering populist governance and red-guard-like behavior of the masses.

Promoting the rule by virtue rather than rule of law constitutes another feature of these two types of channeling methods. In most cases, the government would bypass the legal process and administrative institutions and intervene the problem solving or remedy process directly. The CCP regime is not able to enforce popularity through free national election. But this direct vertical communication effectively boosts the public trust and support. Hence, the state heavily relies on these two types of interactions despite the fact that they are more confrontational and riskier. Moreover, the Chinese public seems to prefer the non-democratic channeling institutions and direct dialogue with the state over administrative process and litigation because, as long as they can successfully attract the attention of the state elites and induce intervention, they often get what they want in a timely manner, sometimes even more than what they may have gotten by going through formal legal procedures.

NOTES

1. The data are from both Edelman trust barometer and the WVS.

2. According to an ancient Chinese legend, about 4,000 or 5,000 years ago, Yu the Great successfully combated the recurrent flooding of the Yellow River by strengthening dams to block the water on the one hand, dredging rivers and building channeling networks to divide the floods on the other.

3. The data are from the Immigration and Refugee Board of Canada.

4. The administrative rule states that the setting of local police stations parallels the administrative setting of township and street level offices. http://www.mca.gov.cn/article/sj/tjjb/qgsj/2018/201806041601.html.

5. The data come from the statistics of the Ministry of Civil Affairs of the PRC. See more detail from: http://www.mca.gov.cn/article/sj/tjjb/qgsj/2018/201806041601.html.

6. The data come from the annual statistics of the CCP. See more detail from: http://www.xinhuanet.com/politics/2018-06/30/c_1123059570.htm.

7. See *History of Song (Song Shi):* https://ctext.org/wiki.pl?if=gb&chapter=992782.

8. See http://www.law-lib.com/law/law_view.asp?id=564 for the Organic Law of Urban Residents Committees in 1989; See http://www.npc.gov.cn/wxzl/gongbao/1987-11/24/content_1481517.htm for the Organic Law of Villager Committee in 1987.

9. See http://www.xinhuanet.com/politics/19cpcnc/2017-10/28/c_1121870794.htm for the Constitution of the CCP.

10. See the article "'Internet Public Opinion Analyst' Job Training Program Starts in Beijing." *People.com,* September 5, 2013. http://society.people.com.cn/n/2013/0905/c1008-22814404

.html.

11. See   http://old.moe.gov.cn/publicfiles/business/htmlfiles/moe/s6637/201207/139880 .html for the related order issued by the Ministry of Education in 2004.

12. See the article "China Gears up for Employment of 8.2 million College Graduates." *China   Daily*,   May   24,   2018.   http://www.chinadaily.com.cn/a/201805/24/ WS5b06cc57a31001b82571c23a.html.

13. See the article "China Sees Steady Graduate Employment Rate in 2017: Survey." *Xinhuanet*, June 11, 2018. http://www.xinhuanet.com/english/2018-06/11/c_137246978.htm.

14. Mencius and Xunzi were important Confucian philosophers. Mencius has been often regarded as the "second sage" after Confucius himself.

15. The data in this book about Chinese netizens and the Internet come from Annual Chinese Internet Public Opinion Analysis Report 2007–2017 by people.com. See more detail from: http://yuqing.people.com.cn/GB/401915/408999/index.html.

16. See Freedom House's reports on freedom of the press from 2002 to 2017. The index measures media censorship with 0 refers to most free and 100 means least free. https://freedomhouse.org/report/freedom-press/2002/china.

17. In 2003, Sun Zhigang, a graphic designer with a college degree from Wuhan, was placed in a custody and repatriation center by the police in Guangzhou where he worked due to lack of a temporary residence permit. He was attacked by staff and inmates and died three days later. His death caused a nationwide criticism of the custody and repatriation system.

18. See http://www.gov.cn/zhengce/content/2016-08/12/content_5099138.htm for the related State Council order in 2016.

19. The data come from the statistics of the Ministry of Civil Affairs of the PRC. See more detail from: http://www.mca.gov.cn/article/sj/tjjb/qgsj/2018/201806041601.html.

Part II

The Second Domestic Dimension

Is Chinese Society Ready for Regime Change?

Chapter Five

Stability at Risk?
Party Elites and Factionalism

Factionalism is a persistently defining feature of China's elite politics. The complex internal power struggles, personal alliances, and factional alignments at the top, among and between retired elites, incumbents, and prospective new leaders, have been shaping the landscape of leadership politics since the reform. Factional activities are widely acknowledged as detrimental to political rationality and stability throughout the world. For example, intraparty conflicts in Japan have caused frequent leadership turnover and thwarted the government's capacity for economic management as well as policy implementation and continuity (Park 2001). In its own history, the CCP regime has suffered the turbulence brought about by the Cultural Revolution, which was mobilized by Mao as a means of power struggle and political purge (Huang 2000; Miller 2015). Though factional infighting has continued throughout the post-Mao era, the Party-state has managed to stay robust with relatively smooth leadership transitions and consistent economic reform and policies. How does the Party-state survive the vicious factional politics and prevent internal conflicts from imploding the one-party political system, at least for now?

This chapter explores that question by analyzing the political interests and perceptions of the Party elites as well as the features of factionalism of the CCP regime since the reform era. We argue that, unlike the ideologically based sharp rifts in the Mao era, the political cleavage in the reform period is primarily interest-driven and power-seeking, having little connection with any distinct ideology or political goal. Limited institutionalization, collective leadership, and meritocracy have played important roles in ameliorating the negative effects of factionalism. Moreover, bridging the provincial-central state division by patronizing local officials and cadres and using public support as leverage in factional politics have also brought a silver lining to the gloomy tussle among Party elites. The chapter also examines President Xi's actions to crack down on corruption, regarded by some scholars as a cynical power play to purge the factionally disloyal in the Party, as well as his abolishment of presidential term limits, considered a big setback for political institutionalization in China. The impact of Xi's prolonged rule on factionalism and political stability in China is also discussed.

EVOLUTION OF CHINESE FACTIONALISM
IN THE POST-DENG ERA

Factionalism has been officially denounced by the CCP following the disastrous Cultural Revolution and the collapse of Mao's personality cult (Francois, Trebbi, and Xiao 2016). In 2014, under the background of a nationwide anti-corruption campaign, the Politburo emphasized that "Banding together in gangs, forming cliques for private ends, or forming factions is not permitted within the party."[1] However, factionalism has been an indispensable strategy for retired senior leaders attempting to retain influence, and for incoming elites to consolidate power in the one-party political system. Despite official condemnation, factional conflicts have been "an inevitable and integral aspect of leadership politics" (Miller 2015, 2).

Before Xi Jinping's incumbency, it was widely acknowledged that Chinese elite politics had been dominated by two major factions: the elitist and populist coalitions.[2] The elitist coalition, originally derived from "*Shanghaibang*" (Shanghai gang), emerged in the Jiang Zemin era. Being selected by Party leaders headed by Deng suddenly to replace Zhao Ziyang following the Tiananmen Square protests, Jiang had to face a complex situation alone with inadequate connections and support (Nathan 2003, 8). As Jiang's power in the Party grew, the "Shanghai gang" evolved to include not just Jiang's former associates in Shanghai such as Zeng Qinghong, Huang Ju, and Wu Bangguo, but also other important members not from Shanghai, such as Jia Qinglin, Li Changchun, and Zhang Dejiang. This elitist coalition has been closely associated with "princelings," the descendants of prominent and influential senior revolutionary communist leaders of the PRC, during the Jiang and Hu administration. In the 18th Politburo Standing Committee (PSC), the highest ranks of Party leadership, four out of seven belonged to the elitist coalition. There have been several informal groups and circles that kept patron-client ties with the elitist faction. For example, the "*Shiyoubang*" (Petroleum gang) was nurtured and led by Jiang's first Shanghai staff chief Zeng Qinghong and Zhou Yongkang, who had extended his career across several important governmental sectors in China: oil, land, and the national police apparatus. Zhou was a member of the 17th PSC and later was convicted during Xi's anti-corruption crackdown (SCMP 2014a). The "Petroleum gang" consisted of some top officials who began their professional careers in the petroleum business.

In 2002, China experienced the first smooth leadership transition since reform. But after a decade of power accumulation, Jiang's elitist coalition reached its peak during the early days of the Hu-Wen administration. During the 16th PSC, at least six of nine members belonged to the elitist coalition. Meanwhile, another informal intraparty faction, the populist coalition, emerged along with the rise of their patron Hu Jintao. Many leading figures including Hu Jintao and Li Keqiang began their careers in the Communist Youth League and the faction has therefore been labeled as "*Tuanpai*" (Youth League faction). Unlike the elitist faction, most members of the *Tuanpai* come from humbler family backgrounds and tend to have had leadership experiences in the inland provinces, making them more amenable to the public and often in support of policy favor the vulnerable social groups, in contrast to the elitist faction (SCMP 2014a).

The relatively clear division between the elitist and populist factions has been blurred following Xi's escalation to the top power. The emergence and growth of Xi's own network of patronage has replaced the bifurcation in China's politics with tripartite dynamic of factions headed by Xi and his two predecessors. Xi strived to build his own inner circle following Jiang and Hu's examples after he gained power by promoting former associates he trusted from his earlier leadership bases in Shaanxi, Fujian, and Zhejiang provinces, for example, the "*Shaanxibang*" (Shaanxi Gang), which includes Xi's friends and associates in his formative years in Shaanxi such as Wang Qishan, and the "*Zhijiang Xinjun*" (New Zhijiang Army), composed of former associates during Xi's term in Zhejiang province like Chen Min'er and Cai Qi (Li 2013). In the meantime, Xi has been undertaking the most influential anti-corruption campaign since 2012, gaining him public support and largely weakening the factional groups of Jiang and Hu by convicting some important figures in Jiang's clique such as Zhou Yongkang and Xu Caihou, and in Hu's group like Ling Jihua, the former aide of Hu during his presidency and an important figure in the *Tuanpai*. The members of Jiang's clique on the PSC dropped from three in the 18th NCCPC in 2012 to only one in the 19th five years later (Table 5.1).

NATURES AND FEATURES OF FACTIONAL POLITICS

Interest-Driven and Power-Seeking Factions

Unlike the factional politics in the Mao era and at the beginning of China's reform period based on the ideological gap between "proletariat revolutionaries" and "powerholders taking the capitalist road," and political differences between "reformers" and "conservatives," respectively, the Party elite contentions in the post-Deng era are more driven by self-interest and power-seeking (Miller 2015). The complex factional structure and ties have been built and interwoven primarily based on patron-client relations with limited ideological or policy traction (Cohen 2012a; Miller 2015; Zeng 2013). For instance, Jiang is a relative reformist who promoted economic liberalization and privatization, in particular his "Three Represents." But some of his loyal cronies, such as Zhang Dejiang, are more conservative and favor development of the state-owned economy (Li 2013). Officials rely on their patrons and related factional connections for advancement and promotion. Their political careers and affiliated faction will face major setbacks if the power of their patron(s) declines due to age, health, or conviction for corruption. For example, Jiang Zemin's age, 93 now, coupled with the rise of Xi and his affiliates, rendered the once powerful elitist coalition inevitably heading toward a low ebb. Some princelings who used to be associated with Jiang's group have since found a new patron as Xi's power grows. The "Shanxi Gang" was itself sacked along with the fall of its boss Ling Jihua (SCMP 2014b).

In addition, the unique Chinese *guanxi* has exerted duel effects on the Party elite dynamics. On one hand, personal connections such as families, friends, associates, veterans, and alumni serve as underlying bricks to shore up the unity of the factions. This *guanxi* is very different from the factional ties which emphasize loyalty, alliance, and mutual protection. On the other hand, *guanxi* also links members from different factions, creating space and opportunity for negotiations and flexibility, making the various elite circles in China liquid and relatively loosely organized (Bo 2007). For example, Miller (2015) questions the affiliation of Liu Yunshan, a firm crony of Jiang's camp but who also maintains connections with Hu; and Li Yuanchao, widely regarded as a solid follower of Hu Jintao, though also a princeling with a political career background in Shanghai and Jiangsu. Another example is Yu zhengsheng, a princeling who played an important role in cracking down on Bo Xilai, the former mayor of Chongqing, himself another princeling associated with Jiang's camp. Yu was also regarded as Jiang's protégé during the Hu-Wen administration. But Yu and Xi Jinping's families have known each other for decades. Yu soon shifted to become one of the important figures of the "iron triangle" of Xi's newly rising inner circle (Li 2014a).

Consensus beyond Division

Though seemingly divided at the top leadership in the post-Deng era, the political elites in China all agree on one critical bottom line: nothing should threaten the Party's grip on power. The elites' political struggles are only possible while they hold the reins of power. The 1989 Tiananmen prodemoc-

Table 5.1.   Factionalism in the 16th to 19th Politburo Standing Committees

	Jiang	Hu-Wen	Xi	Uncertain
16th PSC 2002–2006 (9)	Jiang Zemin Wu Bangguo Jia Qinglin Zeng Qinghong Huang Ju Li Changchun Luo Gan	Hu Jintao Wen Jiabao	N/A	
17th PSC 2007–2011 (9)	Wu Bangguo Jia Qinglin Li Changchun Zhou Yongkang	Hu Jintao Wen Jiabao Li Keqiang	Xi Jinping*	He Guoqiang
18th PSC 2012–2016 (7)	Zhang Dejiang Liu Yushan Zhang Gaoli	Li Keqiang	Xi Jinping Wang Qishan	Yu Zhengsheng**
19th PSC 2017–2021 (7)	Han Zheng	Li Keqiang Wang Yang	Xi Jinping Li Zhanshu	Zhao Leji *** Wang Huning****

Note: *Xi Jinping was considered associated with Jiang's camp before the 18th PSC; **Yu Zhengsheng was regarded as one of the "iron triangle" of Xi's faction (Li 2014). But Yu is a member of princelings, also associated with Jiang's camp before the 18th PSC. ***Zhao Leji is considered relatively neutral. ****Wang Huning is also considered relatively neutral, with connections with Jiang, Hu, and Xi.

racy movement served as a wake-up call that constantly reminds the Party elites how dangerous it could be if the top leadership is deeply split along fundamental political or ideological lines. The collapse of the Soviet Union caused huge repercussions in the society of communist China, particularly within the Party elite. They were eager to understand the causes of the communist regime collapse and desperate to take any measures necessary to avoid a similar fate of overthrow. The political elites in China are convinced that wrong leadership decisions, failure to deliver economic reforms, and ideological erosion by Western liberal ideals and the U.S. policy of "peaceful evolution" all contributed to the fall of the largest communist system in the world (Meisels 2013). In response, the Party leadership has reached consensus on the Party's two paramount guidelines to maintain its rule: steadfast economic reform and zero tolerance of any political challenge. Deng's cautious reform principles have been unanimously respected and implemented: "Economic reforms are not juxtaposed with a democratized political system; state governance will never follow the Western model of tripartite separation of powers; and every major reform policy has to be channeled through the existing authoritarian bureaucracy" (Ho 2012, 515). Though belonging to different factions, survival instincts make the Party elites share common concerns regarding social uprisings and economic reform, and assertive attitudes toward any threat to the status quo. Beja (2006) suggests that major national unrest, such as the Xidan Democracy Wall in the late 1970s, can happen when an insoluble intraparty rift exists. Resultant relaxation and even support from the top would greatly encourage the protestors. In China, power struggles over political and ideological projects have disappeared from the leadership since 1992, following Deng's Southern tour (Beja 2006). Since then, China has enjoyed the longest period in the history of the PRC with no major national protest movements (Chan, Backstrom, and Mason 2014). The temporary alliance of Jiang, Hu, and Xi to punish and oust Bo Xilai, a protégé of Jiang, best exemplifies this consensus beyond division. Bo Xilai's high-profile campaign to promote Maoist and patriotic values in public and mobilize hard line leftists at all levels of society directly challenged the compromised balance among the top leaders as well as the regime's stability; it immediately made him a threat to all the Party-elites across different factions (Shi 2012).

Collective Leadership, Institutionalization, and Informal Partisanship

Following the death of Mao, Deng Xiaoping institutionalized future leadership transition and established a mechanism of collective policymaking in an effort to preempt strongman rule in the reform era (Miller 2015; Nathan 2003). The regularization of political turnover and collective leadership were further enforced in the aftermath of the Tiananmen movement and the collapse of the Soviet Union. After Jiang formally and peacefully took over the leadership with Deng's blessing, and Hu Jintao was informally named by Deng to succeed Jiang 10 years later, the institutionalization of succession politics, though bounded, has taken firm hold in China. It was routinized that power transition from one leader to the next would happen every 10 years, consisting of two five-year terms of the presidency for each leader. In 1997, the retirement age of 70 was instituted by the Politburo to limit senior leaders from remaining for another term in the PSC. In 2002, another informal rule was established by consensus in Politburo, calling on those leaders reaching age 68 to retire before a new term. Wang Qishan, a close ally of Xi, did not enter the 19th PSC because he was 69 years old at that time. Zeng (2013) finds that age combined with institutional rules were significant in determining the appointment of leaders in the 18th NCCPC in 2012. Though it was speculated that the retirement rules were used by Jiang to target two rivals Qiao Shi and Li Ruihuan, the age limits have effectively promoted intraparty mobility and vitality. As such, norm-bound political institutionalization has yielded "orderly, peaceful, timely, and stable successions" (Nathan 2003, 7) of Party leaders for three generations, largely boosting regime stability.

Every five years, the NCCPC elects seven or more members of the PSC as the top leadership team to run the country. Every election the lineup ensures the public the unity and solidarity of the regime's regularized collective leadership, a political legacy of Deng that remains today. Scholars believe that the structure of elite politics in China is characterized by power-balance and secret decision-bargaining rather than zero-sum "winner-takes-all" policies (Li 2016; Bo 2007). Power decentralization makes negotiation and compromise among factions important and regularizes policymaking at the top. Furthermore, Li (2013, 36) argues that "something approximating a mechanism of checks and balances in the decision-making process" has emerged in China's factional one-party polity. He may be optimistic about the power-balancing trend of China's elite politics, given Xi's centralizing move toward one-man rule after the 19th NCCPC. Nevertheless, over the past decades, there were signs of factional power balance and consequent positive effects on policymaking. For example, the rise of the *Tuanpai* has successfully shifted the reform trajectory balance from focusing largely on economic liberalization and privatization, particularly in the East Coast regions, to issues of social equity, income inequality, environmental problems, and development in the inland West and countryside.

A Mix of Patrimonial Bureaucracy and Meritocracy

The conventional judgment suggests a dichotomy of meritocracy and clientelism as two incompatible types of government bureaucracies, based on Weber's distinctions between bureaucracy and patrimonialism (Weber 1946; Evans 1995). However, China's well-established and functioning Confucian civil service examination system, one putative measure of merit since the Tang dynasty has made its long-standing imperial bureaucracies an exception. Apparently, this inherited political wisdom has been incorporated by the CCP into its ruling mechanism nowadays. Unlike the Maoist period, when political loyalty and personal connection were regarded as the basis of official recruitment and promotion, selection based on merit has become one of the most important features of China's bureaucratic system in the reform era in response to increasing demands of technocratic and professional capacity in policymaking and administration (e.g., Bell 2015; Edin 2003; Wright 2015). From the *Guokao*, China's national civil service exam, to Party's cadre evaluation system, to its strict meritocratic criteria in selecting and promoting high-ranking officials and even top leadership, the Party-state has successfully embedded meritocratic feature into its otherwise patrimonial bureaucracy, largely contributing to the regime's continued dynamism and viability. Nathan (2003, 10) points out that "There have always been both meritocratic and factional elements in promotions within the Chinese party-state." Bell (2015) even considers China's political meritocracy as an alternative system to Western liberal electoral democracy.

Empirical studies support the assertion that factional tie plays a large role in political advancement (e.g., Shih, Adolph, and Liu 2012). But none of them identifies political affiliation as the dominant factor. Other variables, such as age, education qualification, even institutional rules, have exerted equally important, sometimes even more important, positive effects on ranking in the Party elite (Shih, Adolph, and Liu 2012; Zeng 2013). Age is often regarded as a proxy of accumulated political capital and experience as officials endure years of intraparty political struggle, implying they are more competitive (Shih, Adolph, and Liu 2012). A college diploma has become an "entry ticket" to the political elite club, thanks to the "four modernizations of cadres" (*ganbu sihua*) project launched by the Party in 1982. The percentage of the Politburo members that had obtained college education jumped from 4 percent in 1982 to 96 percent by 2012 (Zeng 2013). Over 84 percent of the 19th Politburo members held masters or PhD degrees, and four of them have had experiences of studying abroad.[3] The impact of family ties on political advancement is mixed. Some studies find substantial effects of princeling status on political advancement (Shih, Adolph, and Liu 2012); others report no linkage between princeling status and higher party rank of the political elites (Choi 2012; Zeng 2013). The obscure role of blood ties indicates that, contrary to the conventional perception, princeling status isn't the predominant standard of appointment and promotion, and the populist power in the Party leadership has been strengthened gradually. Nepotism and favoritism exist but are hardly prevailing phenomena because administrative skill, technical knowledge, educational background are equally important as political capital and a prerequisite for membership of top elite club. For example, even with Jiang's promotion and assistance, some of his close allies and supporters, such as his bodyguard You Xigui with little administrative experience and political credit can only rank at the bottom among the Alternate Central Committee members (Shih, Adolph, and Liu 2012, 176). In addition, political loyalty remains an important ranking criterion in promoting elite cohesion in a single-party regime. Lee (2015) finds studying in party schools, which provides indispensable political theory training, increases the opportunities being promoted. And patronage from one powerful senior leader or another is critical in political advancement, given all other factors are equally controlled. Overall, the meritocratic facets of the CCP regime's otherwise patrimonial authoritarian bureaucracy has made its officials more strategic, scientific, sophisticated, and well-planned, and largely enhanced the party's governing capacity, effectiveness, and endurability.

The Role of Factionalism in Bridging Central Local Division

The central vs. local division has been a long-standing concern of the Party-state, given China's large territory and huge population. The fiscal and political decentralization along with the economic marketization since the reform has transferred great power to localities. Provincial and local governments in China have gained relatively high autonomy and discretion over policy formulation and implementation. To protect local revenue sources and compete for business investment with other provinces, some local governments even circumvented or disregarded grand policy guidelines and regulations from above (Baum 1992, 497). Many administrative reforms and measures have been carried out by the Party-state since the 1990s to address this typical principal-agent problem, such as the cadre responsibility and evaluation system (Edin 2003).

Beyond bureaucratic control, political factionalism has been playing an important role in bridging the gap between the central government and local officialdom. A close scrutiny of the career experiences of top leaders in China in the reform era sheds light on the vertical factional connections between the central and local governments. For most senior leaders, previous regional leadership experience has been a critical and integral part of their political advancement. At that stage, they usually have already established mentor-protégé relationships with their patrons in the political elite circle at the top. Due to the Party norm of rotating cadres through different geographical areas (*ganbu jiaoliu zhidu*), the majority of them served as provincial level chiefs in at least two different regions (Table 5.2). Six of Seven of the 19th PSC members had leadership experiences at the provincial level. On the other hand, as Li (2014b) observes, "Top leaders have also drawn from the pool of provincial leaders in building their factional inner circles and regional power bases." In the provincial governments, the top two leaders, provincial party secretary and provincial governor, are often from two different factions (Francois, Trebbi, and Xiao 2016). For protégés at the local level, they always align their interest and loyalty with their patrons at the top, largely helping reduce provincial subversion and ensuring implementation of the directives and policies from the central government. For example, when Wang Yang, now a PSC member, was Guangdong party chief, he peacefully solved the Wukan incident by pacifying the protestors with a free election and sided with the villagers by criticizing the local officials for land grabs and failure to redress villagers' grievances (Cohen 2012b). As a firm member of the *Tuanpai*, Wang's move followed the Hu administration's policy on land acquisition and guideline of social management rather than protecting local government's interests. For the patrons at the top, establishing a provincial network of political protégés enables them to maintain control of the local officialdom and enhances regional integration.

Grassroots Support as Leverage of Factional Struggle

Though there is no fundamental political or ideological cleavage among
Chinese political elites, members of various factions do have different policy

Table 5.2.   Provincial Leadership Experience among Members of the 19th Politburo in 2017

Members	Areas of provincial-level leadership experience	Total
Xi Jinping	Fujian, Zhejiang, and Shanghai	3
Li Keqiang	Henan and Liaoning	2
Zhao Leji	Qinghai and Shaanxi	2
Wang Huning		0
Wang Yang	Anhui, Chongqing, and Guangdong	3
Han Zheng	Shanghai	1
Li Zhanshu	Hebei, Shaanxi, Heilongjiang, and Guizhou	4
Ding Xuexiang	Shanghai	1
Wang Chen		0
Liu He		0
Xu Qiliang		0
Sun Chunlan	Liaoning and Fujian	2
Li Xi	Shaanxi, Shanghai, and Liaoning	3
Li Qiang	Zhejiang and Jiangsu	2
Li Hongzhong	Guangdong, Hubei, and Tianjin	3
Yang Jiechi		0
Yang Xiaodu	Xizang and Shanghai	2
Zhang Youxia		0
Chen Xi	Liaoning	1
Chen Quanguo	Henan, Hebei, Xizang, Xingjian	4
Chen Min'er	Zhejiang, Guizhou, and Chongqing	3
Hu Chunhua	Xizang, Hebei, Inner Mongolia	3
Guo Shengkun	Guangxi	1
Huang Kunming	Zhejiang	1
Cai Qi	Zhejiang and Beijing	2

Source: Data are from *Xinhuanet* (http://www.xinhuanet.com//politics/19cpcnc/2017-10/
25/c_1121856249.htm).
Note: Following the method of Cheng Li (2014b, 3), provincial experience is defined as
service as vice governor, deputy party secretary, party standing committee member, or
above. The first seven leaders are members of the 19th PSC.

preferences and priorities. Most members of the populist coalition come from less-privileged families and often prefer less economic-driven policies to tackle problems accumulated since the reform, such as social injustice, economic inequality, or environment degradation (Li 2013, 37). For example, the former Premier Wen Jiabao, an ally of Hu Jintao, regarded wage collection for migrant workers as the subject of his personal crusade. Premier Li Keqiang, a leading figure of Hu's camp the *Tuanpai*, focuses more on social welfare programs and clean energy promotion than solely economic development. The efforts of the members of the populist coalition to voice the concerns of the marginalized lower class and vulnerable social groups do contribute to tension relief and win them popular support from the grassroots. To the populist coalition, popularity among the ordinary Chinese people is an important force to balance the sociopolitical and economic advantage of the elitist coalition, adding their leverage to the factional struggle at the top (Yang 2015, 35).

STRONGMAN RULE OR CONTINUITY OF FACTIONALISM

On March 11, 2018, about 3,000 delegates of the NPC voted almost unanimously to abolish term limits for the president and vice president of the country. The news stunned the world and incurred fear and criticism in the West, predicting that China led by Xi Jinping is heading back toward an unaccountable totalitarian regime and cultish state reminiscent of the Mao regime. Pessimists believe that Xi has undertaken more repressive measures to constrain the public political space and eliminated other leadership factions by selective anti-corruption campaigns, monopolizing China's government with an emerging "strongman" rule while completely marginalizing the established collective leadership (e.g., Shirk 2018; Pei 2017; Minzner 2018).

But will Xi Jinping become the second "Chairman Mao" and bring China back to a monolithic dictatorship? Considering the profoundly different political, economic, and social conditions, domestically and internationally, in contrast to China under the Mao's reign decades ago, it seems too early to draw such a dim conclusion.

First, many believe that Xi's repealing the presidential term limits has eroded the norms of collective leadership and Party power transition established by Deng following the death of Mao. This political move is important because it appears to be a big step backward in terms of intraparty institutionalization and injects uncertainty into China's elite politics. However, the impact has been somewhat exaggerated, because term limits is never the most effective factor to constrain personal power centralization in China. Moreover, the presidency is *per se* a symbolic head of state position without actual legal power; the two positions with real power—the party chief and military commission chairman have never had term limits. The critical factor that has contributed to collective rule and political decentralization since the early 1990s rests on the absence of strong political figures like Mao and Deng, whose power were largely rooted in their revolutionary past and firm control of "the barrel of a gun" (*qiangganzi*). In fact, as the revolutionary veterans in the Party turn older, the growing factionalism and party's rigid organizational structure and advancement norms have created a hostile environment for the rise of an all-powerful leader. In addition, even with the term limits, important political figures in China have been very influential within the successive party leadership many years after they left the office. Although Deng was the one to promote institutionalization of leadership succession, he was the *de facto* ruler in China almost until his death in 1997. Jiang and Hu still exert influence as powerful patrons even after they have long retired.

Second, the basis of Xi's leadership legitimacy is very different from that of Mao or Deng. Xi's political power since the very beginning of his incumbency was mainly derived from three sources. His education from one of China's top universities and excellent performance and consistently good reputation as provincial governors have been critical to his advancement. Beyond merit, the princeling background has also worked in his favor to build connections with the elitist coalition. As the son of Xi Zhongxun, an influential revolutionary leader, Xi Jinping has benefited from his princeling connections, which aligned him with the elitist faction and played an important role in his ascension to the CCP's top ranks. It was under the help of Jiang that Xi was added to the Central Committee of the Party as an over-quota member (Nathan and Gilley 2002). His experience as an "*zhiqing*" (urban educated youth in the countryside) having climbed the political ladder from the very bottom, and most importantly, political credit he gained from his father's alliance with Hu Yaobang, former chairman and party chief who promoted many *Tuanpai* officials, including Hu Jintao (Liu and Ip 2013), made him equally favored by the populist coalition. As such, connection and access to both factions became Xi's unique advantage that helps him reach the apex of political power. However, as a compromise leader, his power was at first dependent and fragile.

After he took over the power, Xi Jinping launched an extensive anti-corruption campaign. He was criticized for purging his political rivals by cracking down on corrupt officials selectively, particularly high-profile figures in both Jiang and Hu's camps. His anti-corruption campaign was unprecedented, because it targeted both low-level party cadres and senior political and military officials, such as Zhou Yongkang, a retired PSC member, the former chief of the Party's Central Political and Legal Affairs Commission, and a Jiang's ally; Ling Jihua, Hu's former aide and former chief of the Party's General Office; Xu Caihou and Guo Boxiong, two former vice chairmen of the Central Military Commission, China's top military body, both Jiang's protégés; and Sun Zhengcai, the nominal Hu's successor supported by Jiang (Albert and Xu 2018). The number of the full and alternate members of the Party's Central Committee arrested for corruption in the five years between 2012 and 2017 is 35, equal to the total number of counterparts punished by the Party in the previous six decades between 1949 to 2012.[4] Regardless of the political purpose, the anti-corruption campaign has won Xi Jinping nationwide popularity and heightened his top leader status in the Party. The competing factions of Jiang and Hu have been greatly weakened.

Although Xi publicly denounced and forbade factionalism in the party, like all his predecessors, he is fully aware of the importance of factional politics in consolidating his relatively fledgling power. Xi has endeavored to form his own faction "*Xijia jun*" (Xi family army), which is mainly composed of his princeling friends, alumni, and former associates at the provincial level. In the 19th Politburo, 15 out of 25 members (60 percent) are arguably affiliated with Xi. The reshuffle of the PLA's top echelons since 2012 reflects Xi's power expansion in the military by promoting protégés such as Xu Qiliang and Zhao Youxia, into important positions in the army (Lam 2017).

Ostensibly, Xi is much more powerful than Hu even in the latter's second term as party chief. Nevertheless, the fact that Xi's power base relies heavily on his personal connections and blood ties indicates Xi is still incomparable to the all-powerful political figures like Mao and Deng.

Third, Xi's power is not as unbounded as some China observers and Western media claim. There have been signs of nascent power balances and checks even after 19th NCCPC, an important landmark of Xi's leadership consolidation. For example, the paradoxical factional composition of the 19th Party's PSC suggests a compromised result and the continuity of the tripartite collective leadership, though it is more lopsided in the second term of Xi's rule (Li 2017). Wang Qishan, Xi's close ally, had to retire due to the age limit rules; and Jiang and Hu still have representatives in the highest Party decision-making body. As "parachuted" leaders, Xi's protégés also confront increasing difficulties in local governance. For example, the brutal mass eviction of migrant workers in Beijing led by the capital's party chief Cai Qi, Xi's protégé, created harsh criticism from society and even within the Party (Mai 2017). The disastrous history under Mao makes China a society second least tolerant of strongman leadership, compared to its neighbors with similarly strong Confucian influence (Figure 5.1). The growing personality cult and adulatory propaganda about Xi have raised concerns and spurred resistance from the ordinary people and intellectual elites, at a time when China is facing growing domestic and international challenges. For example, in July 2018, a young woman protested over Xi's "tyranny" by splashing ink on a poster of Xi; the related video went viral soon after. Xu Zhangrun, a law professor at Tsinghua University delivered a scathing critique condemning Xi's hardline policies and the government's tilting toward dangerous one-man rule (Buckley 2018a). It is intriguing to observe that a series of conces-sional actions have been undertaken to ease the social tensions; the author-ities started to take down posters of Xi after the ink-spraying incident (Nagai 2018), and research focusing on Xi's early years in the village of Liangjiahe in Shaanxi was called off (Lam 2018).

Some China observers believe that Xi represents the princelings, the "red aristocrats," and attempts to spearhead a revival of communist orthodoxies that carrying over from their parent revolutionary generation (e.g., Lian 2018). However, the princelings are better characterized as a loose group with diffuse interests rather than a highly unified ideology-driven faction. Some of them own businesses, becoming part of the emerging bureaucratic bourgeoisie (Ho 2012). In September 2018, an online article calling for end-ing the private economy induced panic and anxious speculation in China among the rising capitalists and the middle class that Xi intended to constrain capitalist economy. In late September, in response to fears in the business society, Xi was compelled to give a speech expressing his support for both SOEs and the private sector (The Economist 2018). There are other princel-ings that still revere Deng and believe that his domestic liberal economic

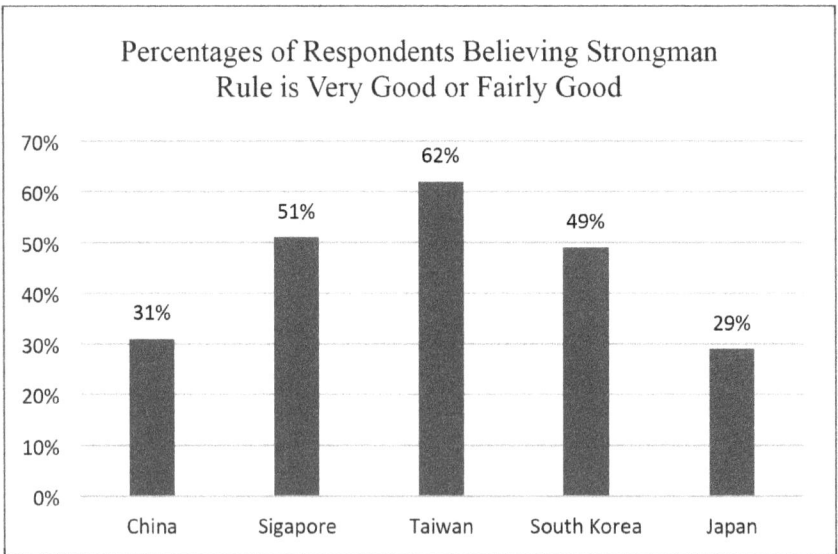

Figure 5.1.   Percentages of Respondents Believing Strongman Rule Is Very Good or Fairly Good Source: Author Generated. Data are from the WVS Round Six (Inglehart et al. 2014).

reform and international strategy of "keeping a low profile" should be continuously implemented. The growing trade war with the United States and the paralysis of negotiations have heightened the tension between the two largest economies in the world, causing rifts within the political elites at the top in China. Some important Party members criticized that Xi's assertive response to the trade war and cocky domestic boasting and nationalistic rhetoric have placed China in a dangerous and vulnerable position regarding Sino-U.S. relations (Buckley 2018a). In a speech given in the Disabled Person's Federation in 2018, Deng Pufang, the eldest son of Deng Xiaoping urged the Chinese government to "keep a sober mind and know our own place" (Yan 2018), a clear message showing his dissatisfaction with Xi's departure from Deng's fundamental reform policies and strategy.

Factionalism is usually associated with political instability and irrational policies. In a political system lacking an all-powerful man, playing factional politics is the only effective strategy for political elites to survive and rise through the ranks. In China, factional elite politics has coexisted with decades of peaceful socioeconomic development and three smooth leadership transitions since the late 1980s. Chinese factionalism has been impacted by the country's unique political, cultural, and socioeconomic context. The most important element that has prevented a catastrophic irreconcilable rift within the Party is the interest-oriented nature of all political factions. Since Deng, dangerous political or ideological rivalry has disappeared in China's leadership politics; this environment generates pragmatic and flexible factions, making almost every decision amenable to negotiation and compromise. The second critical factor that offsets the destructive effects of factionalism lies in the consensus of all political elites that nothing should threaten the Party's rule. The third pillar that forestalls extreme nepotism and favoritism and ensures Party robustness is the incorporated meritocracy in an authoritarian bureaucratic system. The constraining effect of these three factors on factionalism has been fortified by the regularization of leadership appointment, promotion and turnover in China. All of these enable political elites in China to maintain a balance between competing factions that is essential for regime stability. In addition, the close factional ties between the patrons at the top and protégés in the local governments effectively bridge the central-local division. And more importantly, factional power struggle also produces incentives for political elites to cater to the demands of the mass public and voice their concerns to garner popular support and political credit.

As for the changes since Xi rose to power, it is premature to predict a consequent strongman dictatorship and political instability in the near future. First, Xi's prolonged rule will give him time to address domestic and international challenges and fulfill his pledge of "China Dream" and building "*xiaokang shehui*" (a moderately prosperous society) in the critical period of China, as many are concerned about sharp policy shifts and discontinuity that would be more likely due to leadership turnover. Second, retaining power even after retirement is common in the elite politics of China. In this sense, abolishment of the presidential term limits simply exposes otherwise hidden facts. Xi will strive to maintain influence in the Party after he leaves office no matter whether the term limits are removed or reinstated. Third, as a compromise leader, Xi's power is relatively weak and dependent, in contrast to that of Mao or Deng. The fact that he has formed his own inner circle indicates factionalism is still very relevant. Moreover, there are signs of backlash both from society and the Party that may play an important role in constraining Xi's power consolidation. And most importantly, positive changes are being observed in response to the rising opposition voices, at least for now. It is too soon to conclude that Xi's power is constrained by criticism either from the public or the Party. However, it is doubtless that increasing domestic challenges and international pressures will make Xi prioritize political stability and be cautious on his path to power centralization.

NOTES

1. See the article "*Dangnei Jinzhi Labang Jiepai* (Forming Factions Is Not Permitted within the Party." *Xinhuanet,* December 29, 2014. http://www.xinhuanet.com/politics/2014-12/29/c_1113818162.htm

2. It is worth noting that though it is widely accepted, the existence of certain factions and who belongs in which faction are mainly based on educated speculation.

3. See the article "Education Qualification of Members of China's 19th Politburo." *Free Radio Asia*, November 24, 2017. https://www.rfa.org/mandarin/zhuanlan/yehuazhongnanhai/gx-11242017131235.html

4. See the article "Xi's Anti-Corruption Campaign." *BBC*, October 23, 2017. https://www.bbc.com/zhongwen/simp/chinese-news-41719314.

Chapter Six

Unexpected Allies

Coopted Capitalists and the Middle Class

Beyond the state-centric approach, liberals and Marxists have traditionally emphasized the critical role of social forces in regime change. They believe that the social cleavages and class alliances shaped by historical legacy and socioeconomic context largely determine the transition course that a regime heads to (Moore 1966; Moraze 1968; Luebbert 1987; Rueschemeyer, Stephens, and Stephens 1992; Bermeo 1997). The importance of the bourgeoisie or the role of working class and peasantry have been highlighted in their work respectively in explaining the variation of regime formation. Democratization occurs not simply as a natural consequence of economic prosperity and wealth accumulation *per se*. It is driven by dynamic and complicated class struggles and social interaction. Therefore, regime change is more "an outcome of actions, not just of conditions" (Przeworski and Limongi 1997, 177).

This line of enquiry is applied in the analysis of the following two chapters. The question of whether the CCP regime will survive or fall is explored from the angle of a state's legitimacy base: the people. Along with dazzling economic development, Chinese society has evolved in the past four decades from a proletarian/peasantry dominated state into a hierarchical social system with multifarious strata. Beyond the existing working class, intellectuals, and peasants, a new social cohort including private entrepreneurs and the middle class has arisen from within. Theoretically, all these social actors could initiate regime change and shed tremendous influence on the transitional process. Therefore, they deserve further scrutiny, but in a China-specific context.

CAPITALISTS AND MIDDLE CLASS IN REGIME CHANGE

Social Agent of Western Democratization

The role of capitalist and middle class in Western democratization has been explored by many scholars. They all identify the propertied class as the indispensable social agent of democratic transition. Marxists believe that affluent town dwellers and businessmen, who represent more efficient productivity, spearhead the development of parliamentary democracy. Historical sociologists such as Moore and Moraze emphasize the crucial role of capitalists in determining the development path of particular societies. In his inimitable maxim "no bourgeoisie, no democracy," Moore (1966) asserts a causal relationship between the existence of an urban bourgeois class and democratization. Modernization theorists, led by Lipset (1959), postulate that economic development engenders a growing middle class, who are prodemocracy and would exert more pressure for political liberalization if democracy does not yet exist. Huntington (1968) refutes the proposition that democracy is a natural product of economic growth, arguing that the middle class is the underlying force that promotes democratization.

The line of reasoning of capitalists and the middle class's democratic propensity is based on four arguments: First, democratic inclination of the bourgeoisie is primarily an economic imperative because their material interests have been largely infringed by the absolutist state, which is associated with the traditional feudal force of landlords and aristocrats. The new propertied class who has accumulated wealth and power through industrialization have been impelled to impose democratic constraint over the state which is the biggest barrier of capitalist advancement (Moore 1966; Moraze 1968). Second, rapid economic growth brings in more business, education and job opportunities, enlarging and empowering the private entrepreneurs and the middle class. As the primary beneficiary of the economic development, the propertied class has the incentive to engage in politics and promote rule of law to protect their own benefits and properties. Their education background, economic security, and political confidence enable them to take more time and resources to participate in public affairs, exerting demands on the regime (Lipset 1959; Dahl 1971). Moreover, in line with Maslow's hierarchical needs theory, when the per capita income reaches certain threshold, the individual is released from the bound of basic physical needs and becomes intrigued by the post-material values, such as self-expression or a sense of autonomy. It is believed that members of the middle class experience this value shift when they rise as the lion's share of the population in a prosperous urbanized society. Thus, the middle class constitutes a sizable social force bearing values and beliefs at odds with that of the restrictive authoritarian regime, pushing for political reform (Nathan 2016). Finally, the prodemocracy leaning of the middle class also results from the perception of its strength relative to the upper capitalist class and the lower classes of workers and peasants. Unlike business entrepreneurs, members of the middle class are bereft of economic or political resources as well as patron-client ties with political elites. Therefore, they opt for representative institutional settings not only as a moderate resolution of possible conflict with the lower classes, but also a reliable tool to defend their rights and interests from potential state encroachment (Glassman 1997).

All of these theoretical arguments are mainly rooted in Western experience and democratic evolution. A historical review of European political liberalization shows how the propertied class generated the dynamics of democratic transition. Parliamentary reform and universal suffrage have been achieved in the West through a series of political developments that unfolded over more than a century, composed of roughly two stages. The first stage is at the early period of capitalist development. It began with the rise of the bourgeoisie and its struggle for economic freedom from the feudal state. The advancement of capitalism collided with the traditional values and norms in a feudal society where the absolutist state constrained and threatened the very basic material interests of this newly emerged socioeconomic force. The urban business class advocated to protect private properties, promote individual rights, and to limit the power of the aristocrats. In this first phase, European capitalists successfully mobilized their bourgeois economic power and toppled the monarchical feudal states. The second stage occurred in the advanced period of capitalism. Industrial revolution and advancement of the capitalist economy nurtured a strong organized working class. Along with the collapse of feudalism and the predominance of the capitalist system, the fierce battle between the feudal state and the bourgeoisie shifted to a struggle between the capitalists and the proletariat. Western European democracy was by and large a parliamentary institutional setting that was created and imposed by the propertied class in order to defend their material interests. Therefore, two objects, to struggle for political freedom to defend their material interests in the early period and to ensure a stable social environment for further capitalist advancement in the second stage, formed a strong impetus for the capitalists to promote a democratic system in the West.

Late Development and Contingent Democrats

The diverse development courses of many countries in the developing world suggest that the inevitability of the propertied class's prodemocracy inclination no longer stands in a more complicated late-development circumstance. For example, in Southeast Asian countries such as Indonesia and Malaysia, economic sponsorship from the patrimonial authoritarian states, strong waves of labor unrests, plus compelling ethnic conflicts have pushed the propertied classes to shy away from democratic projects (Morley 1999). In Latin America, the middle class has played a subdued, if not adversarial, role in democratic transition (Stephens 1989). Even in South Korea and Taiwan, two "Young Tigers" in the third wave of democratization in the 1980s, the role of the middle class has remained mixed (Bellin 2000).

The conventional understanding of a correlation between the rising of the propertied class and democratization is mostly derived from the Western experience and context. The "unilateral approach" posits a single universal political development path, only supporting the endogenous theory of evolution of the propertied class's prodemocracy orientation. It neglects the importance of the exogenous dynamics which shift the political alignment of the propertied class from prodemocracy to anti-democracy or vice versa. Many scholars demonstrate the cross-section and time-series effects of various contextual variables on political stances of the capitalists and the middle class toward regime change. Similar socioeconomic upward mobility can lead to opposite political results in different countries. Even in the same country, the political stance of the propertied class toward democratization does not necessarily remain constant. The situational factors that account for the variation include, but are not limited to, the economic strategy of the state, the social position of the lower classes, and prevalent levels of fear regarding sociopolitical instability. Besides, other variables, such as fragmentation of the propertied class and the perceived level and efficacy of socioeconomic welfare, also contribute to the variation (e.g., Rueschemeyer, Stephens, and Stephens 1992; Stephens 1989).

The most popular exogenous explanation of the propertied class's political contingency in developing countries highlights a far more competitive and complex global economic environment the late developers encountered than those of the early industrializers. A more integrated global economy, with higher entry costs, and relative capital and technology deficiencies force the late developers in the developing world to rely on strong state sponsorship and intervention in an attempt to catch up with early industrializers and build their own national competitive capacities. As Alexander Gerschenkron (1962) and Peter Evans (1995) suggest, this peculiar condition of late development often results in a collaborative private sector, heavily dependent on the relatively powerful state. Furthermore, developing countries have experienced various levels of economic reform and growth due to domestic development and economic globalization. The exogenous modernization has transformed the feudal state into an industrializing one, no longer hostile to capital, dissipating or moderating the antagonism between the state and capitalists during the transition. In contrast to their counterparts in the West, private entrepreneurs in late developing countries find themselves more in line with the state in terms of economic interests and development strategy. Therefore, it has been argued that the private entrepreneurs and the middle class are "contingent democrats" (e.g., Bellin 2000; Li 2010; Chen and Lu 2011). Whether they champion democracy or not depends on the level of perceived security of material interests. Unlike their Western ancestors, who struggled for economic freedom from the state through democratic revolution or transition, the private entrepreneurs and the middle class in developing countries tend to be more conservative and supportive of authoritarian states to advance their personal benefits and profitability.

Beyond the logic of state-dependency, the political contingency of the middle class and private entrepreneurs is also attributable to their sense of insecurity due to lower class mobilization and resultant instability. Pervasive poverty and deepening income inequality heighten dissatisfaction and grievances of the lower class, which has gained mobilization capacity in the past anti-colonial campaigns and communist-influenced labor movements in the developing world. Thus, empowerment of the lower classes through democratic representation grants an institutional weapon to the poor to constrain further capitalist advancement of the affluent and shift wealth distribution in favor of the property-less. This poses imperative threats to the fundamental interests of the capitalists and the middle class in securing and sustaining their own property rights and long-term benefits and profitability (Bellin 2000). Moreover, the private entrepreneurs and the middle class in developing countries are leerier of democratization today than their equivalents in the early transition, because the former enjoy the status quo maintained by the state through selective corporatism and cooptation. Further concessions demanded by the property-less class would likely challenge the established economic and social structure and result in regime collapse. For the propertied class in developing countries, these are often reminiscent of past experiences of popular violence, which usually wiped out the newfound prosperity of the affluent and endangered social stability (Rueschemeyer, Stephens, and Stephens 1992; Owen 2015).

State-dependence and fear of lower class are not the only important variables in explaining the exceptionalism of the propertied class's political orientation in the developing world. Cultural traditions, historical legacy, socioeconomic context, and the international environment all have significant bearing on the manner in which the capitalists and the middle class in developing countries, including China, develop and evolve.

STATE DEPENDENCY OF THE CAPITALISTS AND THE MIDDLE CLASS IN CHINA

Evolution of the Chinese Bourgeoisie before the Reform

The seeds of capitalist development in China began to sprout in as early as the 15th century, almost the same time as in the European countries. Unfortunately, the fledging Chinese capitalists have encountered many more barriers than their counterparts in the West. While in the following centuries capitalist economies had burgeoned and flourished in countries like Britain, France, and Spain, in China, the development of an indigenous capitalist economy was severely retarded by the strong feudal state and bureaucracy, the traditional political culture and policies of "*Zhongnong Qingshang*" (stressing agriculture and belittling commerce), the "close-door" economic isolation of the Qing dynasty, as well as the invasion of the Western capitalism since the middle 19th century. The collapse of the imperial Qing Empire and the establishment of the Republic of China in 1912 created a more amiable environment for economic growth. Marie-Claire Bergere (1989) argues that the bourgeois economy in China experienced a relatively rapid growth during the warlord era, mainly concentrating in the big cities and treaty ports where the existence of the foreign colonial power somehow compensated the weak state capacity in providing the framework of law and order and necessary socioeconomic infrastructures. China had even witnessed the emerging of a nascent "civil society" thanks to rapid commercialization, the quick rise of urban centers, loosening political control and increasing demand for local self-governance due to weakness and fragility of the Chinese state during this period (Strand 1993). However, other scholars argue that the so-called social groups such as chambers of commerce, guilds, and kinship organizations were mainly associated and cooperated with local governments (Chan 2010). The bourgeois sparkle was soon put down when the Nationalists established the Nanjing government in 1927 and began to consolidate state power in part by increasing repression and incorporation of the merchant class (Bergere 1989). The indigenous capitalists were either forced to depend on the Nationalist government or were milked dry and driven out. The development space of the Chinese bourgeoisie was once again restricted by crony capitalism and decades-long political insatiability and violence. In this period, civic associations such as labor unions, intellectual salons, teahouses, and chambers of commerce were mainly discouraged; some were suspected of being associated with communists and were suppressed or disbanded (Chan 2010).

Scholars tend to analyze the lack of civil society tradition in China from the cultural perspective. It is important to recognize that the capitalists and the middle class in China before 1949 never had a chance to be fully developed. As Moore (1966, 467) concludes, the weak "landed upper class by and large did not make a successful transition into the world of commerce and industry." In China, it was the peasantry, not the capitalist class, that emerged as the historical agent of revolutionary change. Fairebank (1983, 51) ascribes the merchant class's dependence on state bureaucratic elites to China's failure of genuine capitalist economic transition. Thus, without a mature and complete capitalist development, China fell short of a large base of bourgeoisie and middle class and a strong tradition advocating autonomous civil society.

The year of 1949 was a significant shifting point for the development of Chinese bourgeoisie. The private economy, which had survived decades-long anti-Japanese war and civil war, had to operate under a new political system which targeted elimination of the capitalist class. Mao proclaimed that there should be only three social strata in a communist China at that time: workers, peasants, and intellectuals who would be eventually absorbed and become part of the working class (Li 2010). In the 1950s, a series of legislations and policies gradually restricted the options of the private sector. For example, from 1950 to 1953, the agricultural reform and collectivization in the rural area redistributed land and most extant means of production to the peasants. By 1950, college students no longer had freedom to choose jobs, but to obey the assignments of the government. In 1952, the government eliminated stock markets and established price controls. By 1956, all the private enterprises had either been nationalized or were under joint state-private ownership, causing the demise of the urban bourgeoisie and the middle class in China. The civic life that had developed before 1949 disappeared, replaced by the waves of the state-directed class struggle movement.

The evolution history of the Chinese bourgeoisie and the middle class is unique. Unlike Eastern European former communist countries such as Poland and Hungary, which had a rich history of capitalist development and a functioning civil society before the communist rule (Frentzel-Zagorska 1990), China had never experienced full industrialization under the Qing dynasty or the Republic of China, resulting in a weak and small urban bourgeoisie before 1949. Moreover, in contrast to other non-communist developing countries such as South Korea or Indonesia, whose capitalists and the middle class derived naturally from industrialization and modernization and have developed uninterruptedly for generations, China has witnessed the extinction and resurrection of the propertied class by the same regime in only several decades.

A New Social Class Created by the State

The underlying reasons that shifted the CCP regime's antagonisms toward the bourgeoisie to its imperative decision to create and expand the capitalist and middle classes were pragmatic and rational. First and foremost, sustainable economic development serves as the strongest impetus. Since the global financial crisis of 2008, the CCP regime has embarked on a painful economic structural transformation, transitioning its export-led manufacture and investment-based economy into a consumption-driven economy powered by domestic growth and internal demand. Affluent private entrepreneurs and a middle class with high disposable income are the key elements of this strategy. By 2015, China's middle class represented 12 percent of total world consumption, and the projected proportion will reach 22 percent by 2030, making China the biggest middle-class market in the world (Kharas 2017). For the state, an ever-enlarging propertied class suggests a growing market demand to be fulfilled, implying a secured promise of sustained prosperity. The trade war further makes it imperative to increase domestic demand. Second, opposite to the conventional Western expectation that quick rising of the middle class causes democratic transition, the Party-state is convinced that the proportion of the middle class in the population could be used as a social harmony factor, because the propertied should prefer stability given their stakes in the status quo. Data from Western countries also suggest that a football-shaped social structure is more stable than a pyramid-shaped one, with its resilient capacity to better survive formidable political or economic crises (Li 2010, 73). As the Gini coefficient closes to 0.5, rising income inequality has been perceived by the Party-state as a critical challenge to regime survival; increasing middle-class income is essential to counteract this challenge. The government's intentional effort to enlarge the middle-class population could pacify the lower class, making the poor hopeful for future livelihood improvement and thus more dependent and politically supportive (Li 2010). Third, the middle class and private entrepreneurs are usually well-educated and enjoy a comfortable and secure life. They are perfect citizens expected to use their influence to uphold positive social values such as trust, honesty, respect for law and order against the moral crisis due to rising materialism and consumerism; they therefore could serve as a role model in state's effort to "civilizing" its people and creating a harmonious society (Rocca 2017).

Deng Xiaoping's decision to launch economic reform, and his campaign to liberalize people's minds, preluded a large-scale reverse of social class elimination and resulted in the most unprecedented massive upward mobility in human history. Chinese economist Zhang Weiying concludes that China has experienced three major waves of economic privatization, with each phase contributing to a further round of astounding economic growth, nurturing generations of private entrepreneurs.[1] The first wave was initiated in the 1980s, starting with the rural household contract responsibility system, the restoration of private ownership, and the resulting flourishing of small-sized private businesses, so-called *getihu*, and rural township enterprises. By 1992, the number of private enterprises had grown from zero to 139,000.[2] Deng's 1992 Southern China tour rallied the whole country for his further economic reform, ushering in the second wave of development in the 1990s. Many government officials, Party cadres, and intellectuals were greatly inspired and quitted the "iron bowl" jobs to start their own private businesses. In 1992 alone, there were at least 100,000 such cases.[3] Since the early 1990s, the annual growth rate of private entrepreneurs has remained at about 35 percent

(Owen 2015, 186). The reform of the public sector underlined the strategy of "grasping the big and letting go the small," and nationwide privatization of SOEs in the late 1990s has provided perfect opportunities and environment for business start-ups and triggered another round of state employee's "*xiahaichao.*"[4] By 2002, the number of private enterprises had jumped to over 2.4 million (Dai 2002). In the beginning of the 21st century, the development of communication technologies and membership in the World Trade Organization (WTO) have signified China's deeper integration into the global market and induced the third wave of economic development. In the past two decades, China has witnessed the emergence of a new generation of private entrepreneurs; most of them with study-abroad experiences and technological backgrounds. By the end of 2017, privately owned businesses reached approximately 65 million, and the number of private enterprises has increased tenfold, reaching 27 million (Zhao 2018). The private sector contributes more than 50 percent of tax revenues, 60 percent of GDP, and 80 percent of urban employment (Zhu 2018).

Unlike the Western bourgeoisie, born and developed naturally along with independent advancement of the capitalist economy, the private sector now in China is the brainchild of the Party, created and fostered by a series of intended reforms and economic policies initiated, despite conservative resistance, by Deng Xiaoping. From Deng's "let some people get rich first" to "private economy as a necessary complementary part to the state-owned economy" advocated in the 13th NCCPC; from "private sector is an important component of the socialist economy" postulated in the 15th NCCPC during the Jiang administration, to "the private sector is equally important as the state-owned sector" recognized in the 17th NCCPC during the Hu administration, to "the private sector should enjoy equal rights, opportunities, and rules as the public sector" emphasized in the 18th NCCPC during the Xi administration, the communist party has gradually opened up political space to revitalize the Chinese capitalist class.

In the 1980s and 1990s, the term "middle class" was mainly used to describe newly emerging private entrepreneurs, intellectuals, managers, and professionals. Along with the exponential growth of the private economy, promoting and expanding the middle-income social stratum has become an important agenda for the Party-state since the early 2000s. In 2000, Jiang Zemin formulated the theory of "Three Represents," advocating a broadened Party base to include entrepreneurs, intellectuals, and technocrats. In the 16th NCCPC in 2002, Jiang launched a new policy goal of "expanding the middle-income group" to build a "relatively prosperous society." Ten years later, in the 18th NCCPC, Xi Jinping updated the goal and announced China would increase GDP per capita to $10,000 and its middle-income population to over 600 million by 2020 (Allison 2017a).

According to the World Bank, the population living only on less than $5.5 per day in China has decreased dramatically since 1999, from 89 percent to 27.2 percent in 2015.[5] Sustained rapid economic growth over the past decades paved the way for the emergence of China's middle class. The national average wage has been doubling almost every five to seven years since the late 1990s, jumping from 6,470 yuan in 1997 to 74,318 yuan in 2017.[6] The expansion of China's higher education system since the late 1990s has greatly increased the college enrollment rate from 9.8 percent in 1998 to 42.7 percent in 2016, making previously elite higher education far more accessible for the general public (Liu and Wang 2015). In 2017 the number of college graduates reached 8 million, nearly 10 times higher than it was in 1997 (Stapleton 2017). In the past five years, about 20 million students graduated from universities, injecting a large educated and skilled labor force into China's emerging technology-based industries. The number of white-collar workers in China reached at least 175 million in 2017.[7] The Party-state has also issued a series of financial, taxation, and welfare policies to enlarge the middle class and promote domestic demand.

Besides salary increase, higher education expansion, and other policy promotions, the growth of the stock market and especially housing reform have also enormously contributed to the quick rise of the middle class. After 1949, the communist state nationalized almost all the private lands and real estate properties, and the private housing market disappeared. In the early 1990s, the CCP regime initiated nationwide housing reform. Housing is no longer viewed as a welfare benefit assigned by the work unit or a public service provided by the government, but as a commodity with a market value that could be privately owned by individuals. The marketization of urban dwellings and the individual's private homeownership were achieved mainly through the following four routes. First, the government terminated the public housing distribution system in 1998 and replaced it with a commercial housing (*shangpin fang*) market, cash subsidies, a housing provident fund, and a mortgage financial service. The existing state-owned housing was sold to individual households at substantially discounted prices. Second, the "*jingji shiyong fang*" (economical housing) program, focusing heavily on government subsidized urban housing since the 1990s, has satisfied the housing demand of much of the urban low and middle-income population. Third, many urban residents have been compensated with new "*chaiqian fang*" (relocation settlement housing) with equivalent square footages when their decades-long apartments were demolished and relocated or rebuilt during the nationwide urban reconstruction movement embarked on by the Party-state since the 1990s. Some rural residents have also been compensated with urban "*chaiqian fang*" during the growing urban expansion and annexation, particularly in the East Coast metropolitan areas. Fourth, some employees in public institutions, such as university faculty and staff, still enjoy housing provision as working benefits. The development of the housing market and the soaring housing values since the early 2000s played a critical role in enlarging the middle class and private entrepreneurs. The average price per square meter reached 8,000 yuan in 2018, four times than the price in 2000. According to *Forbes*, seven of the world's top 10 most expensive cities for residential property are in China (Seales 2017). In metropolitan centers with many millions of residents, such as Shanghai, Beijing, and Shenzhen, the average housing price has skyrocketed more than 10 to 20 times since 2000. Many urban residents have entered into middle- and upper-income strata by quick wealth accumulation directly derived from homeownership and real estate investment and industry.

Under such unprecedented state sponsorship, the size of the private entrepreneurs and the middle class in China has exploded. According to McKinsey & Company, a consultancy, the size of the middle-class households, which is defined by an annual income of $11,500 to 43,000, has expanded from 5 million in 2000 to around 225 million in 2016. It is estimated that the number will continue to climb and reach 275 million by 2020, comprising 75 percent of urban households.[8] If using the World Bank cutoff of $10 per day for middle income as a yardstick, about 40 percent of the population, around 550 million, has fallen into the middle- and upper-income strata by 2018. Although scholars have not reached a consensus on a precise definition of the middle class, they all concur in a general profile of the Chinese propertied class through a combined lens of income, consumption, education, and occupation. The Chinese middle class has been generally portrayed as those in the middle- or upper- income strata with growing financial assets and property, adequate disposable money and time to meet their needs for consumption and leisure pursuits; people who are well-educated, engaging in white-collar jobs with better conditions and certain autonomy in their work, and enjoying health care and social security welfare (Li 2010, 248; Nathan 2016; Owen 2015). Li (2010, 143) classifies the Chinese middle class into four social categories: private entrepreneurs or capitalists, old middle class, including small business owners and self-employed, new middle class, composing of professionals, managers, and government cadres, and a marginal middle class, consisting of low-wage white-collar and other workers with wages crossing the low-middle income threshold. We adopt his methods to define the propertied class because this classification clearly reflects the evolutionary and hierarchical feature of the new social elites. Thus, the terms "private entrepreneurs" or "capitalist class" refer to businessman owning big or media-sized firms, while the term "middle class" in this study covers the old, new, and marginal middle class Li refers to.

The private entrepreneurs and the middle class in China are distinguished from their counterparts in other developing countries or in the post-Soviet Union and Eastern European states, because they were wiped out completely in history, and then recreated and nurtured, by the CCP state from the ground zero. The CCP regime has designed and supervised the rebirth of the propertied class under the rubric of creating a "*xiaokang*" society and boosting the regime legitimacy. Hence, the socioeconomic traits and political discourses of this newly emerged social force have been tremendously shaped and molded by the Party-state (Li 2010). An analysis of the consequent structural features of the capitalist and middle class helps to better understand their state-dependency and ambiguity toward political reform and regime change.

First, a large number of private entrepreneurs and members of the middle class in China either have bureaucratic and administrative backgrounds or currently work in various levels of governments, SOEs, and public institutions such as universities and hospitals that are controlled by the state. As the result of waves of "*xiahaichao*" in the 1990s, many former government officials and managers of SOEs have become the leading forces of Chinese private entrepreneurship. For example, among the top 30 private entrepreneurs on the *Hurun* Global Rich List in 2018, over half had work experiences as managers or officials in the public sector.[9] Studies show that there are significant percentage of private entrepreneurs who were already party members before becoming business owners (Li 2010, 296). Most entrepreneurs of the township and village enterprises, who were usually local level government cadre, formed the first generation of the private business elites in rural China (Odgaard 1992). Many studies show that government officials, cadre, and other state apparatus employees account for a significant share of the expanding middle class (e.g., Li 2010; Nathan 2016). Chen and Lu (2011, 712) find in a survey that about 60 percent of their middle-class respondents were employed in the public sector. The practical consequence of the structural feature suggests that this lion's share of the private entrepreneurs and the middle class is more likely to develop a sense of dependency on the Party-state because the latter preponderantly influences their business or career opportunities, promotion, working benefits, and retirement welfare.

Second, it took centuries for the West to witness the evolution of the bourgeoisie, whereas upward mobility and socioeconomic reconstruction in China have been compressed into just four decades. Industrialization and urbanization are not natural products of endogenous development in China. Unlike their Western counterparts, who were the outcome of division of labor, achieving their social status independently through education, knowledge, skills and specialties, and professionalism, the Chinese nouveau riche and swelling middle class have quickly obtained their novel identity mainly thanks to state promotion and sponsorship. For example, many people have gained their wealth through the boosting housing market, regardless their education level or occupation. Li finds that about 65 percent middle class members come from farmer or worker families and 57 percent of them had blue-collar working experiences (Li 2010, 24). Most of the newly emerged propertied class are economically practical and politically indifferent. They represent more of a consumptive than a sociopolitical force. As Andrew Nathan (2016, 10–11) points out that most of Chinese middle-class members are still "in the process of forging a way of life, in part by self-consciously emulating what they understand of Western consumption habits" and "political participation is a distraction."

Third, the newly emerged capitalist and middle class are economically and politically fragmented, without a unified class identity. Many scholars find it very difficult to define this propertied social group in China because its members range from disparate income levels, various occupations, different education attainment, and miscellaneous family origins and political backgrounds (Li 2010; Nathan 2016). They are representing different, sometimes even conflicting, interests and resultantly, various political stances. This heterogeneity within the capitalists and the middle class has greatly eroded its power and position as a socioeconomic group. Furthermore, China is bereft of independent social structures such as churches or other civic associations that could provide a forum for the middle-class members to reach out the likeminded and establish common values and class identity.

Rational Calculation in a Unique Chinese Context

Developmental State and Favorable Policies and Benefits

Beyond the distinct evolution history, the development of the propertied class in China has encountered similar late development circumstances as other developing countries. Most studies ascribe the state-dependency and indifference toward democratization of the burgeoning propertied class in China to the country's late developer status in a competitive global economy. Few pay attention to the fact that communist China has also been considered by some of the Western politicians as a political threat, an economic rival, a cultural adversary, and an ideological enemy. This cognitive hostility could transfer into unfavorable and restrictive economic or diplomatic policies, making China's already disadvantaged late development environment more stringent and rigorous. The United States and Western European countries have imposed export controls in the name of national security to limit technology transfer to China involving areas such as aerospace, automotive, defense, information technology, telecommunications, and software industries for decades.[10] Western developed countries have also applied increasingly strict scrutiny on Chinese investment from both SOEs and private investors due to national security concerns. For example, Germany blocked Aixtron's sale to a Chinese private company in 2016. In 2017, a privately owned Chinese telecom giant, Huawei, was denied access to the U.S. market. In 2019, the Trump administration further accused this fast-growing high-tech company of posing a national security risk and imposed a contracting ban on it. In sum, China's embryonic capitalists and middle class face intensified disadvantages due to these dual contextual drawbacks.

Under these circumstances, the CCP regime has taken a developmental state strategy since the reform, in which the state utilizes all its resources to explicitly promote and sponsor domestic industrialization and marketization through an export-oriented economic model in an effort to rapidly accumulate national wealth and capacity. The development of capitalist industry is closely associated with state prosperity. The private entrepreneurs and the middle class in China have received substantial government support mainly through two dimensions.

First, the CCP regime has directly nurtured and sponsored the growth of private enterprises and small businesses by providing various capital and financial resources including but not limited to government subsidies, bank credits and low-interests loans, and tax reductions and exemptions. By 2011, the Party-state had distributed over 56 billion yuan in various government subsidies to support small- and medium-sized enterprises (SMEs), the majority of which are privately owned.[11] For example, a private company focusing on robot production received various government subsidies for years and the amount reached 167 million yuan in 2016, accounting for 40 percent of its revenue in that year.[12] The taxation policies have been developed in favor of business growth. The state has been using export tax rebates as leverage to promote the competitive capacity of domestic products in the international market since 1985. To reduce the impact of the trade war with the United States on the domestic export industry, the state has increased the export tax rebates to up to 13 percent for hundreds of products since 2018 (Koty 2018).

Second, the growing capitalist and middle-class cohorts have also enjoyed a favorable development environment sustained by the Party-state. The government has introduced a number of policies and reforms to reduce the administrative and procedural barriers for investment and business. For example, the business system reform since 2014 has greatly simplified the registration and approval process for new businesses. A Five-in-One business license and online registration system has been introduced to significantly shorten application processing time since 2016 (Shira 2017). The state has also built thousands of business incubators to offer private entrepreneurs with start-up infrastructure and services. In 2011, the state issued an order to set aside 30 percent of government procurement budget for purchasing goods and services from SMEs.[13] Chinese capitalists and small business owners have been enjoying a rich supply of cheap labor greatly thanks to the discriminatory *Hukou* system, planned urbanization, and largescale layoffs of SOE employees. The government-planned urban encroachments have provided the private economy, particularly the real estate industry, with affluent land resources at low cost. More importantly, Chinese capitalists and small business owners have also benefited from the Party-state's efforts to protect the market position for its domestic infant industries. The number of Chinese automobile companies on the list of the Fortune 500 Companies has increased from zero in 1998 to two 10 years later, and six in 2018, partly thanks to import tariffs.[14] The exponential growth of the Chinese Internet industries such as e-commerce and social media is ascribed to the fact that most Western websites are blocked by the Firewall. Three tech giants JD, Tencent, and Alibaba have worked their way up onto the Fortune 500 list in 2018. The rejection by Google of censorship in 2009 has forced its share in Chinese market to drop from 33 percent to less than 2 percent, creating a huge market space for other indigenous companies to mushroom. In addition to domestic protection, the quick rise of China's global economic power and presence has greatly met the growing demand of the domestic private entrepreneurs and the middle class for investment abroad. Overseas private investment has increased from $120 million in 2005 to $65.8 billion in 2016 (Chang 2017). Finally, the CCP regime has endeavored to build a supportive legal environment for the market and its major actors. In 2004, the Chinese Constitution was amended to protect private property rights. Since then, a series of laws governing property and business contracts have been issued to fortify and interpret this fundamental principle of capitalism. The resolution of capital and labor disputes has been gradually institutionalized (Yang and Zhao 2015). In 1992, the state established the Securities Regulatory Agency to protect the interests of shareholders by supervising the stock exchange market and investigating and prosecuting securities fraud. However, the efforts of legal reform have been mainly limited to the business field to primarily satisfy the needs of foreign investors and private enterprises (Wang 2015).

Patrimonial State and Cronyistic Relation

It is still under debate whether China is qualified as a truly developmental state because although the Party-state plays a decisively sponsoring role in rapid economic development, the level to which this state intervention is institutionalized is questionable in contrast to its Eastern Asian predecessors, like Japan and South Korea. Rather, the relationship between the CCP regime and the propertied class is subject to some features of patrimonialism. According to the crony capitalism index configured by the *Economist* in 2016, the wealth of China's billionaires accounted for 7.3 percent of the GDP, among them 44 percent from crony sector which is highly vulnerable to political interference and favoritism, suggesting a relatively high degree of cronyism in China's economy.[15] Dickson (2003) uses "crony communism" to define China's close state-market relationship. Doubtless, the patrimonial feature and cronyistic relation have profoundly affected the political orientation of the capitalists and the middle class in China.

Although the current economic system has by and large departed from a planned economy, the Party-state is still in control of crucial social and economic resources. The basic services such as electricity, water, gas, banking, transportation, and communication remain administratively allocated. Private enterprises have often had to rely on special pleading to gain access to the local municipal services they need, especially if they wish to expand their activities (Zheng 1994). More importantly, one's party membership and affiliation with the public sector matter a lot when it comes to attaining critical resources such as bank loans, subsidies, information, and preferential tax credits. According to the Chinese Private Enterprise Survey in 2008, former government officials and public-sector managers comprised over 50 percent of the private entrepreneurs (Zhang 2012). Among those private companies that have transitioned from SOEs since the late 1990s, about half are owned by party members who worked in the public sector before privatization (Dai 2002). The personal connections (*guanxi*) and social networks are of special concern to private entrepreneurs in China. In a survey when private entrepreneur respondents were asked to name their closest friends, cadres and government officials have the highest percentage, 52 percent, while workers and farmers only account for 5 percent (Li 2001). Another survey shows that about one third of the relatives of the private entrepreneur respondents were officials or cadre in the public sector (Dai 2002).

Compared to education and occupation, a person's family origins and personal connections (*guanxi*), in particular the part associated with the government and public institutions, play a more critical role in obtaining and maintaining his/her middle-class status in China. For example, private housing redistribution has heavily favored those who were closely affiliated with or have politically loyal to the Party-state (Tomba 2014). When the government holds the absolute power to reallocate state-owned housing and land resources, housing reform has turned into a tool to transfer political privilege into material benefits. Individuals with higher rank and position in the hierarchy of public sector often gained larger and higher quality apartments with better location and later received more discounting when they purchased their dwellings (Li 2010, 196). Besides, government employees also receive superior medical insurance and pension funds, and a faster rate of salary increases than employees in other sectors (Tomba 2014).

State Containment and Accommodation of Lower Class

Despite its impressive progress in the recent decades, China in many respects remains a relatively poor society facing formidable socioeconomic and ecological constraints. The biggest challenge resides on its growing uneven distribution of social wealth. Decades ago, the reformist leadership began to use an uneven development strategy, breaking from Mao's egalitarian legacy, contributing to the quick emergence of the propertied class. However, it also has resulted in a huge wealth gap between rich and poor. While the number of millionaires and billionaires continues to rise in big cities, a significant percentage of poor people barely make a living in inland rural China. According to the World Bank, about 43 million people in China still live in extreme poverty, with yearly income lower than 2,300 yuan, equivalent of less than 95 cents a day (the poverty line set by the Chinese government) (Hernandez 2017). Income inequality is becoming a highly potential liability to social stability. For the fledging capitalists and the middle class, the large amount of the property-less population and widening income gap are like a time bomb, posing threat to their newfound wealth and long-term benefits. They fear that their interests will be overwhelmed by those of the capital poor who are clearly the majority of the country. Moreover, China has a recent revolutionary legacy that featured the destructive capacity of lower-class mass mobilization and subsequent disastrous social disorder. What happened in the former Soviet Union, Eastern European countries, and Middle Eastern countries are vivid lessons that have convinced the Chinese business elites and the middle class to link political change with social turmoil and instability. Thus, the least the propertied class wants is political empowerment of the poor through democratization. Many studies find that private entrepreneurs prefer stability over political rights and democracy (Dickson 2016; Li 2010). College students usually represent the most radical force in a society. In our survey, we also find about two-thirds of the student respondents believe stability is more important than democratic practices.[16]

How to contain the massive working poor and keep them submissive and acquiescent is critical for the propertied class to continue to enjoy economic prosperity based on the further exploitation of a docile workforce. Acemoglu and Robinson (2000) argue that democracy is a result of elites' tradeoff between being constrained in power to certain degree by a democratic setting versus endless lower-class unrests and the high costs of repression. In most cases, such as Argentina, the elites chose a one-time generous offer to a full democracy rather than being trapped in an infinite loop of protest and concession, or repression. Clearly, the market cannot tackle these sociopolitical problems. The propertied class in China seems to have found an alternative route to solving the problem. They choose to rely on the Party-state to accommodate the poor, to counter opposition or obstruction and manage concomitant social conflicts, and to maintain a stable social and political order for sustainable economic development. Over the past several decades, the Party-state has not only sponsored economic development, but also taken great pains to accommodate and contain the lower class in an effort to create a stable sociopolitical environment for economic growth. From the *Hukou* system to minimum wages to "New Countryside Construction" strategy, the Party-state has pacified and contained the workers and peasants on the one hand, and on the other has continued to distribute limited resources preferentially toward the affluent urban centers along the East Coast, where the emerging capitalists and the middle class are disproportionately concentrated.

Thus, the political orientation of the private entrepreneurs and the middle class is further explained by the indispensable role of the Party-state in economic advancement, murky cronyistic state-business relations and the state capacity to contain and appease the lower class. When the propertied class remains the primary beneficiary of state-sponsored economic development in a late-development context, it is their survival instinct to align their material interests with that of the politically supreme Party-state. Apparently, the economic development in China has yet gone far enough to undermine the decisive power of the authoritarian state in directing economic activities and untethering the propertied class as an autonomous sociopolitical force, as happened in another East Asian developmental state, South Korea (Bellin 2000). We believe that the shifting of the political orientation of capitalists and the middle class won't be replicated in China. Unlike South Korea, a sizable and rising communist China would never become a strategic ally of Western developed countries. This unique disadvantaged international context will keep Chinese capitalists and the middle class bounded to the state. Furthermore, given that a murky cronyistic relation with the authoritarian regime plays a critical role in boosting the capitalists' profitability and the affluence of the middle class, it is not surprising that political reform and democratization, which emphasizes the principle of rule of law and transparency and which would destroy the shady state-business link, presents little attraction for most Chinese business elites and the middle class. Over and above that, a shockingly widening wealth disparity has kept the fear of the propertied class vivid and forces them to rely on the Party-state's capacity to contain the poor. It is the rational choice for the private entrepreneurs and the middle class to opt out of democracy which may bring political disorder and destroy their privileged position in the current political and economic system.

INTERACTION BETWEEN THE PARTY-STATE
AND THE PROPERTIED CLASS

Interaction between the CCP regime and the private entrepreneurs and the middle class in China has usually been described as a top-down and lopsided state penetration, with interference through manipulative cooptation and corporatism. The Party-state has provided patronage to selective constituent groups in exchange for their compliance and support. But as Li (2010, 5) points out some members of the propertied class are "the clients of political patrons, but many more are self-made people." When autonomy is focused on as the only criterion to study Chinese civic activism, whereby meaningful functions and contributions to regime accountability are ignored, the Western "civil society" standard has lost its persuasiveness in the Chinese context. The stereotypical profiling of state-society relations based on a Western confrontational framework has greatly restricted the understanding of the real effect of the interplay between the state and the propertied class and how this affects regime legitimacy. Recently more empirical studies show that the interaction between the Party-state and the capitalist and middle class bears a tendency of increasing collaboration and interdependence. To survive, the Party-state has endeavored to improve its governance, being more responsive to and dependent on society, particularly the privileged propertied class. On the other hand, the business elites and the middle class have seized the opportunities, taking various means to strategically engage in bottom-up political channeling to fulfill their material and psychological needs.

Political participation of the private entrepreneurs and the middle class has frequently been studied as a behavioral outcome of a series of contextual and historical factors, such as state dependency or fear of the capital poor and instability. In this section, we explore the interaction between the Party-state and the propertied class as an independent variable based on a "state-society interdependent" model. Given a relatively amenable administrative environment, the privileged bottom-up channeling has largely enhanced the political efficacy of the propertied class and consequently increased their political support to the authoritarian regime.

Party Membership and State Cooptation

The reformist communist regime has made efforts to recruit members of the capitalist and middle class into the ruling party. Although the Party had banned the admission of private entrepreneurs to membership for about a decade in light of the prevailing bourgeois thoughts in the late 1980s and the pro-democracy movement in 1989, the restriction has never been strictly implemented (Dickson 2007). The "Three Represents" theory elaborated by Jiang Zemin in 2001 following the large-scale privatization since the late 1990s has officially confirmed the Party's resolution to coopt business, cultural, and intellectual elites. The CCP would open its door wide to recruit "outstanding elements" from the growing private sector and a rising propertied class does not necessarily represent a political threat to the party leadership. The share of private entrepreneurs with Party membership has increased from about 13 percent in 1993 to 38 percent in 2007 (Dickson 2016), which is far higher than the percentages of Party members in other social groups such as workers and farmers. Although a large number of private entrepreneurs were already party members before starting their own private businesses, the ascendency of party-member concentration in the capitalist class indicates increasing willingness and efforts by the business elites to become affiliated with the ruling party. According to a survey by the Chinese Academy of Social Sciences in 2013, over 40 percent of the private entrepreneur respondents expressed their intention to join the communist party. By 2017 over 73 percent of (roughly) 1.87 million privately owned enterprises have allowed the existence of the basic communist party units, compared to only 27 percent in 2002 (Long 2012).

Besides party membership, it becomes more frequent that business, cultural, and intellectual elites have been coopted into various levels of legislative and consultative institutions across the country. Celebrities from both mainland China, Hong Kong, and Macau have been actively involving in various levels of the PCs and the PPCCs (Jeffreys 2016). The number of business elites in the system of the PC and the PPCC has arisen dramatically for the last two decades. Zhang (2017, 2) finds that, following the government and party cadres, the private entrepreneur deputies have made the second largest deputy groups in many local PCs, especially in the eastern coastal developed provinces. At the national level, more influential Chinese billionaire entrepreneurs such as Pony Ma from Tencent, Robin Li from Baidu, and Lei Jun from Xiaomi have been elected as the PC and the PPCC delegates. In 2017, there were over 200 of the richest private business giants coveting seats of the national PC and PPCC (Mitchell 2017). In addition, business, cultural, and intellectual elites have been encouraged to join various social organizations such as the Chambers of Commerce (*Shanghui*), the China Federation of Literary and Art Circles, the All-China Youth Federation, and various writers' associations, all of which are supervised by or affiliated with the CCP regime.

Proactive Civic Activism: Policy Entrepreneurship, Lobby, and Consultation

Along with deepening economic reform and openness, the CCP regime has also offered expanding space for political participation of the business society and the middle class. It is worth noting that this political loosening is not just a perfunctory gesture to cope with the increasing participatory needs of the propertied class. It is widely acknowledged that China's civic associations have not been able to flourish because they are confined by the state. However, two important points must be considered. First, the Party-state desperately wants to improve its governance. This strong resolution results in a relatively progressive and flexible stance of the authorities in dealing with the participatory demands and advocacy voices from the propertied class. Taking the health care system reform as an example, the state has greatly opened to public policy inputs in a conscious effort to satisfy the public's basic needs (Korolev 2017). Second, the Party-state increasingly depends on the expertise, knowledge, information and resource of business, cultural, and intellectual elites in handling the increasingly complex socioeconomic problems and diverse social demands. The public space has been increasingly depoliticized and dissident intellectuals have been "replaced by experts, whose legitimacy for action in society is based on 'scientific' knowledge" (Beja 2006, 63). This dependence has guaranteed more discretion for policy stakeholders, albeit within the general boundaries set by the state, making the interaction between the state and the propertied class dynamic and collaborative. Studies also find that the Party-state grants more autonomy, even access to policymaking, to certain social organizations in exchange for their services in public goods provision (Teets 2013; Howell 2012).

Consequently, this flexible environment has nurtured a mushrooming development of political engagement by civic associations, advocacy groups, public intellectuals, business elites, and activists, who have managed to both produce social capital and hold the state accountable to some degree within the confines of a tight regulatory regime. Scholars have defined this pursuit of civic participatory initiatives from varying angles, such as policy entrepreneurship, interest-group lobby and advocacy (e.g., Kennedy 2008; Yu, Yashima, and Shen 2014; Liang 2017), or deliberative consultation (e.g., Teets 2013; Truex 2017; Deng and Liu 2017). Some activities overlap or are closely related to others.

Lobbying by interest and advocacy groups is an important practice in liberal democracies to facilitate citizens' direct inputs in legislation. Although China remains a one-party dominant authoritarian state, organized interest lobbying has become more important as a means for the propertied class to shape public policy outputs (Kennedy 2008; Yu, Yashima, and Shen 2014; Liang 2017; Steinberg and Shih 2012). Schubert and Heberer (2017) find that private entrepreneurs in China have been increasingly active in collective and strategic ways to defend their interests against unpopular policies. Given their expanding representation in various levels of legislative and consultative bodies and the extensive sociopolitical networks they have across party-state units and administrative agencies, the large elite enterprises have exerted substantial influence on various industrial and business policy formulation, from policies on the steel and consumer electronics (Kennedy 2008) to oil production regulations (Downs 2007), from exchange rate adjustment (Steinberg and Shih 2012) to e-commerce lawmaking (Deng and Liu 2017). Besides such specific interest lobbying by business elites, other professional, academic, and civic groups representing the interests of either intellectuals or the general public have also engaged in policy lobbying. For example, Liang (2017) argues that though the general environment is constrained, the intellectual lobbying has still made some achievements;

those such as "C9," the first university advocacy coalition, successfully influenced the policy changes regarding university autonomy to admit students.

Policy entrepreneurship and deliberative consultation represent the changing political pattern of interaction between the state and the propertied class in China. The former refers to an open policymaking process involving actors with critical knowledge and expertise to influence outputs and achieve their own policy ends. The latter highlights the role of citizens in policy making by sharing their opinions and suggestions through formal or informal, online or offline channels. Both act as critical catalysts for changes and engines that similarly drive the institutional adaptations and policy innovations in Western democracies. The Party-state has been incorporating these two policymaking tools as a "mass line" strategy into its governance since the 1990s, establishing an important top-down and bottom-up institutional channel complementary to a political system lacking popular election. The policymaking participants include some government officials and local cadres. But the majority is composed of non-state actors such as NGOs, businesspeople, and public intellectuals including scholars, journalists, editors, lawyers, and other professionals (Zhu 2016). Though in many cases, the opinions and suggestions are just reference points, the special structure of interactive communication and level of transparency of the policymaking process have empowered the participants to impose some constraints and guidance on the state.

In sum, the bottom-up proactive political participation by the propertied class bears the following features. First, it is a privileged channeling mechanism. The majority of the participatory activities occur in the urban areas and among the business, cultural, and intellectual elites. Business organizations, professional groups, and academic associations account for over 85 percent of the total social organizations in China (Chan 2010), leaving little room for collective associations representing interests of the working class and peasants. Even within this mechanism, the participation process is hierarchical. The actors with more resources such as expertise, knowledge, information about constituencies, and more experienced with better reputation, or who have influence in specific policy fields such as industry or environment, receive more attention and opportunities to participate and yield effective influence (Han 2016; Yu, Yashima, and Shen 2014; Zhu 2016; Zhan and Tang 2016). It is worth noting that there are other two factors that have impact on the efficacy of this system: a close relationship with the government and a strong capacity to mobilize the public. For example, the inputs from environmental NGOs are often regarded more valuable by the government due to their ability to establish linkages to the mass public.

Second, both individual activists and organized participants are more or less controlled, supervised, or at least affiliated with the Party-state (Han 2016). Independence from the state is a luxury in terms of civic activism in

China. That being said, the vast majority of the civic associations are not created solely to "compulsorily and monopolistically" represent the constituencies assigned by the state (Han 2016, 29). And most of them enjoy certain "operational autonomy," having freedom in leadership selection and turnover, fundraising channels, and day-to-day operations (Han 2016; Teets 2014). Many studies find that the participants rarely fight for maximum autonomy. On the contrary, having a close relationship with the government helps them leverage more support, information, and opportunities of engagement to pursue their own or members' interests and goals (Han 2016; Yu, Yashima, and Shen 2014). Zhan and Tang (2016) find that NGOs with connection to the government are more likely to shed influence on policymaking than those without linkage to the state. Based on their empirical study, Yu, Yashima, and Shen (2014) argue that the participators with consultant status assigned by the state lobby the government more often than those self-established advocacy groups. Furthermore, the participators are often service-oriented, knowledge-based, and self-disciplined, consciously or not consciously limiting themselves to depoliticalized areas, avoiding broader sensitive political issues like human rights.

Third, despite the lack of autonomy, most of the participators have taken advantages of the existing institutional settings and established effective channeling with the state. They are able to fulfill their own interests and policy goals or represent their members and constituents by shaping policy outputs (Han 2016; Yu, Yashima, and Shen 2014; Ergenc 2014). Although this bottom-up political participation is subject to strict state control and surveillance and therefore explicitly limited in many aspects, the effects of such successful participatory activities profoundly affect the relationship between the state and the propertied class. The active participators from the capitalists and the middle class gain strengths and reputation through successful public mobilization and state interaction, and subsequently improve their political efficacy to a large extent. Yao and Han (2016) find that a group of cultural elites have played a significant role in promoting urban heritage preservation by successfully mobilizing the urban residents and the media and navigating the government with their expertise and mediating capacity to achieve their policy goals. Most propertied-class participators believe that with their in-depth knowledge, expertise, information, and resources, they are indispensable for the government in policy adjustment, formulation and public goods provision, and therefore push the state to head in a promising development direction (Ergenc 2014; Zhu 2016; Beja 2006).

Passive Political Participation: Rightful Contentions of the Propertied Class

If policymaking engagement of private entrepreneurs and segments of the middle class is proactive political participation, involving strong demands for inclusion and representation, then organized contentions of the propertied class for their violated interests indicate a quite different participatory pattern. Over the past two decades, China has witnessed an alarming upsurge in social rights–protection unrest by the members of the propertied class mainly in cities. Among them, mass protests for environmental protection and homeowner rights are on the front line of the urban civic contentions.

In the wake of widespread industrial pollution and ecological degradation, the propertied class has endeavored to put up organized demonstrations and protests to defend their environment in opposition to air pollution, fouled water, the construction of chemical plants and incinerators (Steinhardt and Wu 2016; Miao 2016). For example, large-scale urban residents' protests and planned demonstrations at chemical plants over pollution fears and health concerns have broken out in cities like Shanghai, Xiamen, Dalian, Ningbo, Chengdu, Kunming, just to name a few.[17] Moreover, street demonstrations have echoed online protests as well as collective policy advocacy by environmental NGOs and activists. Proactive policy involvement and passive political participation have reinforced mutually. Most of the environmental protests have been sympathized and tolerated by the government (Li 2010). In light of the rising environmental uprising, the Party-state has reacted with stricter environmental protection laws and regulations to resolve or ameliorate the problem of industrial externalities. The government has written pollution reduction goals into its Five-Year plans. Since enactment of more stringent environmental protection laws and regulations and putting pollution reduction as development goals, the government has shut down and penalized more than 30,000 factories and firms and over 5,700 officials (Corne and Browaeys 2017).

Since the late 1990s, another contentious movement, city dwellers' protests, has swept urban areas in China along with the rapid growth of homeownership. Homeowners and homeowners' committees, self-organized bodies representing and consisting of neighborhood homeowners, have organized various activities from petition to litigation and even collective contentions to defend and protect their ownership and interests against issues such as government demolition, unpopular housing regulations, or conflicts with property management companies. Studies find that the homeowner activists have started to develop horizontal connections beyond the boundaries of individual neighborhoods and imposed collective influence on related policy inputs and law formulation, though this tendency is still limited to big cities like Beijing and Guangzhou (Chung 2015; Xia and Guan 2014). Occasionally other types of urban protests, primarily driven by various accidents and events, have erupted, such as protests against the chemical-warehouse explosion in Tianjin in 2015, parents' street demonstration on a vaccine scandal in 2018, and nationwide protests of fans after a humorous online video app was banned by the authorities for "vulgar content" in 2018. In contrast to the environmental and homeowner rights-protection movement, these protests usually occur less frequently and with very short duration and limited influences.

The passive rights-protection activism has generally been driven by specific interest-violations over "not in my backyard" issues such as living conditions, children's education, home demolitions, or pollution. These issues critically impact the quality of livelihood of the urban propertied class and are thus tightly related to their very basic material interests and needs. It is not surprising to observe some horizontal connections derived from the deeply shared expectation and insecurity, such as the homeowners' cross-neighborhood coalitions in Beijing. The horizontal association is more of an effort to organize different consumer interests than the formation of general rights consciousness and a sense of unified citizenship identity, as some scholars claim (e.g., Xia and Guan 2014). All the issues the propertied class targets are problems that can be corrected within the existing political system rather than critical institutional flaws that only could be overhauled via dramatic regime change. None of the protests aim at sensitive issues or a broader political agenda. Participants' decision to engage in regime change revolt hinges on whether the odds of success or the reward of revolt are high enough to risk breaking the status quo in which they still hold a critical stake (Lorentzen 2014). As Nathan (2016, 12) argues, the issues that the propertied class protests over "are not scalable to the level of a class interest defined against the existing political order." By the same token, the protests by the urban capitalists and the middle class are less likely to pose a threat to the regime.

It has also been observed that the propertied class protests featured "rightful resistance" which was proposed by O'Brien and Li (2006) as a key characteristic of rural uprisings in China. The urban participators often choose peaceful demonstration and online discussion than violent protests and confrontation with the authorities. They have taken advantage of state rhetoric, policy, and laws to justify their contentious behavior, and mainly aimed at local officialdom. In a survey of middle-class participators in a protest over the proposed expansion of a PX chemical plant in Ningbo, Miao (2016) finds that the respondents proclaimed their loyalty to the Party-state, expressed their respect to the law and regulation, and believed they as the middle class, are the stabilizers of Chinese society and an ally rather than an opponent of the reformist government.

More importantly, these urban social uprisings have been largely tolerated, if not encouraged, by the Party-state. Because of the interest-based nature of the urban protests, their goals seem to fit the long-term development strategy of the state: for example, the environmental movement echoes the state's efforts toward sustainable development; homeowner activism is in line with the government's strategy of community construction and self-governance; and protests over consumer product safety parallels the state's resolutions about market regulation. The protests are usually sympathized with by the authorities because the protested issues often involve critical livelihood crises with impacts on many people; some even affect government officials themselves and their families, and others with relatively high social influence. Thus, these protests act like a watchdog rather than a threat, alarming the state when it infringes too much on the rights and interests of the urban propertied class and pushing the government back to the table for better implementation of state policies.

VALUE SHIFTING OF THE CHINESE
CAPITALIST AND MIDDLE CLASS

Scholars tend to underline the importance of political attitude and social value in explaining the role of the private entrepreneurs and the middle class in the democratic transition process (Almond and Verba 1963; Lipset 1959). The logic of value shaping of the propertied class driven by economic growth and social prosperity is supported by Maslow's classic psychological model of human needs. It states that once an individual is no longer constrained by basic physiological needs, he is free and motivated to pursue more advanced psychological and social desires, especially the senses of belonging, esteem, and self-actualization (Maslow 1943). Following this line of reasoning, it is widely acknowledged that as a society becomes wealthier, traditional demands for material benefits are gradually replaced by compelling urges for individual freedom and rights as well as more political participation and self-determination, which are regarded as the critical catalyst of democratization.

However, this theory is incomplete. It makes sense to assume that human beings will seek more individual rights and liberty after becoming rich in a Western context, given that individualism and a distrust of state have long been embedded in its culture and history. But the higher level of psychological and social needs pursued by individuals in developing countries after they are pulled out of poverty are not necessarily identical to those in the Western societies, considering the significant differences in cultural and historical experiences. Historical legacies and cultural evolution have a significant and persistent bearing on people's political attitudes and perception. For example, according to the WVS in 2012, the percentages of respondents who believe it is bad to have a strong authoritarian leader were 43 percent in China and 30 percent in Taiwan, compared with much higher rates of positive answers in Germany (75 percent) and the United States (63 percent) (Inglehart et al. 2014). In this sense, it is misleading to expect the members of the Chinese capitalist and middle class to develop the same civic features of individual freedom-seeking and aversion to authority as their counterpart in the West, obviating the influence of the distinct Chinese history and culture. The formation of the post-material values of the propertied class in China bears the mark of their unique civilization and reflects their political and cultural environment.

Having said that, the Chinese capitalists and the middle class have been keeping abreast of global cultural currents, particularly those from developed countries. Looking at Western modernity and prosperity, the Chinese people, mainly the propertied class who has gained many opportunities to be exposed to the outside world, self-consciously accept and emulate what they understand and like about the West, from consumption habits to democratic ideas, though few of these are derived from their own knowledge and experiences. The WVS shows that over 70 percent of the Chinese respondents who perceived themselves as middle class believe that it is good to have a democratic system. However, over 67 percent of this group also think China is already being democratically governed to some degree today (Inglehart et al. 2014). This result is consistent with other survey findings (e.g., Shi 2015; Dickson 2016).

Apparently, the "democracy" that most of the Chinese propertied class perceive is very different from the one in the West. The WVS shows over 68 percent of the Chinese middle-class respondents regard the government's tax function to redistribute social wealth as an essential characteristic of democracy; while over half of them define democracy as people obeying their rulers (Inglehart et al. 2014). Studies find that most members of the propertied class in China support democratic values and individual rights, especially those directly related to the protection of their financial assets and property from the arbitrary governments (Tang 2016; Chen and Lu 2011). However, many of them show no enthusiasm about engaging in government affairs and political activities. The members of the propertied class seem to be clearly aware of the "the distinction between the desirability of a concept and the feasibility of its implementation" (Miao 2016, 171). They are supportive of the idea of democratic self-governance, nevertheless, in real life they are reluctant to participate. According to a survey about community activities in Shanghai in 2016, over 83 percent of the resident respondents expressed their willingness to participate, but only about 30 percent have taken any action. The participatory rates at community public hearings and residents' committee meetings are only 12 percent and 11 percent, respectively.[18] Most scholars explain this *laissez-faire* based on a conventional "society against state" paradigm. For example, they ascribe the gap between democratic perception and behavior to the cynical attitudes toward the civic activities because the members of the propertied class believe their political participation is meaningless under strict state control (Heberer and Gobel 2011). Other scholars contrast the political indifference of most members of the propertied class with those dissidents and human rights activists in China, considering the latter as the pioneers for the former. They believe that most members of the Chinese middle class are categorized within the lower-middle income band, hence are in the middle of the stage of climbing the social ladder by scraping out more wealth accumulation. In this sense, they are still very much occupied by their Maslovian material needs and physical well-being and thus unwilling to engage in political activities. Along with the advancement of the capitalist economy, the Chinese capitalists and the middle class would break their reliance on the state, overcome the sense of insecurity surrounding wealth and property, and act like their counterparts in the Western democracies (Nathan 2016; Chen and Lu 2011). However, not all members of the propertied class are apolitical. The WVS observed that about 43 percent of the Chinese middle class respondants believe politics is important in their life and about half claim they are interested in politics (Inglehart et al. 2014). This segment of the middle class is very likely involved in civic activism, as we mentioned in the last section, mainly the business, cultural, and intellectual elites. How should their activities be perceived? Scholars try to include existing civic activists, who are enthusiastically engaging in political activities while accepting and complying with the boundaries set by the Party-state, in this scale of democratic activism in China. They contend that the civic activism under state confinement could be regarded as a stepping stone for a real civil society in the future because the activists are gaining more democratic experience and confidence to fight for more public space with the monolithic regime (e.g., Nathan 2016).

Nevertheless, the explanations based on the assumption of a confrontational state-society relation is questionable in the Chinese context. The argument of prevailing cynicism conflicts with the high rates of institutional trust in China reported in surveys. The prediction of eventual democratic pursuits by the apolitical members of the Chinese propertied class after the capitalist economy becomes fully developed is unrealistic because China's economy is not pure capitalism; it features a "Comcapitalism" model that not only highlights reform and liberalization, but also emphasizes the indispensable role of the Party-state in economic development. Furthermore, it fails to address the question why the political-psychological evolution of the Chinese propertied class is independent of the country's cultural and historical context. And the "stepping-stone" explanation trying to account for the collaborative and compliant attitudes and behavior of the current civic activists is irrational. If the members of the propertied class have already somehow negotiated a space with the relatively responsive and proactive Party-state to fulfill their policy goals, defend their interests, and hold the government more accountable to some degree, why should they bother to fight for regime change, which cannot guarantee their privileged position, very likely would cause social instability and cost their newfound wealth, and doubtlessly subordinate their interests to a much larger lower class?

In this section, we propose an alternative model of value shifting of the propertied class in China. Once the members of the propertied class arrive at an affluent status, they do begin to pursue more advanced needs, but not necessarily targeting a democratic end following those in the West. The political values and attitudes of the private entrepreneurs and the middle class in China have been deeply shaped by the country's unique historical, cultural, socioeconomic, and even international political environment.

The ancient Chinese maxim "Cultivate the moral self, and then regulate the family, govern the state, and lead the world to peace" (*xiushen qijia zhiguo ping tianxia*) summarizes the typical hierarchical moral expectation of the traditional Confucian culture for average people. It closely links personal interest with that of a nation and country, highlighting collective responsibility and orderly obligations to the family, people, and country as the essential element of individual "self-actualization." This value expectation mechanism, coupled with the concept of the "Mandate of Heaven," has set the fundamental tone of a harmonious state-society interaction given a benevolent government, and is deeply rooted in the mindsets and conscious of the Chinese people.

The traditional cultural principles may explain why some members of the propertied class focus on the interests and benefits of the individual and family and remain political indifferent at this early stage of value system development. Before someone possesses strong moral capacity to engage in politics for the country or to provide for the general public, he should cultivate himself and take care of his family first, leaving the government for problem-solving. The Party-state and society appear to have reached a balanced contractual relation. When most of the members of the propertied class trust the state, as demonstrated by various survey results in China, the apolitical political attitudes also could be interpreted as traditional dependency on the government to solve most of the problems. For example, the WVS shows that over 60 percent of the Chinese middle-class respondents believe that government should take more responsibility to provide for the people (Inglehart et al. 2014). Additionally, Beja (2006) points out that the increasing complexity of modern social problems have estranged the mass public from participating in civic activities. The contractual relationship and inertia to depend on state for problem-solving may address the "fire-alarm" pattern of political participation by many propertied class members: join the collective contentions only when their interests are at risk. Guan and Cai (2015) find that residents are driven to participate in the residents' committee election because they are aware that the formation of the homeowners' committee, which represent their endangered interests, is greatly influenced by the former. It indicates many members of the propertied class are more attracted to those interest-related civic activities to better defend their rights and benefits.

Members of the propertied class in China seem to highly value collective responsibility and obligation to the country rather than individual rights and liberty. It is not to say that they do not care about their personal rights. Over the last four decades, Chinese people, in particular the propertied class, are getting increasingly conscious of their basic political and social rights accompanying the modernization of the country. Rather, collective responsibility and obligation has been put in a more morally advanced position than individual rights. And only those most self-motivated socioeconomic elites could cultivate and possess the moral capacity to speak for the people and assist the government for better governance and stability. Thus, obsession with political stability by the propertied class in China is not just a result of rational calculation, but also has been reinforced by their deeply rooted perception that stabilizing society is their most important collective responsibility as social elites. The WVS shows that two-thirds of the Chinese middle-class respondents think they would never participate in any protests (Inglehart et al. 2014). A recent empirical research posits that more educated people are less likely to participate in protests in China (Ong and Han 2019). Rocca (2017, 5) finds the average Beijinger considers the capacity to behave harmoniously as the most important character of the middle class. Although the democratic and human rights activists such as the late Nobel Laurfate Liu Xiaobo and their efforts to challenge the authorities for individual rights and liberty have gained extensive news coverage of the Western media, they have attracted very little attention from the Chinese public. At a human rights event in 2018, Liu Xiaobo's wife expressed her pessimistic about the democratic consciousness of the Chinese people. She didn't believe that Liu would have had the power to rally the public if he returned to the public's sight (Guo 2018). It is surprising to observe that the aforementioned civic activists, who are labeled by some scholars as at the middle of the democratic activism scale, temporarily compromised with the state and trying to fight for autonomy gradually, have also acted indifferently toward the democratic actions, such as the *Charter 08* movement in 2008. A year after the movement, the number of signatures has only reached 10,000 (Lin 2009). But it makes sense if those civic activists are more influenced by the traditional culture and values, as we proposed. If their primary psychological and social needs rest on collective responsibility and obligation to the country and society rather than to individual rights and liberty, and they are satisfied with the current fruitful interaction with a relatively benevolent state, then they choose not to rally with the democratic pioneers because they did not share the same impulses and even believe that the democratic movement can threaten the stability of Chinese society.

Many scholars are focused on signs of political change and democratic advancement in China and tend to be occupied by confrontational activities of a very small group of prodemocracy activists and dissidents, while consciously or unconsciously ignoring the much larger group of state-friendly civic activists who collaborate with the government via various bottom-up channeling methods to promote interests and benefits for themselves and the members or constituencies they represent. Nathan (2016, 14–15) recognizes the puzzling fact that there are few heroic dissidents in China. To answer the question, he categorizes the whole middle class into four groups based on a Western "society against state" assumption and claims that there is no big difference among these groups because they are all too realistic to fight against the regime. He does mention there are two groups "acceptors" and "ameliorators" who are working within or with the system and believe they contribute to progress of the regime in their own way. Most scholars group these pro-state activists with the rest of the propertied class and criticize that this social class as a whole lacks important citizenry characters such as social awareness and concerns, public morality, and civic virtues (Li 2010). Nevertheless, these descriptions do not fit the historical image of these active members of the propertied class in China: mainly business, cultural, and intellectual elites, who have enthusiastically participated in waves of critical movements in history from anti-imperialism nationalist uprisings in the early 20th century, through the communist insurgency and revolution in the 1940s, to the prodemocracy campaign in the 1970s and 1980s. It is also unfair to dismiss the efforts of the civic activists just because they are believed to be coopted by the state and engage in politics under the supervision of the government.

These business, cultural, and intellectual elites generally consist of scholars, lawyers, media workers, journalists and editors, professionals, white-collar officers, well-educated businesspeople and entrepreneurs, college students, activists and volunteers in NGOs, former government officials and cadres in various levels of governments, and managers and specialists in other public sectors (Zhu 2016). They interact with the state individually or collectively, effectively shaping the landscape of policy making (Zhu 2016; Yao and Han 2016), government accountability (Ergenc 2014; Lorentzen 2014), and public goods provisions through multifarious proactive channeling means such as policy advocacy and lobby, NGO participation, public hearing, and public service volunteering. They do possess a certain social consciousness and public morality, civic virtue, a capacity for analytical thinking and reasonable argument, and an idealist belief that they contribute to the betterment of the country. What they seek to self-actualize is the perfection of the moral capacity of collective responsibility and obligation to the country and people. Therefore, their social elite identity is often associated with a counselor role in assisting and pressuring the state for better governance and responsiveness, and a spokesperson role in being concerned with public affairs and representing the mass public (Beja 2006, 66). Therefore, they are more sensitive toward corruption and less tolerant of malfeasance and power abuse of the government than other groups. The resentment toward official corruption motivated the business, cultural, and intellectual elites into the prodemocracy movement in the late 1980s. Xi's anti-corruption campaign has lately greatly satisfied this propertied class group and largely eased tensions between the state and intellectual elites which had accumulated over the past decades.

In addition, members of the private entrepreneurs and the middle class, in particular the business and intellectual elites are extremely patriotic, and sensitive to national security issues. Some Western scholars attribute the nationalist sentiment of the newly emergent middle class to their lack of economic and status security at the early stage (Lipset 1959; Huntington 1993). But this theory is again incomplete due to its failure to consider the level of importance of the civilization, history, and culture in the minds of average Chinese people. As Rocca (2017, 142) points out they are "fierce nationalists, always quick to defend the honor of the nation." For the business, cultural, and intellectual elites in China, patriotism and nationalism are the most important route to fulfill their moral collective responsibility. The WVS shows over 80 percent of the propertied class respondents in China are proud of their nationality. And about 75 percent of them claimed their willingness to fight for their country, comparing to 57 percent in the United States, 35 percent in Argentina, and 63 percent in South Korea (Inglehart et al. 2014). It is not surprising to observe that Xi's "China Dream," which promulgates an ambitious political manifesto to realize the great rejuvenation of the Chinese civilization and build a strong and wealthy country, has been greatly echoed by the members of the propertied class. In a 17-city survey, Lu (2015) finds that the urban residents highly support the "China Dream." The recent trade war between the United States and China has been viewed as a compelling threat and bully from the West, facilitating the growth of a popular loyalist and patriotic response from the business, cultural, and intellectual elites (Li 2018).

Although the evolution of the capitalists and the middle class in China shares several common features with those of other developing countries, there is uniqueness of this development trajectory that contributes to political indifference toward democracy and regime change. China doesn't have a previously existed civil society that could be reignited when a possibility emerges. Nor does China have uninterrupted capitalist economic development, which could gradually strengthen the capitalists and the middle class. The elimination of the propertied class after the CCP took control eradicated any social capital accumulated before 1949. As such, the Chinese capitalist and middle class was literally given birth and raised by the Party-state in the post-Mao era in accordance with the regime's goals to maintain stability and legitimacy. It is not exaggerating to say that the political discourse and socio-political traits of the newly emerged propertied class have been shaped and molded by the Party-state. One important consequent structural feature is that over half of the capitalists and members of the middle class are formal government officials and cadres and employees in public sectors, implying a cozy cronyistic relationship between the state and the propertied class.

As a late developer and communist country with a distinct civilization, China confronts an international environment featuring not only fierce competition and protectionism, but also an atmosphere of rivalry, distrust, and even hostility. Subsequently, the state has initiated the economy reform, not only acting as an agent of political order but also responsible for facilitating socioeconomic development. The survival instinct makes the capitalist and middle class tightly cling to the Party-state. As a developmental state, the CCP regime has dedicated to the economic development and generously provides various benefits, resources, opportunities, and protection to the capitalist and middle class. The patrimonial feature of the system further makes the connection to and affiliation with the government a necessary condition for individual and family success. The propertied class has also depended on the state to accommodate and contain the lower classes, keeping them weak, unorganized, and less threatening to the capitalist advancement and social stability. The ongoing trade war with the United States has justified the necessity and importance of a powerful proactive Party-state, further strengthening the nexus between the state and the propertied class. The deeply entrenched, indispensable, and murky state dependency has positioned the private entrepreneurs and the middle class as an ally of the state, depriving them of any incentive to challenge the authoritarian regime and break the status quo.

Third, over the past decades, the one-dimension top-down state corporatism has been dramatically changed and reconfigured into a much broader array of collaborative and interdependent interaction between the state and propertied class in China. The CCP regime has realized the imperative of depending on the business, cultural, and intellectual elites for information, resources, and expertise in policymaking and public good provision. It becomes reactive and strategic. More channeling routes, though under state control, have been provided to the propertied class to promote their political participation, to voice their opinions, concerns, and grievances. Regardless of the expectations of scholars, the vast majority of the members of the propertied class have enjoyed this "supervised public space" offered by the Party-state. They are pragmatic and strategic, too. Autonomy never poses as a problem to the civic activists, no matter whether they act individually or collectively, proactively or passively, as long as their participatory efforts are efficacious. Indeed, almost all the civic activists in China prefer closer embeddedness with the state to compete for attention, resources, and opportunities so that they could better fulfill their policy goals and defend their interests. The pragmatism and mutual interdependence defy the conventionally perceived "society against state" assumption. The effective bottom-up channeling mechanism and responsiveness of the Party-state seem to satisfy the participatory needs of the propertied class and meet their minimum criteria for a benevolent government. Therefore, at least at this point, a contractual interdependent relationship between the state and the propertied class has reached equilibrium.

Finally, because of the huge historical and cultural difference between China and Western countries, it is very likely that the value shifting process of the propertied class may head toward a different end than the Western models. Being well educated and living a decent life, they will become more interested in civic morality and virtue and concerned about public affairs. But they won't necessarily prioritize the individual rights and liberty largely derived from a unique Western culture. The formation of the value system will likely be profoundly influenced by historical, cultural, and socioeconomic factors primarily derived from the indigenous knowledge and experiences. In China, the traditional Confucian culture has long highlighted collective responsibility and obligation to the state and people as the most noble and highest level of self-cultivated morality. History has proven that these values and perceptions are squarely rooted in the minds of the business, cultural, and intellectual elites. In this sense, the members of the propertied class may accept and even look up to the democratic ideas and system because they perceive democracy along with science and modernity as the most attractive features of advanced Western developed countries. Of course, the self-assumed rosy image of democracy is fragile as they acquire more information and knowledge about Western countries and the chaos of some Western regimes (Huang 2015a). Highly valued post-material perceptions such as freedom of expression and association are quickly replaced by more conservative pro-state thinking whenever external threats to the country are perceived (Reilly 2016). More importantly, members of the propertied class in China never prioritize democratic ideas because deep in their hearts an ideal society of "*xiaokao* and *datong*" (moderately prosperous and great harmony and unity) and a contractual state-society relationship based on the "Mandate of Heaven" are more attractive, suitable, and earnest, whether from the consideration of national security concern, cultural inheritance and continuity, or the socioeconomic context of contemporary China.

To put it succinctly, our proposition and analysis about the political orientation of the Chinese capitalists and the middle class presents a very different expectation for their future political evolution in contrast to many conventionally, especially Western, perceived predictions. The majority of the propertied class appears to think the Party-state has fulfilled the social contract adequately. It seems irrational to assume that after they gain more experience in political engagement, the business, cultural, and intellectual elites would pursue more autonomy which has never been regarded as a critical goal for them. It is also unrealistic to predict that, as the Chinese propertied class grows richer, they would eventually create pressure for democratization. First, no empirical evidence indicates that the existing members of the upper and upper-middle income strata in China have ever enthusiastically fought for democratization. Second, given the Party-state's dedication and commitment to the contractual goals, there is no incentive for the propertied class to give up a functioning political system and fight for democracy, which has proved problematic in most developing countries and even in the Western liberal democratic world.

NOTES

1. See the article "*ZhongGuo Xiangzhen Qiye de Qianshi Jinsheng* (Evolution of Chinese Township Enterprises)." *People.com*, April 24, 2007. http://finance.people.com.cn/GB/1045/5657214.html.

2. The data are from the article "*Zhongguo Minying Jingji Fazhan Jinru Xinde Lishi Jieduan* (China's Private Economy Has Entered New Historical Period)." *Qiushi*, March 31, 2017. http://www.qstheory.cn/dukan/qs/2017-03/31/c_1120706998.htm.

3. See the article "*Lishu ZhongGuo Xiahai Jingshang Guanyuan* (Chinese Former Officials Went to Business)." *China Weekly*, October 21, 2009. http://news.sina.com.cn/c/2009-10-21/181718878437.shtml.

4. The term refers to the phenomenon of quitting jobs, mainly in the public sector, and going into the "sea" of the business world in the 1980s and 1990s in China.

5. According to the World Bank, $5.5 is the cutoff of the poverty line of upper middle-income countries. The data are from the World Bank Poverty & Equity Database. See http://povertydata.worldbank.org/poverty/country/CHN.

6. The data are from the PRC's NBS website. See http://www.stats.gov.cn/was5/web/search?channelid=288041&andsen=%E8%81%8C%E5%B7%A5%E5%B9%B3%E5%9D%87%E5%B7%A5%E8%B5%84; http://www.stats.gov.cn/tjsj/ndsj/2001c/e0520c.htm.

7. The estimation is based on a report about China's white-collar netizens. See http://www.199it.com/archives/125019.html.

8. See the article "225m Reasons for China's Leader to Worry." *The Economist*, July 9, 2016. https://www.economist.com/leaders/2016/07/09/225m-reasons-for-chinas-leaders-to-worry?cid1=cust/ednew/n/bl/n/2016077n/owned/n/n/nwl/n/n/NA/n.

9. See 2018 Hurun China Rich List http://www.hurun.net/EN/Article/Details?num=E406EB5BC439.

10. See https://www.millercanfield.com/resources-341.html for the U.S. export control laws applicable to China provided by the website of Miller Canfield, November 2013.

11. See details from the website of Ministry of Finance of the PRC http://www.mof.gov.cn/zhuantihuigu/czjbqk2011/czzc2011/201208/t20120831_679874.html.

12. The data come from the company's financials that were made public online. See http://www.cninfo.com.cn/finalpage/2018-03-23/1204506834.PDF.

13. See details from the website of the Ministry of Finance of the PRC. http://www.mof.gov.cn/zhuantihuigu/czjbqk2011/czzc2011/201208/t20120831_679874.html.

14. The data are from Fortune China 2018. http://www.fortunechina.com/fortune500/c/2018-07/19/content_311046.htm.

15. See "Comparing Crony Capitalism around the World." *The Economist*, May 5, 2016. https://www.economist.com/graphic-detail/2016/05/05/comparing-crony-capitalism-around-the-world.

16. See the appendix for more details about the survey.

17. The data are from the Environmental Justice Atlas. https://ejatlas.org/conflict/protest-against-gaoqiao-paraxylene-px-plant-relocating-in-jinshan-shanghai-china.

18. The data are from the community survey by the Shanghai municipal government in 2016. http://www.shanghai.gov.cn/nw2/nw2314/nw24651/nw39559/nw39606/u21aw1145444.html.

Chapter Seven

The Marginalized Social Class

Workers and Peasants

In 2011, the residents in Wukan, a fishing village in China's Guangdong province, staged a rebellion against corrupt local officials over the sale of communal lands. The whole village was temporarily controlled by angry villagers calling for a new fair villagers' committee election. In 2018, the workers at Jasic Technology, a private company in Shenzhen, took to the streets to protest inhumane working conditions, unfair dismissals, harassment, and retaliation over their legitimate efforts to form a self-governing labor union. Since 2016, army veterans have staged several protests, demonstrating their grievances over low military pensions and poor veteran treatment in various parts of the country. These mass incidents along with many others have been internationally reported and regarded as the tip of the iceberg, suggesting a brewing nationwide lower-class uprising. While hope and enthusiasm regarding Chinese democratization have been rekindled among Western scholars and China observers, few have closely examined the significant recurring details in these protests. In the Wukan incident, the protesters insisted calling for direct interference from higher authorities; in the Jasic labor unrest, the workers refused help from overseas labor organizations, instead seeking support from the Maoists to confirm their proletarian rights in the communist regime; in the veterans' movements, the demonstrators proudly waved national flags to express loyalty to the Communist Party and its authority, catering to the government for grievance redress (Buckley 2018b).

If the pro-state risk-averse capitalists and the middle class are leery of democratization, could the marginalized working class and peasants be counted on as a sufficiently angry and discontented social agent to topple the authoritarian regime, as their predecessors did 70 years ago? Or are the growing grassroots contentions merely a way to voice demand and grievance within the system and reach out to the CCP authorities which the demonstrators still considered legitimate? How have the working class and peasants dropped from a privileged dominant position to the bottom of Chinese society over the past decades? How do we understand the political orientation of this marginalized lower class in China's booming economy? In this chapter we explore these questions by analyzing the evolution, current condition, political perception, and economic interests of the Chinese working class and peasants, as well as the increasing labor protests and rural unrest. We argue that the political stance of the lower class is determined by its economic, social, political, cultural, and structural characteristics, derived from a unique Chinese context. Being largely marginalized by the market reform, the members of the property-less class are weak, divided, and primarily dependent on the state, and thus unlikely to pose a threat to the CCP regime.

THE ROLE OF THE PROLETARIAT AND PEASANTRY IN REGIME CHANGE

The Property-less as a Social Agent in Early Democratization

While some scholars define Western democratization as an elite-led liberal triumph from above, others cast doubt on the rationality of the propertied class risking their privileged stance in a majority-rule system advocated by themselves. Instead, the role of the industrial proletariat has been portrayed as the champion of a bottom-up democratic movement to fight for political inclusion and repressed material interests (Marshall 1950; Thompson 1963; Therborn 1977; Rueschemeyer, Stephens, and Stephens 1992). It is argued that the primary goal of the bourgeoise was to introduce a representative government to defend capitalist interests and prevent the state from infringing on their civil liberties and political rights. The capitalists originally opposed the very fundamental idea of a true democracy to share political rights with the property-less class through institutional settings (Bellin 2000, 176). Once they have attained prosperity and hold an increasing stake in the status quo, the propertied class is usually the first to be satisfied with the state's democratic concessions, realizing further demands could exacerbate social tension and lead to instability, which could endanger their interests and benefits. In light of the vivid disparity between their backwardness in a capitalist socioeconomic system and their tremendous contribution in the economy, the working class is the most committed agent for political empowerment and legislative representation to redress their unequal treatment and grievances (Rueschemeyer, Stephens, and Stephens 1992; Owen 2015). Thompson (1963) describes an epic historical evolution of how the English workers developed genuine class consciousness, and, though betrayed by the middle-class reformers, took great pains to fight for universal suffrage. In the United States, the labor radicalism and upheavals had forced great concessions from the government, producing democratic transition in the early 20th century (Helgeson 2016).

In contrast to the importance of the working class in early Western regime change, the role of the peasants in democratization is largely neglected, or even regarded negatively. The Enclosure Movement in Britain and France, an agrarian movement toward commercial agriculture, has deconstructed the peasantry, resulting in a politically impotent rural force (Rozental 1956). The sweeping industrial revolution of Western Europe attracted farmers to leave their land for the cities, transforming them into urban workers. Therefore, peasants in countries like England, France, and the United States played no significant role in the capitalist democratic transition (Moore 1966). Furthermore, Moore even suggests an adversarial effect of a strong peasantry in a democratization process in both early industrializers such as Germany and Japan and in relatively undeveloped economies like Russia and China. He hypothesizes that a combination of a weak landed aristocracy and urban bourgeoisie with a powerful peasantry has derailed the social transition in all four countries, resulting in very different types of regime formation than the capitalist democratic route (Moore 1966).

Contingent Democratic Role of Lower Class in Developing Countries

Moore's analysis of the social origins of dictatorship and democracy also implies that lagged industrialization leads to a typical social structure of weak commercial agricultural elites, underdeveloped urban bourgeoisie, and a fragile working class versus a large-sized strong peasantry, making any political transition to democracy unpredictable and less stable (Moore 1966). The volatile political discourse of the multifarious social forces across countries and time in the developing world proves the proposed complexity and variation. Not only are the capitalists and the middle class contingent democrats, the political preferences of the working class and peasants also vary with political, socioeconomic, cultural, historical, and even international factors. In some cases, the property-less class has been the most determined supporter of the democratic project. For example, for workers in South Korea, the harsh working environment, being ruthlessly exploited in an export-led economy, and state hostility toward organized labor due to historical legacy left them no choice but to steadfastly embrace democratic reform (Bellin 2000, 200). However, in other cases, the property-less class was reluctant to champion democratization. For instance, in Malaysia and Singapore, state interference, repressive labor legislation, and suppression of the leftists largely constrained the workers' interests in collective actions (Neu-reiter 2013). In Nepal, a country with 82 percent of the labor force employed in agriculture, the peasants chose to support the Maoist insurgency against electoral democracy because the former promised them land reform and relief from clientelist dependency on landed elites (Joshi and Mason 2008). The most intriguing cases are those that witnessed the change of political orientation of the property-less class given shifting conditions. For example, the working class in Mexico enjoyed a corporatist relationship with the state in exchange for political support until the 1982 debt crisis which forced the government to move toward a neoliberal export-led economy featuring bud-get contraction, privatization, reduction in government subsidies, and caps on wages. Losing the cozy dependent status, more Mexican workers have be-come advocators of democratic transition to fight for their interests and bene-fits (Tilly 2013).

All these cases have shown a common pattern of the political contingency of the working class and peasants in the developing world. Various combina-tions of later development, export-led labor-intensive economic models, and international financial regulations have created a structurally disadvantaged position for workers and peasants in most of developing countries, resulting in deep state dependency. The weaker the capitalist economy, the stronger the dependent relationship between the lower class and the state. Beyond the logic of state corporatism, the political stance of the lower class is also a function of its perceived position with other social forces in society, the capacity of the state to contain and accommodate it, the country's historical legacy and political culture, and the international environment.

THE EVOLUTION OF THE LOWER CLASS
AND STATE-DEPENDENCE IN CHINA

From Aristocrats to the Bottom of Chinese Society

Strong Peasantry and Weak Working Class before 1949

To fully understand the role of workers and peasants in the development of China's political, social, and economic landscape, it is necessary to explore their historic evolution and consequential characteristics. The working class has never been strong in contemporary Chinese history. Chinese capitalist economy developed slowly in the early 20th century due to various internal and external barriers. The economy was primarily dominated by imperialistic foreigners and compradors and later by bureaucratic capitalists closely asso-ciated with the Nationalist government, until the CCP took control in 1949 (Bergere 1989). Accordingly, Chinese society did not undergo a concentrated period of capitalist accumulation and advancement from which a muscular industrial proletariat could emerge and rise. It is estimated that around 1949 there were only a total of 2.4 million industrial workers and about 4 million employees in other economic sectors such as service, mainly in big cities like Shanghai, Beijing, and Nanjing (Dai 2002).[1] The majority of the population in an agrarian China before 1949 lived in the countryside, constituting a prevailing social structure of peasant class. Given a weak landed aristocracy, the overwhelming number of peasants plus their dependence on a centralized feudal bureaucratic state fundamentally determined the trajectory of China's regime formation in the first half of the 20th century (Moore 1966). Furthermore, the victory of the communist movement largely depended on Mao's strategy of "encircling the cities from the rural areas and then capturing them" rather than relying on the working class in the cities as the former Soviet Union did in its proletariat revolution.

Aristocratic Status and False Sense of Authority from 1949 to 1978

Constitutionally, the workers and peasants represent the leading force in a newly established communist society. However, in reality, this constitutional power of the property-less class is illusionary. The means of production are supposed to be owned and controlled by the working class and peasants in a modern communist regime, but the autocratic leaders and the Party often dominate almost every aspect of society. In a non-communist regime, the interests of working class and peasants are at least theoretically represented by left-wing parties like communist party or labor party. However, if the left-wing party becomes the only party in a communist regime, serving the lower class is no longer its exclusive political agenda. So was it in China. After the CCP took over, the workers and peasants lost their independence and had a false sense of authority. The land reform evolved to nationwide collectivization of the rural lands and establishment of the people's commune in 1953. Since then, peasants were deprived of freedom to make decision about their production and products and treated as "collective slaves." For the workers, the capital-labor struggle turned into a lopsided working-class state interaction. The All-China Federation of Trade Union (ACFTU), the officially recognized trade union, represents the interests of the communist regime more than those of the workers. The Party-state claimed that the regime is the only representative of the working class and peasantry. However, wages and incentives were determined by the central government as a matter of national policy with state rhetoric focusing on moral encouragement rather than on material reward. During this period, freedom of strike, which was stated as a fundamental constitutional right of citizens, was in thrall to collective responsibility for maintaining socialist economic order. Despite these restrictions, before Deng's economic reform, the condition of the working class and peasants was relatively sound compared with the rest of society. Although lacking political rights and freedom, they, especially industrial workers, did enjoy many benefits in a planned economy, such as universal free health care, free education, full employment, public or work-unit housing, and retirement pension. For example, according to the World Development Report, free health care covered all urban dwellers and 85 percent of the rural population in China by the end of 1970s, when the period of economic reform began (Berkley et al. 1993).

Declining Social Status since the Reform

The economic reform and openness set the peasants free from the counter-productive collective communes, and greatly spurred the productivity of the workers. However, at the same time, it has gradually marginalized the previous aristocratic classes into a structural and strategically disadvantaged position. As a peripheral economy in a competitive liberal global environment, China heavily relied on a model of export-led and investment-based industrialization in the early stages of the reform, managing to ramp up the economy and achieve prosperity by taking advantage of global division of labor and foreign demand. A vast and quiescent labor force backed up by a massive and docile rural population is the focal point of the Party-state's development strategy. The CCP regime's economic prosperity was built on the exploitation, repression, and exclusion of the Chinese labor. The leftists, losing power due to the stagnant economy before the reform and further silenced by Deng's 1992 Southern China tour, lacked political strength to provide support for the sidelined workers (Yang and Zhao 2015). Ever since the reform, the working class has experienced an increasingly difficult time.

FDI liberalization was one of several early reform strategies adopted by the Party-state. For foreign investors, a cheap, self-disciplined, and non-unionized labor force was extremely attractive. By the early 1990s, foreign enterprises and joint venture companies had sprouted up all over China's East Coast. These firms, which focus on labor-intensive production in Guangdong, Fujian, Jiangsu, and Zhejiang, have absorbed a huge amount of young and inexperienced migrant workers since the 1980s (Yang and Zhao 2015). To court foreign investors, many new practices, very unpopular for the urban workers in the public sector, such as short-term labor contracts and sharp reductions in welfare provision by enterprises, have been encoded into labor laws and regulations designed for the FDI without trigging furious opposition (Gallagher 2002, 355). Indeed, these established laws and regulations were soon applied to other economic sectors, normalizing and legalizing practices such as workforce casualization and separation of business and social functions of firms in China.

The nationwide privatization and bankruptcy of many medium- and small-sized SOEs with resultant massive layoffs since the 1990s have further emasculated the Chinese proletariat. Many urban industrial workers lost their traditional privileges, retirement pensions, health care, job opportunities for their children, and in many cases housing—all of which had been covered by the state employers during the era of command economy. It is estimated that about 40 percent of the labor force in the public sector, around 45 million people, was laid-off during this "restructuring," causing a net equivalent loss of 40 percent of formal urban jobs (Hurst 2009).

Trade unions have played an important role in China's turbulent communist revolution by mobilizing urban workers and organizing labor movements. Shortly after the founding of the communist regime, the government affiliated ACFTU and its subordinate local and enterprise branches were defined as the only representatives of workers by the Trade Union Law. As semi-government entities, the leadership of ACFTU and subordinate agencies are no longer elected by workers they represent but appointed by Party-governments. Therefore, they are now just empty shells in terms of representing and defending workers' interests and rights. The Party-state relies on the official trade unions to collect information, control workers, preserve social stability, and promote economic growth. Along with bankruptcies and privatization of SOEs, the official trade union system has itself been eroded since the late 1990s. In the early twenty-first century, the ACFTU members accounted for only half of the total urban labor force, dropping from almost 100 percent before the reform (China Labor Bulletin (CLB) 2005).[2] An investigation in 2004 showed that about 60 percent of the total 480,000 foreign firms did not install trade unions and by 2003, only about 33 percent of the workers in the private sector were unionized.[3] Nevertheless, even if a labor union is established in a private-owned firm, in accordance with the labor law, it represents the interests of the management and the state more than the workers.

Moreover, the workers' legal right to strike was removed by the 1982 Constitution due to economic stability concern. By 2017, the percentage of industrial workers in the Communist Party has dropped from about 19 percent in 1978 to only 7.4 percent.[4] Workers in China have been gradually losing representative power in the political system. Since strike and protest are illegal, and the union is functionless, the majority of the workers lack mechanisms to channel their discontent and fight for their own rights and interests. They are rapidly falling to the bottom of China's social strata.

Waves of Rural Migrants to Cities

The modernization and industrialization of many developing countries have always been accompanied by fast urbanization and social reconstruction. In Taiwan, the peasant population downsized from 66 percent in 1970 to 30 percent in 2000, and in South Korea from 72 percent in 1960 to 20 percent in

2000.[5] China is no exception. The rural population has dropped from 82 percent in 1978 to 42 percent in 2017. Urban modernity and the industrial transformation process have attracted hundreds of millions of migrant workers to leave the rural hinterland and flood into cities for job opportunities, higher payment, and a better life. By 2016, the number of migrant workers has reached 282 million, accounting for 60 percent of the urban workforce in China (NBS 2009–2017). These migrant workers have become the "backbone" of the export-led economy, tremendously contributing to the stunning development and urban prosperity. It is estimated that internal labor migration has contributed around 21 percent of total GDP in recent years (NBS 2009–2017).

The massive migration of rural population to the cities began to warrant attention when the enormous "*mingongchao*" (influx of migrant workers) almost paralyzed the rail system in South China before the lunar New Year of 1989. In fact, the rural to city migration had begun years earlier. The dissolution of the people's communes and the implementation of the contract responsibility system have greatly boosted the rural productivity. The surplus labor in the countryside began rushing into newly emerged village and township collective enterprises in the neighboring areas in the early 1980s. Since 1984, the Party-state has shifted the reform center from rural area to the cities. The immense inflow of the foreign capital and expansion of the private economy in the urban areas, particularly the East Coast cities, has dramatically increased the demand for cheap labor. Accordingly, the *Hukou* system has been loosening. Abolishment of the food quota system has made it possible for migrant workers to stay longer in the cities. And the urban service sectors have also begun to allow employment of migrant workers since the 1990s. All of these have contributed to the continuous massive migration. The "floating population" jumped from 30 million in 1989 to 100 million in 1997. The privatization of SOEs has induced another wave of influx. To prioritize the employment of laid-off urban workers, some coastal cities and provinces such as Shanghai, Guangdong, and Jiangsu had to issue policies to limit the hiring of migrant workers. There were several setbacks in rural migration due to economic recessions or strict urban policies, but all turned out temporary. Since the early twenty-first century, every year an average of 6 to 8 million more rural young people have joined the army of the "floating population" (NBS 2009–2017).

The working conditions of migrant workers has been harsh. Most are in labor-intensive industries or service sectors such as manufacturing, construction, sanitation, and other menial works that are unattractive for residents in the cities. They work longer hours with lower pay than urban workers, in unconfortable working environments and with few employee rights. There have been frequent news reports about the miserable conditions of migrant workers in foreign-owned factories such as Foxconn, Mattel toy, or Ivanka

Trump's clothing-maker shops (Harwell 2017). Migrant workers have also suffered rampant problems due to nonpayment or late payment in private enterprises. A survey in 2006 showed that less than half of the migrant workforce was getting paid regularly (Lee and Friedman 2009).

Although migrant workers have been essential for China's economic growth over the past decades, they have never been beneficiaries of the Party-state's preferential policies and development strategies. The government has only set out to tackle migrant worker–related problems in a bid to better promote the economy and social stability. For example, the original plans focused on how to ease the pressure of the rural migration on transportation and the overburdened urban infrastructure. Then Premier Wen Jiabao's efforts to address the wage collection for migrant workers were mainly aimed at pacifying this new social force (Lee and Friedman 2009).

The prevalence of the *Hukou* system for decades in China exemplifies the CCP regime's effort to constrain the rural poor in a resource-scarce economy. It has legitimately and effectively blocked the rural poor from accessing urban public services and opportunities such as education, training, investment, health care, housing, and pensions. Since 2016, the urban residence permit has gradually replaced *Hukou* as a city-dwelling restriction, particularly for megacities, provincial capitals, and second-tier cities, in order to enable these economic and political centers to absorb qualified skilled and talented outsiders and simultaneously provide generous public services and welfare for privileged urban residents.[6] These policies successfully differentiate and alienate the urban affluent from the rural lower class, particularly migrant workers who have been swamping the coastal cities since the 1990s. In the winter of 2017, the Beijing municipal authorities launched a slum clearance program to drive out unwanted migrants, an example of aggressive efforts by the government to control the massive influx of the poor migrants who are discriminatorily labeled as "low-end population" (A. Li 2017).

Left and Trapped in the Countryside

The rural liberalization has unleashed the peasants from the collective communes. The new agricultural production institution is a combination of Chinese traditional farming and socialism. It has restored the traditional practice of farming based on households but kept the collective ownership of the land, thus assigning or leasing the land to peasants for farming on a per capita basis. In a word, this reform just turned peasants back to "individual producers," and was not well adapted to modern farming that is based on technology and machinery. In China, therefore, agricultural modernization has been occurring slowly. After a short period of significant initial economic improvement in the early 1980s, the rural economy has been losing its energy and stagnating (Zhong 2013).

Compounding these problems, the village and township enterprises and later the private and foreign firms in the coastal regions have absorbed the vast majority of the young male labor force from rural areas. By 2016, over half of the rural population consisted of migrant workers working in towns and cities (NBS 2009–2017). Old people, women, and children accounted for a significant percentage of those left in the countryside. Losing a major farm labor force, the preferential development strategies favoring urbanities, and various agricultural taxes and fees have depleted the agrarian resources and restricted agricultural development, deteriorating the living conditions for the massive rural population. Today there are still many peasants in China that are preoccupied with simply producing enough food to eat, for themselves. Over 40 million rural inhabitants in some remote and inaccessible areas still lived below the national poverty line by the end of 2017. The old healthcare system was abandoned with the disappearance of the people's communes. Over 95 percent of the rural population must pay all medical costs out of pocket in the 1980s and 1990s (S. Yu 2010). The *Hukou* system made it possible for the Party-state to focus its energy and resources on industrial urban centers. However, it also resulted in asymmetrical two-dimensional development, with inland rural regions lagging far behind the east metropolitan areas. By 2017, the average disposable income of an urban resident reached 36,396 yuan, 2.7 times that of a rural villager (NBS 2009–2017). People living in the countryside have been denied access to the economic prosperity they once fought for.

Conditions and Features of the Working Class and Peasantry

Fragmented Chinese Labor and Diverse Interests

The *Hukou* system, by classifying the population in the countryside as a category inferior to that in the cities, has resulted in a huge human development gap between these two groups. Further, incomplete market reform, featuring a significant percent of SOEs, contributes to the dichotomy of employment with vivid difference between workers in public and private sectors. The Party-state's uneven development policies have also created great disparities across regions and industrial sectors. All these contribute to internal heterogeneity of the workforce in China. Apparently, the socioeconomic, geographical, and political conditions in China have never been conducive for the development of a radical and cohesive working class. Decades of divided policies have led to significant cleavages between various Chinese labor subgroups. These subgroups have faced varied challenges and opportunities, and have developed divergent, if not conflicting, interests and perceptions.

One important cause of diversity in the Chinese workforce lies in the employment opportunities and policies in different sectors and industries. In 1978, all workers worked in SOEs or collective work units. The unified working class was significantly weakened as economic privatization progressed. The large-scale layoffs in SOEs in the 1990s eventually broke the old working class into three groups. The first group is composed of older and low skilled workers or those in bankrupted SOEs, who were laid off and later retired or became self-employed. The second group consists of highly skilled workers, who have been attracted by the rapid-growing private economy and decided to voluntarily leave and found better jobs in foreign firms or private enterprises. Some of these entered the low-middle income strata and become the "marginalized middle class." The third group, primarily urban residents, consists of those who survived waves of layoffs, and along with new recruits in large SOEs, becoming the only working class in the public sector. By 2015, the number of workers in this group had dropped to 34 million, accounting for about 15 percent of the total urban workers. As organized labor, they are concentrated in critical industries such as motor vehicles and parts, oil and gas exploration and production, petroleum refining, chemical, metals and minerals, and telecommunication. These workers enjoy relatively better wages, benefits, insurance and pensions, working environments, and job security. A report about average wages in 851 large SOEs nationwide indicates that workers in the public sector earned about 109,900 yuan in 2012, almost four times of the average annual income of migrant workers that year (NBS 2009–2017).[7] Though the minority in the Chinese labor force, workers in SOEs are the ones with the "iron rice bowl" and benefit from their dependent relationship with the Party-state. They have little incentive to challenge the regime, in fear of losing their relatively privileged status.

The urban-rural division within the workforce has been the root of many unequal features. Most social services and welfare are contingent on one's household-registration status. The reform, by diverting social functions from the work units to local municipalities, has reduced the burden on businesses and continued to guarantee workers' subsistence beyond wages. However, this arrangement did not include migrant workers. Now, over half of the urban workforce are peasant migrants, most of them denied access to the basic resident-only public welfare and social services. For example, almost all substantial welfare benefits in Shanghai, such as the housing subsidies for low-income households, a minimum living standard guarantee, and health-care for seniors and people with disabilities, require local residency.[8] Moreover, the migrant workers have been excluded from the benefits of the housing reform focused on urban dwellers. Not surprisingly, the migrant and residential workers have very different stakes in the social status quo. In addition, most migrants' work in the private sector is temporary, part-time, or casual employment, putting them in a more disadvantaged position with little bargaining power.

In a survey to compare how the different public groups benefited from the reform, Lu (2010, 113) finds that unskilled workers were the relative losers in China. The majority of the migrant workers are young, with low education and no skill. They hold the lowest rung in the system comparing to the rest of the workforce. However, they are also the most easily satisfied. Most of them came from areas with prevailing poverty. In contrast to the life in the remoted hinterland, their incomes and living standards in cities are a great improvement. A national survey in 2017 showed that over 90 percent of the migrant workers were satisfied with their lives (NBS 2009–2017).

Socialist Countryside and Peasants' State-Dependency

Traditionally, the peasants have been tightly dependent on the state for subsistence and protection in China. This state-dependency was tremendously enforced as the CCP regime bounded peasants closely through collective people's communes since 1950s. After the economic reform, the farmers were allowed to produce as they could and sell extra product in the free market, but all lands were still collective or state properties, indicating the persistence of a dependent relation between the peasantry and the Party-state. The peasants have continued to rely heavily on the government for income, local public service and welfare provision, infrastructure, disaster relief, flood and drought mitigation, various government subsidies, and even market protection.

Although the economic reform seems to discriminate against the inland western regions and caters more to the development needs of the coastal areas, that doesn't mean the Party-state hasn't made efforts to conciliate and accommodate the marginalized rural population. To the contrary, the CCP regime's "Comcapitalism" development model is characterized by a strategy targeting a structural balance between the rich and the poor, the business and the society, and the rural and the urban. While Jiang concentrated on economic liberalization, the following Hu-Wen administration focused more on social equity and economic sustainability. Since the early 21st century, the Party-state has begun to tackle the "*sannong wenti*" (three rural problems)—*nongye* (agriculture), *nongmin* (farmers), and *nongcun* (rural area) that have accumulated since the reform.

The government launched a "Go-west" campaign in 2000 to promote economic development of China's western inland regions by focusing on infrastructure construction, FDI, environmental protection, and education. By 2016, about $914 billion had been invested there in 300 major projects, mostly in infrastructure and energy.[9] A series of monumental reforms addressing the most acute rural problems have been launched since early 2000s.

A new rural cooperative medical system was established in 2003, aiming to cover the vast majority of the rural population by 2010 (S. Yu 2010). The Party-state has initiated a grand program of "building a new socialist countryside," assertively committing itself to rural development in each following Five-Year plan since 2005. The government has invested over 6 trillion yuan from 2003 to 2012, and over 1 trillion every year since 2011, in rural areas.[10] The agricultural tax was abolished in 2006 and the state has dramatically increased various subsidies for agricultural production, rural infrastructural construction, and peasants' livelihoods. The same year, a law was passed to provide and rigorously enforce nine years of free education in the countryside. In 2007, a rural minimum living allowance system was introduced to ensure a basic living standard and reduce poverty. The government has also built a rural social pension insurance network since 2009 and expanded it nationwide in 2012 (Shu 2018).

These policies have profoundly influenced life for the rural population. Though the rural living standard is relatively low comparing with that in the cities and the "three rural problems" still remain critical, the substantial progress in improving living standards and the Party-state's sustained efforts and pervasive propaganda have influenced most peasants, making them believe their country is heading in the right direction and optimistic about their future. In the WVS in 2012, over 75 percent of the Chinese respondents who identified themselves as lower class (not include working class) were very satisfied or moderately satisfied with their lives (Inglehart et al. 2014).

In addition, the peasant class has become more internally diverse. The reform has brought more freedom and options. The number of real farmers has been decreasing dramatically, only accounting for 36 percent of the total rural population. Others have left for the cities or have been working in township enterprises. The rest is composed of relatively rich and privileged local government cadres, rural intellectuals, or self-employed entrepreneurs and managers (Zang and Chen 2015). This new internal structure of rural population is hierarchically based on the stake each group holds in the political system. Therefore, the interests of the peasants are no longer unified.

One thing in the Chinese rural areas of note is the rural election system. In one sense, it is a form of democracy because rural residents are able to participate in local politics and air their voices over local decision-making. However, the grassroots village level election system is more like a bounded "local autonomy" rather than a "democracy" (Manion 1996). First, the rural election system was initiated from above; it is not a natural institutional setting derived from below. Second, the election system is confined to the village level, separating from the state administration; there is no sign that the electoral process will be extended to the township level nationwide. Third, the elections have been supervised, and sometime intervened in, by local governments, which control major economic and political resources and thus able to influence the voters' preferences. People in the rural area largely lack appropriate education and adequate political skills or qualifications. Under such circumstances, free village elections mean nothing more than populist dictatorship by the majority in discrete places in the countryside, posing little threat to the CCP regime.

LOWER CLASS ORGANIZED CONTENTIONS AND THE RESPONSE OF THE PARTY-STATE

Labor Movement and Rural Unrest

Waves of Working-Class Movement

Lacking a functional union bargaining mechanism has made collective contention the last powerful resort for Chinese workers in an asymmetrical capital-labor relation. Over the past decades, the communist regime has witnessed a fast-growing working-class movement fighting for its interests and rights. Labor collective resistance, usually reflecting a contentious relationship between workers and employers, has been closely associated with major economic policy change and economic slowdown in China.

The privatizations and bankruptcies of tens of thousands of SOEs since the late 1990s have caused massive layoffs of state employees who had enjoyed job security and benefits since the beginning of the communist regime. Most redundant workers and staff in SOEs were forced to "*maiduan gongling*" (buyout of working years) as a severance package and became unemployed in their 40s and 50s. In 2000, only 35 percent of the laid-off workers had found new jobs; the percentage dropped to 26 percent two years later. Over 85 percent of the reemployed had to work temporarily or as contract workers with low pay and no benefits or insurances (NBS 2009–2017). Their resultant dire living conditions and a strong sense of betrayal have given rise to waves of workers' collective open confrontations in the late 1990s and early 21st century. These protests usually took place in Northeastern and Midwestern China, where many old industrial centers were concentrated. The workers demanded government guarantees of employment and minimum living standards, returned backpay wages, better severance packages, and punishment of corrupt managers responsible for the enterprises' bankruptcies. For example, in the Daqing oil field, a renowned symbol of China's revolutionary industrialization, about 50,000 workers protested against low severance package and government action to stop paying insurance premiums and heating bills (Pomfret 2002). The majority of laid-off workers' protests were interest-based, consisting of peaceful collective petitioning or demonstrations, and were sympathized with by society and the political elites (Cai 2006).

The SOE restructuring and labor marketization have enormously weakened the old working class. Since then workers in private enterprises and foreign firms, in particular the migrant workers, have emerged as the major actors in the mushrooming labor protests during the following decades. Lacking an independent bargaining mechanism and social safety net, the migrant workers are extremely vulnerable to ruthless exploitation and arbitrary working-related rules and regulations by management. As economic marketization proceeds, the labor-capital conflicts have grown sharper. The 2008 financial crisis hit China's export-led economy hard, resulting in the closing of over 67,000 factories in the first half of the year (Wong 2008). The Pearl River Delta and the Yangtze River Delta, two most developed regions attracting the majority of the migrant workers, suffered heavily from the sharp fall in foreign trade and inward FDI. Massive factories shut down, making 20 million migrant workers unemployed or unable to find a job (CLB 2000–2017) and igniting widespread labor disputes and protests over delayed or unpaid wages, particularly in the East Coast provinces of Jiangsu, Zhejiang, and Guangdong. A 2010 strike over pay and working conditions at the Foshan Honda car plant in Southern China marked a milestone in the history of labor conflict, turning migrant workers' resistance from a "passive and individual actions" model, which usually takes the form of committing suicide or threatening suicide to express desperation over sweatshop working conditions, to a more "active and collective" model aiming at gaining better payment and respect through orderly staging of strikes, and even collective negotiation and bargain (Guo 2014, 426–427). The increased labor wages in the coastal regions, coupled with the slowdown of China's economy, have forced up production costs and driven many labor-intensive firms to move to the inland provinces or even other countries with cheaper labor. The government has begun to tackle the problem of industrial overproduction since 2012, cutting production in industries like chemicals, steel, shipbuilding, and solar power. In the meantime, the Party-state has embarked on an ambitious economic transition from an export-led economy to a consumption-based one focusing more on innovation and technology. For example, in Dongguan, a city known as "world factory" due to its strong processing and export-oriented production and with migrant workers accounting for 75 percent of its population, the government has invested 200 million yuan each year from 2014 to 2016 to help enterprises implement advanced industrial automation (Keegan 2018). Under such circumstances, the traditional labor-intensive manufacturing industry in the coastal regions has been impacted severely, resulting in a new wave of labor protests since 2014. According to the CLB, about 1,200 labor protests and strikes have been recorded from 2011 to 2013. The number of recorded labor unrests rose to 1,379 in 2014, and to over 2,770 the following year (Griffiths 2016; CLB 2016).

Rising collective resistance was not limited to the manufacturing sector. It also spread to other industrial and service fields such as transportation, education, and wholesale. For instance, China's stressed-out taxi drivers have staged waves of strikes across the country since the early 2000s, protesting over rising fuel prices, low fares, and transportation apps that are squeezing their business profits. Teachers, particularly in the inland areas, as well as sanitation workers, veterans, and bus drivers have all joined the rising lower-class unrests over the last decades, mainly demanding higher wages, insurance coverage, and better working conditions.

Overview of the Rural Organized Contentions

In rural China, desperate peasants often resort to collective action to redress their grievances over issues such as excessive agricultural taxes and fees, deteriorating pollution of water and farmland, land acquisition with unfair compensation and murky process, and malfeasance and corruption of local cadres. In the 1990s and early 2000s, tax revolts organized by overburdened farmers prevailed in rural China, especially in the remote inland areas. For example, in 1999, in Fengcheng city, Jiangxi, tens of thousands of peasants protested violently over excessive taxes and ransacked the local government offices (Tong and Lei 2014). The large-scale riot shocked the central government and led to major agricultural tax reform in the following years.

Around the turn of this century, rapid urbanization, industrial expansion, and associated infrastructure projects across the country made land allocation an increasingly critical factor in China's quest for economic prosperity and social stability. The rising demand for industrial land by urban capital stimulated profit-seeking local governments and agrarian capitalists to deprive peasants of their land leaseholder rights and convert large amount of farmlands for non-agricultural use. It is estimated that urban sprawl has caused about 2 million farmers to lose their farmlands every year (Huang et al. 2017). And the total number of landless farmers will likely reach 100 million by 2020.[11] For many, farmlands are their only source of livelihood, yet they are only compensated with a very small percentage of the revenues generated through sales of those confiscated lands. Over 90 percent of the profits go to township and village governments (Chan, Backstrom, and Mason 2014). Predictably, forced and illegal land acquisition and unfair compensation became another major cause that fueled a new round of rural resistance and contention in the 21st century. Land disputes now account for over 60 percent of the tens of thousands of protests in China every year (Economy 2012). In 2011, the angry villagers of Wukan stood up against unjust land grabs and demanded free villagers' committee elections, setting a model for their counterparts in the rest of rural China.

The third most widespread cause of rural discontent and protests rests on growing pollution and dam construction in the countryside. The rural environmental complaints and unrest have soared up along with the rising concerns over air, land, water, and noise pollution. The number of the environment disputes increased from 51,000 in 2004 to 128,000 in 2005 (Ma 2008). For example, over 500 local residents in Hongxiao village, Zhejiang, staged a violent protest over pollution caused by a nearby solar panel factory and resulted in its closure by a government order in 2011.[12] In 2005, thousands of villagers in Huaxi, Zhejiang province protested against pollution from nearby factories (Yardley 2005).

State Accommodation and Containment

Taking Care of Critical Grassroots Social Issues

Facing serious social uprising, with almost 500 protests every day, how has the Party-state managed to maintain order? Clearly, heavy coercion alone cannot solve the problem; sometimes brutal repression provokes greater anger and discontent and escalates conflicts. The CCP regime's attitude and strategy toward these lower-class "mass incidents" has changed from repressive to a more proactive tone. In 2004, the Party-state issued *Opinion on the Work of Actively Preventing and Properly Handling Mass Incidents*. For the first time, the lower class's collective resistance to address economic concerns and redress grievances was defined as a "non-antagonistic contradiction arising from harm to personal livelihoods and interests," though still illegal (Biddulph 2015, 10). The general guideline highlighted the depoliticization of social unrest and destigmatized the "disruptive social order" narrative. While the state security apparatus is still ready to suppress violent contentions, the authorities have begun to take a softer and more sophisticated approach using tolerance, persuasion, education, and responsiveness to handle the grassroots resistance (e.g., Yang 2015; Chan, Backstrom, and Mason 2014). To appease protesters and contain the conflicts, on one hand, police force is deployed to block the road and control the conflict scene, while news and information are censored to prevent it from spreading and known by the mass public. On the other hand, the governments often make a series of concessions such as postponing the SOE's restructuring process, punishing corrupt officials, paying off delayed wages for firm owners who have escaped, and issuing temporary government cash subsidies to unemployed workers and farmers (CLB 2000–2017). For example, in 2008, about 7,000 workers in Dongguan staged a sit-in outside the township government, protesting over unpaid wages due to sudden bankruptcy of several factories. The uprising was put to an end when the local government managed to pay the workers 24 million yuan of their total owed wages.[13] Though the soft problem-solving strategy alone cannot fix systemic flaws, it has greatly contributed to social stability, at least in the short run.

Since the Hu-Wen administration, the government has shifted from solely focusing on economic reform to managing a structural balance between economic growth and social equity, namely the rich and the poor. *Minsheng*, or people's well-being, has become the catchword of consecutive government work reports and Five-Year plans. Chinese leadership has constantly highlighted the importance of caring for people's livelihoods, expanding employment, improving the social safety net, reforming the income distribution mechanism, poverty reduction, and environmental protection as working priorities. A series of substantive policies and legislations have been issued targeting the roots of some prominent and rampant social problems, largely easing the social tension.

In response to rural discontent and unrest over excessive local taxes and surcharges, the central government began to address the problem in the late 1990s. In 2002, the Party-state officially enacted the tax-for-fee reform and replaced various fees levied on farmers with one single agricultural tax (Kennedy 2007). In 2004, the central government further lowered the agricultural tax and expanded government subsidies for agrarian production (Yang and Zhao 2015). And the agricultural tax was rescinded in 2006, resulting in a dramatic decline of tax- and fee-related resistance and riots in China's countryside (Tong and Lei 2010). With regards to rampant illegal and forced rural land acquisition and low compensation, the central authority and even the Supreme People's Court have repeatedly called on local governments to protect the rights of farmers, to ensure they receive fair share of the profits from the land conversion, and to cease the activities if facing extreme opposition (Cody 2006). In 2004, the government ordered a decree to freeze the conversion of arable land into non-agricultural uses for half a year due to concerns about falling grain production and overheated housing markets. A series of rules and regulations have been issued to intensify the control of land conversion since then. Heurlin (2016) finds that the central government has been actively responding and addressing many of the protestors' grievances by adopting policy changes as well as enforcing local officialdom for implementation. Since 2014, the central government has initiated a rural land ownership reform program to separate farmland ownership rights, contracted rights, and operating rights. Since legally the lands are still collectively owned, the village and township governments could easily appropriate land for sale or conversion without the consent of the affected farmers. The reform clearly identifies the rights the farmers have over the collective land and imposes market values on contracted and operating rights of the land, allowing the farmers to financially benefit from these rights by either transferring the operating rights, mortgaging the contracted rights to banks, or investing it in exchange for fees or shares.[14]

Though large-scale resistance and demonstrations by laid-off workers have prevailed across the country for almost a decade, the SOE restructuring and massive layoffs were carried out without a substantial political crisis that endangered the regime's rule (Cai 2006). The relatively acquiescence is ascribed to the limited power, resources, and by characteristics of the labor movement we will discuss later, as well as to the Party-state's effort to accommodate and contain the laid-off workers' collective contentions. From 1998 to 2005, the Party-state issued dozens of orders and decrees, requesting and directing provincial and local governments to help with laid-off workers' living conditions and reemployment by all means (CLB 2000–2017). Some substantial policies have been implemented to help the laid-off workers, including subsistence support, free vocational training, tax exemptions, extended small security-backed loans, and capital investment for job creation (Lu and Feng 2008, 64). Since 1998 the government has separated and removed social welfare provision from SOEs to a newly established social security system and demanded that laid-off workers should be guaranteed income support, basic social security and unemployment insurance, and a minimum living standard. The population receiving an urban minimum allowance has skyrocketed from 11.7 million in 2001 to 22.4 million by the end of 2006 (Lu and Feng 2008).

In light of the deplorable and powerless condition of most migrant workers and their increasing collective resistance and discontent, the Party-state has undertaken a sequence of policies and legislations to rectify their disadvantaged and discriminated status. It begins to recognize that migrant workers are critical for national economic growth and social stability. In 2006, the central government issued the *Opinions of the State Council on Solving Problems of Migrant Workers*, specifically addressing the problems of these "second class" citizens including low and unpaid wages, long working hours in poor working conditions, lack of social security, work-related disabilities, substandard housing, and children's education (Gleiss 2016). Minimum wages cross the country have grown at an average rate of 11 percent since the state promulgated new minimum wage regulations in 2004.[15] The following year, three important labor legislations were promulgated: the *Labor Contract Law*, the *Labor Mediation and Arbitration Law*, and the *Employment Promotion Law*. It is believed that China may now even have some of the most protective labor laws in the world (Gallagher 2017).

Besides building of the administrative and legal institutions through which the migrant workers could redress their grievances, the role of the government in capital-labor conflict has also gradually changed. As the private sector becomes a major part of the economy, the Party-state realizes it is not necessary to always side with the management in a capital-labor conflict. Instead, the government has become more neutral, and often acts as a third party to push for capital-labor negotiation in a labor-management conflict.

Furthermore, the central government has been striving painstakingly to incorporate migrant workers into the corporatist system by emphasizing the role of the ACFTU and its local branches in promoting a tripartite system of collective bargaining and enforcing signed employment contracts (Wen and Lin 2015; Clarke, Lee, and Li 2004). Though official trade unions are inefficient and powerless due to failing to effectively represent workers, the tripartite bargaining mechanism has proved functional where the local government is determined and supportive. For example, in Wenling, Zhejiang province, with the intervention and intermediation of the local government and local branch of the ACFTU, annual collective bargaining between the trade association representing the capital and industry-wide labor union has been institutionalized, largely contributing to stable capital-labor relations (Wen and Lin 2015, 666).

Political Economy of State's Proactive Responses

Apparently, the CCP regime has become far more strategic in dealing with lower-class discontent and resistance. While selectively quelling any unrest that poses a direct threat to its rule, the Party-state by and large inclines to rely on a soft and caring method to accommodate and contain the poor. Why would the authoritarian state choose to tolerate, persuade, and concede while facing challenges from the grassroots, given its overwhelming state repressive capacity? An analysis focused on the political economy of the Party-state's proactive responses toward social uprising helps illustrate how a sophisticated ruling mechanism contributes to the regime's durability.

First, a constant and overwhelming sense of urgency has made the CCP regime obsessed with social stability in order to guarantee its sustainability. On one hand, to prevent violent protests and revolutions, governments must appear legitimate by catering to the needs of the people and making concessions to placate and satisfy them. On the other hand, for the CCP regime, staying in power is the bottom line that no reform, policy, and concession can cross. For example, obviously the root of the fierce rural protests over land acquisition lies in the fact that the farmers do not privately own the land. But land privatization will never be an option for the CCP regime because it means the Party-state would lose control over the farmers. The "three rights separation" (*sanquan fenzhi*) land reform reflects a typical tradeoff by the Party-state between maintaining social stability and staying in control. Another example is Party-state's response toward increasing labor unrest. As a communist party, the CCP knows better than anyone else that the best way to improve migrant workers' miserable condition is to allow independent unions to engage in bargaining with the management. However, in light of labor NGOs' effective roles in organizing strikes and promoting negotiation, the Party-state is more concerned about the threat from a growing labor civil society than the protests of the unorganized migrant workers. Xi's crackdown on labor activists and NGOs is part of a strategic maneuver to contain migrant workers within the state corporatism, in an effort to prevent the growing of independent labor unions with political conscious and mobilization capacity. And by intervening directly in disputes, the government can effectively marginalize the power of labor NGOs.

Second, the Party-state's proactive response to grassroots-organized contentions is also determined by its grand economic development strategy. Zhan (2017) argues that the huge profits generated from the conversion of rural land to industrial use have caused agrarian capital, urban capital, and local governments to form tripartite alliances; these constitute the underlying forces for locally initiated *Hukou* reforms. One critical engine of China's economic transition from an export-led to a consumption-based economy rests on aggregate demand. The government realizes high domestic demand comes from high domestic income. In this sense, increasing the wage of the mass public becomes imperative. And this becomes one of the important reasons for the government to promote minimum wages and employment contract signing, tipping a little in favor of the migrant workers, though it is still very cautious in protecting the interests of the business elites. For example, after the financial crisis, the government postponed a previously planned increase of the minimum wage for two years across the country.[16]

Third, governments' relative responsiveness and tolerance, sometimes even encouragement, in coping with the grassroots uprisings is also motivated by its dependence on the citizens for information and feedback regarding policy implementation, malfeasance of local officialdom, acute social problems, and general public attitudes and sentiments. For example, it was the rampant and ferocious rural riots and protests over agricultural tax and surcharge that informed the CCP regime how urgently rural tax reform was needed. Besides, the rapid emerging grassroots unrest has been useful as a balancing tool to check the ever-stronger policy-influencing power of private businesses. For example, enaction of *Labor Contract Law* was strongly opposed by the private trade associations, particularly foreign chambers of commerce. But frequent labor protests and strikes, most of which took place in the provinces where many foreign-owned or joint ventures were located (Tong and Lei 2010), have kept pressure on the capitalists to compromise.

Moreover, the softer handling strategy used in the state's confrontations with civil disobedience and populist insurrections has been justified by the split of the populist and elitist factions in China's ruling elites. The populist coalition has been relying on the support from the mass public to offset elitist group's advantages by advocating and promoting reforms to tackle the most serious socioeconomic problems of the lower class (Yang 2015).

Features of Lower-Class Uprisings

Will the lower-class uprisings challenge the CCP regime's legitimacy? To answer this question, we need to unravel the last piece of the puzzle, to analyze the features of the lower-class uprisings. The mass incidents in the countryside and urban labor movement share some common characteristics.

Diffuse and Localized Interests

One of the important features of both the working class and peasants in China is their internal heterogeneity. Consequentially, diffuse, and localized interests have made it difficult to form a strong, united, nationwide voice for either group. The majority of the labor protests and rural resistances erupted in a form of individual disputes or spontaneous collective petitioning and demonstration at a specific factory, village, or resident community (Chan, Backstrom, and Mason 2014; Tong and Lei 2010; Fu 2017). As Lee and Friedman (2009, 21) posit that, "There is hardly any sign of mobilization that transcends class or regional lines." For example, strikes by cabdrivers against low fares, high gas prices, increasing competition, and shrinking income have broken out in dozens of cities since the early 2000s. But no evidence shows there has been a cross-regional collaboration between or coordination among the strikes by the cabdrivers. Various specific conditions and demands as well as different government responses have largely localized the taxi drivers' strikes and protests even when they may have similar grievances, claims, patterns, and goals as their counterparts in different cities. The same phenomenon exists in teachers' strikes, migrant workers' protests, and farmers' resistance against land grab. The diffuse and localized interests, as well as media controls, make it easier for the local governments to contain and resolve social unrest on a case-by-case basis in a timely fashion.

Unorganized and Lack of Strategies

Constrained by the overwhelming state repressive power and a continuing ban on independent association, neither workers nor farmers in China are conscious of their collective capacity to challenge the management or the system. In reality, labor protests and rural contentions in China have been generally spontaneous and poorly organized without collective interest articulation or common goals, neither seeking "class-based solidarity nor cross-cutting collaborations" (Chen and Kang 2016, 599; Perry 2009). Furthermore, members of the lower class in China are usually undereducated. The rural population's average level of education is only seven or eight years. Over 73 percent of migrant workers do not have a high school diploma (NBS 2009–2017). Thus, their collective actions suffer from a deficiency of comprehensive strategies and coherent plans, and are often impulsive, fragile, and less sustainable. It is worth noting that there is a more recent tendency for members of the lower class to seek professional assistance from NGOs or public intellectuals in guiding and mobilizing grassroots resistance. For example, some environmental NGOs have offered legal consultation to the pollution victims in rural areas and labor NGOs have provided legal training to the migrant workers and even engaged in workplace labor negotiations (Matsuzawa 2012). During the labor protests at Honda's Foshan factory in 2010, the workers sought help from a labor law expert in Renmin University in developing negotiation strategy and goals of strikes. Nevertheless, this professional support is geographically constrained and only covers limited issues. The majority of the NGOs prefer non-confrontational strategies to avoid being labeled as "political" organizations and face resultant suspension (Fu 2017). The CCP regime's repression of labor NGOs and crackdown on human rights lawyers needed to enforce state control of the lower class, particularly during Xi's administration, have made the chance of migrant workers and farmers seeking guide in protests more tenuous.

Depoliticized and Interest-Driven

Almost all the mass incidents by the lower class in China have revolved around specific economic demands and material interests. The economic-oriented and interest-driven lower-class uprisings target immediate grievance redress or indemnity; they rarely carry out broader agenda aiming at citizen rights or political reform (Guo 2014; Tong and Lei 2010; Yang 2015). Even those who protested over poor quality or corruption of local officialdom often expected the higher authorities to address the problems rather than calling for rule of law or systematic change. The workers blamed the employers for inadequate pay and bad working environments, rarely holding the CCP regime responsible for their miserable situation. In over 8,000 cases of labor conflict recorded by the CLB between 2013 to 2017, the number of labor protests demanding an independent trade union remained single digit (CLB 2000–2017). With material interest as the primary motive of collective contention, those protests and demonstrations are easily managed by the authorities once the minimum economic demands of the participants have been met.

Fail to Connect to Other Social Forces

Since the 1989 Tiananmen Square event, civic uprisings that engulf all major socioeconomic forces have disappeared. The deepening gap between the urban rich and rural poor is not only reflected in economic inequality, but also sociopolitical cleavage. The government's uneven, if not discriminatory, policies represented by the *Hukou* system, have not only allocated capital and resources in favor of East Coast urbanities, but also encouraged privileged and superior feelings by urban residents regarding the rural poor. The migrant workers are labeled by the urbanites as "*mangliu*" (blind flows), a derogatory term usually associated with criminality and poverty. Though they cannot maintain their living standards without the cheap labor of migrant workers, most urban residents believe the rural migrants lack "*suzhi*" (quality), "a term meaning a mixture of level of education, politeness, and urban behavior" (Beja 2006, 67). Tse (2016) finds urban residents with higher education and household income are more likely to show prejudice toward rural migrants, and this discriminatory attitude could be transferred across generations. Urban homeowners are especially concerned about the existence of the rural migrants because they believe the latter are responsible for increasing crime rates in the neighborhood and harm their security and quality of life (Rocca 2017, 184). Lack of emotional attachment makes the urban propertied class indifferent toward the struggle of the lower class.

Bereft of urban registration status and being excluded by the urbanites have largely reduced the peasant workers' willingness and capacity to stay permanently in the cities. A 2014 survey of migrant workers in Shanghai showed that over 55 percent of the respondents did not plan to settle down in the city; they wanted to go back to the countryside to take care of their families or go elsewhere for jobs.[17] The vast majority of the migrant workers have been moving back and forth between their rural hometown and urban workplaces, seeking jobs from city to city. About 20 percent of the migrant workers went back to their homeland to help their family farm in the busy season (NBS 2009–2017). In 2017, the total "floating population" in the four metropolitans in China, Shanghai, Beijing, Shenzhen, and Guangzhou, reached 31 million (Lin 2017), four times the population of New York City. The migrant workers have been an indispensable force making urban life more prosperous, affordable, and smooth, a life they helped build but hardly take part in. On average, only about 38 percent of the migrant workers in the cities view themselves as urban residents. The bigger the city they work in, the less sense of belonging they feel. In megacities with a population over 5 million, usually the most attractive coastal metropolitans for migrant workers, only 19 percent of the migrant workers believed they were part of the city (NBS 2009–2017). And unlike their urban counterparts, besides their family and coworkers, migrant workers have very few social networks to help them reach out to urban residents. In addition, the size of the new generation of the migrant workers, those born after 1980, has increased rapidly. One important feature of these young migrant workers is their high tendency to job hop. In Shenzhen, on average the young migrant workers find new jobs every one and half years (Liu 2010). Apparently, this high mobility largely impacts their enthusiasm for participating in labor movement; they could just leave and find another job if not satisfied.

Rightful Resistance

Rather than questioning the legitimacy of the CCP regime, the peasant pro-testers tend to exploit the contradiction and division between the central and local administrations, legitimize their contentious actions by citing official values, policies, laws and commitments of the state in their fights with the local governments or businesses, and seek intervention and support from higher authorities (O'Brien and Li 2006; O'Brien 2013). In fact, to gain sympathy and support from the government and society, most of the lower-class contentions are organized within a similar framework, justifying direct confrontation as defending existing grand policies, legislations, and official values of the regime against any neglection or improper implementation. For example, in 2002, several thousand workers at the Liaoyang Ferro-Alloy Factory, a SOE in Liaoning province, took to the streets and protested over the corruption of the managers that apparently led to the bankruptcy of their factory. Though attacked by security forces, the leaders of the protest wrote letters to senior officials of the Party-state, emphasizing their loyalty to the Party, and asked for enforcement of the laws against corruption (Fisher 2012). The Wukan villages' rebellion, the veterans' protests, and Shenzhen Jasic labor contention mentioned in the beginning of the chapter all exem-plify the "rightful resistance" nature of lower-class uprisings in China.

In addition, the second dimension of "rightful resistance" lies in the incli-nation of the lower-class members to prefer administrative or legal methods in solving disputes and redressing grievances, such as petitions, complaints, or litigation. The peasants and migrant workers usually avoid direct disrup-tive confrontation unless their problems cannot be addressed through other available options. Collective petitioning is one of the most common methods the peasants adopt to channel discontent (Hurst et al. 2014). When migrant workers encounter workplace disputes, they are more likely to seek help from the government, friends or coworkers, or legal methods (NBS 2009–2017).

Briefly put, the working class and peasants in China are socioeconomically disadvantaged, prioritize physical needs, and lack resources and capacity to mobilize in a growing technology-dependent modern society. Structurally, they are fragmented and unorganized, presenting diffuse, even conflicting, interests. As such, they are unable to form a unified strong force to challenge the CCP regime. Politically, they are well accommodated and contained by the Party-state, at least for now, and therefore identify their interests with that of the central authority. The working class and peasants are generally less educated and culturally conservative, and more receptive to the traditional Confucian values of respect for order and authority. Though at the bottom of society, treated unfairly and marginalized, the lower class seems to pose little threat to the Party-state yet.

NOTES

1. The population of China in 1949 was around 541 million.

2. CLB is a Hong Kong-based Chinese workers' rights NGO.

3. See the article "*Jin Liucheng Waiqi Meiyou Jiangonghui* (About 60 percent of Foreign Firms in China Were Union Free)." *Southern Weekly*, May 11, 2006. http://finance.sina.com.cn/g/20060511/11262559254.shtml.

4. The data come from the annual statistics of the CCP. See http://www.xinhuanet.com/politics/2018-06/30/c_1123059570.htm for more details.

5. The data come from World Development Indicator website: http://data.worldbank.org/indicator/SP.RUR.TOTL.ZS; The data of Taiwan are obtained from http://www.worldometers.info/world-population/taiwan-population/.

6. See the article "*Huji Zhidu Gaige Qude Zhongda Jinzhan* (*Hukou* System Reform Has Made Important Progress)." *Xinhuanet*, February 11, 2017. http://www.xinhuanet.com/politics/2017-02/11/c_1120448026.htm.

7. Part of the data come from a national survey of 851 large SOEs. See http://money.163.com/14/0314/08/9N9IMR1K00255182.html for more details.

8. The Shanghai municipal government posts all the welfare benefits and services it provides for the residents on its website. See http://www.shanghai.gov.cn/shanghai/table.html.

9. The data are from the article "New Five-Year Plan Brings Hope to China's West." *Xinhua*, December 27, 2016. http://english.gov.cn/premier/news/2016/12/27/content_28147 5526349906.htm.

10. See the article "*Zhongyang Caizheng 'Sannong' Touru Nianjun Zeng 21 percent* (State Spending in 'Three Rural Problems' Increases 21 percent Annually)." Ministry of Finance of the PRC, October 30, 2012. http://www.mof.gov.cn/zhuantihuigu/2012sn/201211/t20121107_692859.html.

11. The data are from the article "*2020Nian ShiDi Nongmin Shuliang Jiang ChaoKuo YiYi* (The Number of Landless Farmers Will Reach 100 Million by 2020)." *NetEase News.* March 14, 2009. http://news.163.com/09/0314/05/54BHBOPP000136K8.html.

12. See the article "China Shuts Factory after Pollution Protest." *The Telegraph*, September 19, 2011. https://www.telegraph.co.uk/news/worldnews/asia/china/8773738/China-shuts-factory-after-pollution-protest.html.

13. See the article "*Dongguan Zhengfu Dianfu Liangjia Daobi Wanjuchang 7000 Yuangong Gongzi* (The Dongguan Government Paid off Unpaid Salaries for 7,000 Workers Due to Factory Bankruptcy)." *Sina News.* October 18, 2008. http://news.sina.com.cn/c/2008-10-18/162416479699.shtml.

14. See the article "China Focus: Rural Land Ownership Reform Unleashes Greater Growth Potential." *Xinhuanet*, March 8, 2018. http://www.xinhuanet.com/english/2018-03/08/c_13702 5249.htm.

15. See the article "China's Minimum Wage Laws." *INS Consulting,* May 4, 2018. https://ins-globalconsulting.com/chinas-minimum-wage-laws/.

16. See the article "*Shangti Zhuidi Gongzi Jiang Dailai Sanda Lihao* (Benefits of Increasing the Minimum Wage)." *Xinhuanet*, January 26, 2010. http://jjckb.xinhuanet.com/yw/2010-01/26/content_204556.htm.

17. The data come from an investigation conducted by Shanghai municipal government on migrant workers in Shanghai in 2014. See http://www.shanghai.gov.cn/nw2/nw2314/nw24651/nw42131/nw42178/u21aw1232783.html.

Part III

The International Dimension

Overseas Campaigns for Legitimacy and Prestige

Chapter Eight

The Calculated Strategies of Hard Power and Soft Tread

The CCP's struggle for legitimacy is not limited to the domestic front, as discussed previously. To a great extent, its domestic legitimacy is also correlated to its foreign policies and their perceived levels of success. China's performance on the world stage and its acceptance by the international community are also criteria for the Chinese people to judge the CCP's legitimacy at home. In order to achieve success abroad, it is important for the Party-state to project power by taking advantage of the resources obtainable at home. For this purpose, Beijing has launched a series of campaigns abroad to use its economic and military might. At the same time, the Party-state actively marshals its growing hard power to fight anti-CCP and anti-China forces abroad, it also makes great efforts trying to win overseas sympathizers and collaborators. This chapter is devoted to the study of the measures taken by Beijing in expanding and wielding its newly acquired hard and soft powers.[1] Through many diverse efforts, domestic and international recognition and acceptance of the CCP regime have reached an unprecedented level.

HARD POWER: THE NECESSARY CONDITION FOR THE CCP SURVIVAL

As the largest remaining communist state in the world, the CCP regime in some respects looks like an anachronism that should have been sent into the museum of ideologies. Contrary to most contemporary scholars' predictions, the Party-state survived and succeeded through building and exploiting both hard and soft power. Hard power, in particular, makes the necessary condition while soft power provides the sufficient condition for the Party's survival in a post–Cold War international environment that is unfavorable for a communist regime.

Fending Off International Pressures and Strengthening Domestic Legitimacy

As the only major country that still openly upholds the banner of Communism, China seems to be an aberrant outlier in the mainstream of international political economy. It is also a frequent, and, sometimes, convenient target of the West, led by the United States, on the issues of human rights violations, failed protection of intellectual property, forced technology transfer, manipulations of currency, malpractice in the rule of law and a wide range of other issues. The United States also makes use of the Taiwan issue, the South China Sea, minority suppression in Xinjiang and Tibet to exert additional pressures upon China.

With the rise of China's economic and military power, Beijing has built up increasingly more capital and is enjoying greater leverage in coping with these issues. International pressure on China is becoming less and less effective.

In the military area, Beijing has been devoting more and more of its wealth to updating hardware; its military spending has doubled in less than a decade, reaching second place in world ranking, at roughly a quarter of what the United States spends .[2] With the increasingly strong financial support, China's modernization program has been making steady progress. The country has not only modernized its outdated military hardware but has also acquired new equipment, such as a second aircraft carrier, anti-ship ballistic missile systems, modern frigates, submarines, heavy lift transport planes and radar-evading stealth aircraft. The PLA is evolving quickly into a modern, war-fighting, and offensive-oriented force. Compared to the 1996 Taiwan crisis when China was barely able to do anything while a U.S. battle group led by the carrier "Nimitz" boldly sailed down the Taiwan Strait almost within sight of mainland China, today's China has far more and effective means to persuade the American fleet away from China's coast. As American-born journalist Eric Margolis commented: "Carriers and their escorts cost $25 billion—they are too expensive and fragile to risk" (2011).

It is simple logic to reason: if the military means of the United States such as the mighty carriers, the ultimate expression of American power in the North Pacific region, can no longer pressure China as it did in 1996, what else could check Beijing's ambitions should it decide to seek more adventures?

China today has not only the intent but also the capacity to resist pressure from the West in political, economic, human rights, and even military affairs. Additionally, standing up to the demands and pressures from the West has added domestic effects, especially on issues that can easily fan Chinese nationalism, such as Taiwan and Tibet. The CCP regime boasts itself as the defender of China's sovereignty, territorial integrity, national security, prestige and other national interests. That image has to be corroborated by evidence, so any concessions to outside forces with regard to these issues could instigate a backfire that would burn the Beijing regime itself. For most events, Beijing's presentation of such images, using either solid examples or strong propaganda, is generally accepted *per se* by the Chinese masses, and hence strengthens the CCP legitimacy and position. With stronger economic and military muscles, the CCP regime has become increasingly capable of fending off international pressures and does what it believes necessary to raise its domestic legitimacy and prestige.

Buying Off Opponents and Winning More Friends

As the world's second largest economy with the largest foreign currency reserves and second largest market in the world, the Party-state has free hands in using economic clout to either support certain foreign regimes or cause financial problems to coerce others into aligning with Beijing's policies, particularly on the issue of Taiwan. Any developing country that woos China's financial assistance or investment must accept Beijing's policy bottom line that Taiwan is an inseparable part of China and that the CCP regime is the only legal representative of a China that includes the currently *de facto* independent island. The same principle is applied to developed countries as well if they are interested in investing in China, the largest destination of FDI in the world, or in selling their goods to a 1.4 billion population market.

On the world stage, the CCP regime is always criticized by Western countries for its poor human rights record, lack of democracy and lack of freedoms of expression, assembly, association and religion. However, Beijing can always escape from any United Nations resolution blaming its bad human rights records because of its support by "friends," usually developing countries with close economic ties to China or which otherwise rely on China. China's new OBOR Initiative strengthens its old friendship with countries like Pakistan and helps make new friends like Kazakhstan and Belarus.

One of China's new but controversial friends is Greece, which befriended Beijing quickly in the past few years as China invested heavily in this economically depressed country. Before the Chinese investment, the Greek port of Piraeus, adjacent to Athens and the country's largest port, had been operating poorly and came to the verge of bankruptcy. Intending to make the country a shipping hub between Asia and Eastern Europe as a part of China's OBOR, China's biggest shipping company, COSCO, bought a 51 percent stake in Piraeus for €280.5m in 2016. Since then, the Chinese funds have successfully made the port profitable. In return, Athens vetoed a EU condemnation of China's human rights record at the UN in June 2017 (Smith 2017).

Beijing's financial assets certainly played a role, even though Athens denied it. Anyway, the CCP regime has won many new friends around the world utilizing its strong economic power. Projects like the OBOR Initiative does help raise Beijing's prestige in the world, which facilitates the CCP's self-praising propaganda at home.

EFFORTS IN EXPANDING HARD POWER ABROAD
AND SOFT USE OF POWER

The Hard Side of Hard Power Expansion

China's hard power took a dramatic upturn in the 1990s thanks to its reforms initiated at the end of the 1970s. The foundations laid during the early reforms began to bloom and flower in the 21st century with China's entry into the WTO and the explosive increase in exports of Chinese commodities. The CCP regime launched a series of external campaigns in politics, economy, finance, geopolitics, military, science and technology, etc., of various scales and in different regions around the globe, aiming to further expand its hard power capital.

In finance and economics, Beijing either participated or led in creating a number of new international financial and economic institutions, such as AIIB and New Development Bank.[3] It also successfully expanded its voting share from 3.8 percent to 6 percent at the older financial institution, the IMF, in January 2016 (The BRICS Post 2016). Its currency, the RMB, was also included in the Special Drawing Right basket as the fifth currency starting in October 1, 2016 (IMF 2016), marking a milestone of this communist country's expansion in the world financial system.

In geopolitical and military aspects, the CCP regime's expanding proactive activities are similarly striking. These activities span not only across China's neighborhood, but also distant regions such as Africa, Latin America and the Southern Pacific where China historically had little interest or influence. In China's neighborhood, Beijing intensified its naval activities around the disputed islands of Diaoyu/Senkaku with Japan after Xi came to power. Chinese Coast Guard ships sailed more and more frequently within the 12 nautical miles range where Chinese official ships had rarely ventured before. Beijing's most adventurous and controversial activity is its island building spree in the South China Sea, which prompted the Philippines to launch a lawsuit against China at the Permanent Court of Arbitration in The Hague in 2013.[4] Although China has long claimed the South China Sea islands officially, as early as the 1940s, it then lacked resources to project force into the region except for control of Taiping Island by the Nationalist government on

Taiwan. China's growing capabilities and activities in the South China Sea have caused considerable tensions between Beijing and Washington as well as with other countries in the neighborhood, such as the Philippines, Vietnam and Indonesia.

Beyond the neighborhood, Beijing increased its activities in Africa and Latin America. Initially targeted at oil and other natural resources from Africa to meet its domestic needs, China's investment in Africa has multiplied in quantity and variety, and its trade volume also expanded rapidly, now surpassing that of Europe or America (Burnett 2015). China's influences can nowadays be easily felt across the entire African continent and in almost every sector—politics, economy, infrastructure construction, telecommunication, media, etc. The Chinese navy has been conducting antipiracy operations since December 2008 in waters off Somalia and provides protection to commercial ships sailing in the Gulf of Aden on a regular basis. Moreover, on August 1, 2017, China opened its first-ever overseas military base in the Horn of Africa country Djibouti. Chinese naval ships, including submarines, are being seen more and more in the Indian Ocean.[5] These activities have one ultimate goal—that is, to secure energy, natural resources and raw material for domestic use while expanding markets for Chinese commodities and destinations for Chinese investment.

Chinese activities did not stop in these areas that are easily approachable. The Beijing regime also expanded its activities in the harsh climates of the North and South Poles. On July 28, 2004, China opened its first Arctic scientific research base, Yellow River Station, on Svalbard Island of Norway, and on January 26, 2018, Beijing issued its first White Paper on North Pole activities (Durkee 2018).[6] Although not an Arctic state, these activities indicated China's growing interest in Arctic affairs (Baker 2016). Beijing's explorations in Antarctica also went further and deeper, and in greater scale. China has constructed four scientific stations in Antarctica and plans to build more during its 13th Five-Year plan period. In November 2018, China also started to build its first permanent airfield on the continent, showing Beijing's greater ambition and interest in this frozen land (Chen 2018).

Above earth, China has intensified its efforts to explore outer space. In addition to its projects to send China's "Taikonauts" into earth orbit and rovers and probes to the moon's surface, including one exceptional mission to the far side of the moon, the country has also invested heavily to build its own version of a GPS system: the *Beidou* Navigation System. The system is maturing quickly from a regional to a global one, increasingly comparable to that of the United States.

The signature project of China that has had by far the most significant political, economic, geopolitical, geo-economic, and perhaps military implications for China and the world is the OBOR Initiative. This initiative is gaining traction despite obstacles and setbacks. This project spans across almost the whole world, including the Arctic region, where China sent a fleet to explore shipping lanes from China to Europe so that more economical transportation routes can be put into practical use when global warming allows for more days when shipping can be conducted.

If one takes a further look at the Chinese activities in expanding its hard power, it can be concluded that all these activities have profound implications for domestic politics of China. They are closely related to five goals that are essential for the CCP's legitimacy and long-term monopoly on political power:

1. Long-term and continuous economic growth to create more wealth that in turn will help raise peoples' standard of living and maintain domestic political and social stability;
2. Long-term amicable and facilitative international environment for the country's continuous growth, where Beijing can procure reliable supplies of energy and raw material for industrial and civilian consumption and open markets for Chinese commodities and investments;
3. Creation of conditions for further development by opening up new markets and new sources of raw material and energy;
4. Enhancement of prestige for the nation; and
5. The realization of "Chinese Dream"—the restoration of China's historical place in the world, suggesting a bid for Chinese supremacy.

Hard power is not just the necessary condition and means for the realization of most of these goals, it is an end in itself. By any standard, the CCP regime has made significant progress in developing and expanding its hard power. However, to project its hard power is challenging as well as artistic.

Hard Power Projection—The Hard and Soft Ways

Over the past decade, the world has witnessed several high-profile cases where the CCP regime used its hard power strategically; examples include two cases that happened in 2010, both involving developed countries with strong economies. The case with Japan happened in September when a Chinese trawler ship collided with Japanese coast guard boats in the disputed waters of the Diaoyu/Senkaku Islands. The event resulted in detention of the Chinese crew and the captain Zhan Qixiong by Japan. Under strong pressure from Beijing by cutting off high-level diplomatic talks with Tokyo, restricting Chinese tourists to Japan and reportedly cutting off exports of rare earth elements to Japan, Tokyo succumbed to the pressure and released all of the detainees unconditionally (Harlan and Wan 2010). The other case involved Norway, whose Nobel Committee conferred the Nobel Peace Prize of 2010 on the famous Chinese writer, literary critic, human rights activist and political dissident Liu Xiaobo. This act angered the CCP regime and the event was portrayed as part of a Western plot to sabotage the stability of China. Beijing punished Oslo by canceling all high-level bilateral meetings, including a nascent free-trade agreement, preventing Liu from receiving the award, and imposing restrictions on scientific and artistic exchanges. The CCP regime also imposed selected economic sanctions on Norway, such as restricting imports of its famous salmon (Baker 2016). Beijing similarly used the same technique when leaders of other countries met with the Tibetan spiritual leader Dalai Lama. In the subsequent years, the Norway government made other measures to improve relations with China, including canceling all official meetings with Dalai (Baker 2016).

Although results have varied across different countries and different incidents, the pressure was significant, especially for countries with a great economic stake in China. There is hardly any country in the world which openly challenges China's sovereignty over Taiwan. Taiwan and Tibet are two issues in which Beijing can rouse and foment nationalistic sentiment. The CCP regime's South China Sea island building spree in the past decade was also welcomed and highly regarded at home.

Certainly, China's use of its hard power was not always used in a confrontational manner that made other countries nervous. Beijing has made considerable efforts to show the world the soft side of its growing military, such as by anti-pirate naval patrolling in the Gulf of Aden.

Indeed, the Yemen crisis in March 2015 gave Beijing a hard-waited opportunity to demonstrate to its nationals and to the world the soft side of its military hardware. The Beijing regime redirected its navy battleships performing anti-pirate missions in the Gulf of Aden and Somali waters to Yemen to evacuate both Chinese and foreign citizens (BBC 2015; Panda 2015). In addition to the rescue mission in Yemen, there is also a long list of other overseas peaceful missions Beijing used the PLA forces in, such as deploying PLA assets to Liberia and Sierra Leone to help fight the Ebola epidemic in 2014, dispatching its Peace Ark hospital ship to the Philippines after the deadly Typhoon Haiyan in 2013, and sending the PLA Navy's research icebreaker vessel, the *Xue Long*, to rescue researchers stranded aboard an ice-locked ship in Antarctica in early 2014. China has also contributed a large force to the United Nations peacekeeping missions (Panda 2015). These non-aggressive activities have drawn acclaim and praise from abroad.

Beijing's soft use of its hard power can similarly glorify its image at home. There are a number of widely publicized cases in recent years where the Chinese government rescued its own nationals in distress abroad. Most of these scenarios happened in countries where civil war, natural disaster, or other humanitarian crises had occurred. Each of these events hit the headlines of international and domestic media. Beijing's responses to these situations are regarded as litmus tests of its capabilities as well as accountability to the Chinese people at home. Handled well, they provided the CCP regime opportunities to show its strength as well as its concerns and care for Chinese citizens abroad. If not done properly, the CCP regime would have been seen as impotent and could have given rise to domestic discontent.

The Diaoyu/Senkaku Islands case is such an example showing the CCP regime's high-profile publicity for domestic purposes. After the release of the trawler captain, Beijing sent a chartered plane to Japan to pick up Zhan, which was broadcast and reported on all media in China (Harlan and Wan 2010). This act mollified nationalists who wanted the CCP regime to take a hard stance toward foreign powers and showed the CCP regime's willingness as well as capability to safeguard China's interests and protect its citizens abroad.

The other, and even more notable, case that earned the CCP regime great credit was its swift response to the Libyan crisis in 2011. There, China used civilian and military aircrafts, commercial ships and even chartered foreign cruise ships to evacuate as many as 35,000 Chinese and 2,000 foreign nationals from the danger zone. Considering the thousands of stranded Chinese nationals involved and the great distance from China itself, people unanimously agreed that the rescue missions were a great success. Like the Libya and Yemen rescue missions, a number of other events occurred in which Chinese citizens were promptly rescued by the Chinese embassies, such as earthquakes in Japan (March 2011), Nepal (April 2015) and New Zealand (November 2017), Indonesian volcano eruptions (July 2017), and Dominica hurricane (October 2017), which gave the Chinese government fodder to promote its image.

These positive images are so widely accepted by the Chinese masses that a movie screened in 2017 *Wolf Warrior 2,* which told the story of rescuing overseas Chinese citizens in an unnamed African country, won such popularity that its box office broke China's record (Cain 2017).[7] And this movie successfully attained the 61st place on the list of the world's top 100 highest grosses, becoming the only non-English single territory film to earn such a high rating. Another movie on a similar topic, *Operation Red Sea* showed the Chinese navy's attempts to save Chinese citizens in the Middle Eastern desert, though it was not as big a hit as *Wolf Warrior 2*, hit the box office record in China as well. It also earned spot 154th on the world list.[8] It must be emphasized that both movies were privately invested commercial movies rather than government-sponsored propaganda pieces, such as "*Jianguo Daye*" (The Founding of the PRC) that were shown inside China at about the same time. The high box office rankings are an indication of people's acceptance of these movies themselves for the wonderful acting and special effects, but also the popularity of the government role and image presented; all heroes depicted are Chinese soldiers backed by the Chinese navy protecting commerce in faraway regions in East African coast and the Red Sea.

These stories, based on actual feats already widely popularized on China's media, especially the Internet, have given rise to a great wave of Chinese patriotism and strengthened national pride. The acceptance of the heroes in the movies who are positively associated with the government shows collateral good images of the Beijing regime. Of course, these events would not have happened if China did not enjoy the hard power it does today.

THE DUAL PURPOSES OF SOFT POWER CULTIVATION AND DILEMMA OF PROJECTION

If hard power is the necessary condition for the CCP's survival, then soft power serves as the sufficient condition. With the successful development of soft power, the CCP regime's survivability is more likely. Beijing's efforts have two purposes: the first being to create a congenial international environment for its hard power development and the second to build a positive image overseas that will be imported back to China, showing the Chinese populace its legitimacy in the world.

Sustaining a Congenial International Environment for Hard Power Expansion

China's formal cultivation of soft power began in the mid-1990s, at a time when China's rise was increasingly viewed by both the Western world and its neighbors as a threat to world peace and stability (the "China threat" theory). China had to work hard to convince its neighbors and other countries that it was a peaceful country with neither the intention nor capability to challenge the world order and global stability (Zhang 2007, 111–112).

If China was not seen as a power having the capacity to challenge the international system a decade ago, today more and more observers worry that China is poised to do so if it wants. The CCP regime is facing the same situation it did 20 years ago. In the absence of a proper response from Beijing, they likely will poison the congenial international environment that China still badly needs. This is even more so the case now, with China's deeper integration into the current international system. In the final analysis, preventing the formation of an anti-China military alliance and/or arms races with peer competitors is of the utmost importance.

These goals can hardly be realized through flexing muscles, which also involves potentially quite formidable costs. On the contrary, these aims are more attainable through skillful cultivation, manipulation, and projection of soft power. In the new international context, the CCP regime needs renewed efforts to present a positive picture to the world and ensure a good external environment for its further growth. Furthermore, using soft power has special implications for China's domestic politics.

Successful Overseas Image Building for Domestic Consumption

As the last major surviving communist state, the CCP constantly faces great pressure to legitimize itself. International sanctions imposed in the wake of the 1989 Tiananmen suppression made Beijing look like a pariah regime abhorred by not only its own people but also the international community.

The CCP regime successfully broke its isolation in the immediate years after the Tiananmen suppression by taking advantage of the international situation at that time, particularly the 1991 U.S. invasion of Iraq. It also achieved striking success on the home front by developing the economy, raising the living standards of its people and improving its governance. Nevertheless, China's further opening-up allowed its people more opportunities to interact with the outside world, which raised their expectations for government performance and international approval. Beijing's performance on the world stage, such as relations with other countries and its status in the world community, became new indicators for Chinese people to judge the legitimacy of their government. Thus, China's rapid integration into the world made it important for Chinese leaders to succeed on the international front in order to succeed on the home front.

In the new era, the CCP regime continuously needs to show its people that rather than being an international outcast, the country that it rules is a strong as well as a respected member of international society. Beijing also needs raw material for its propaganda machine to glorify its image and solidify its base of rule.

Hard vs. Soft Power: The Dilemma of Projection and Domestic Legitimacy

Despite China's impressive hard power expansion over the past decade, there are a growing number of people in China in recent years that view their country not as an increasingly powerful state but rather as a victim of aggressive neighbors and the United States as well. By reacting strongly to this sentiment with hard power, the CCP regime will provide new fuels for the "China threat" theory. Yet responding softly will cause backlash at home and endanger the CCP regime's claim as defender of China's national interests. Officially, the Chinese government makes unceasing efforts and employs a multitude of devices to publicize its peaceful and benign intentions. The latter includes speeches from top state leaders, official policy statement, national defense white papers, and so on. Beijing's main objective is to convince external audiences that China will always pursue a peaceful foreign policy no matter how powerful it becomes in the future in order to diminish worries about China's expanding hard power assets.

However, there are increasingly more scholars and Chinese people who counter that the "*Taoguang Yanghui*" (Keep a low profile and bide one's time) policy inherited from Deng's era no longer serves China's national interest.[9] They argue that the policy increasingly is regarded by China's potential opponents as a sign of weakness (Leonard 2008, 83, 90–91). For example, "*Gezhi Zhengyi, Gongtong Kaifa*" (Setting aside Dispute and Pursuing Joint Development) is a policy which flows from *Taoguang Yanghui* and has been used to manage disputes between China and Japan over Diaoyu/Senkaku Islands and between China and various Southeast Asian countries over the South China Sea islands. For the critics, though, instead of encouraging reciprocation, this policy actually spurs some countries, particularly Japan and Vietnam, to encroach on their and China's mutually claimed territory by increasing their military presence in disputed areas. The critics propose that China should make use of its strong economic power to sanction these countries when they encroach on China's rights. Some even advocate that the CCP regime should *liangjian* (draw sword), implying Beijing should use military force.

Outside of China, the most notable "China threat" advocates such as Paul Wolfowitz, Robert Kagan, and John Mearsheimer, actively exaggerate China's capability and its dangers to the world (Leonard 2008, 87). Although an anti-China alliance has not been directly formed, the analogy between China's rise and the ascendancy of imperial Germany and Japan before World War II, evoking the Thucydides Trap theory (Allison 2017b), still cause great harm to China's effort to present a peace-loving image.

China's strategists and policymakers are thus trapped in a predicament. On the one hand, domestic discontent with their "softness" limits their room for maneuvering and they must show certain "toughness" toward China's opponents to placate domestic critics. Furthermore, without showing some "toughness," the CCP regime actually may be regarded as "soft" and exploited. On the other hand, too much "toughness" gives proponents of the "China threat" theory more chances to propagate their arguments. Ultimately, Chinese leaders need to avoid taking toughness so far that it alienates, antagonizes, and scares other countries since this may backfire. It is a difficult balancing act for the CCP regime, given its inflexible position on Chinese territorial legitimacy. In this milieu, continuous soft power tapping can help to build confidence among external audiences. Despite China's much expanded hard power, Beijing has been extremely cautious striking a balance between playing "tough" and "amicable" so that it is able to maintain its domestic support and popularity on one hand while not scaring other countries on the other hand. Using its navy ships to rescue Chinese and foreign nationals from wartorn regions is the best combination of using both hard and soft powers. It is not surprising that similar rescue missions were carried out again and again.

SOFT POWER CULTIVATION EFFORTS

Soft Power Cultivation Policy Enacted

In spite of the growing clamor from academics and the populace in China to abandon *Taoguang Yanghui* in recent years and Beijing's seemingly assertive actions, overall Chinese leaders have not been distracted from their efforts to project a positive image. In fact, there have been hardly any signs the CCP regime has intended to downgrade its image-building project. On the contrary, it has intensified its "charm offensive" in various ways and enthusiastically tries to court other countries (Kurlantzick 2007). Top leaders, spokesmen of the NPC, the Foreign Ministry, the Military, and China's major state-controlled media outlets such as CCTV, China Daily, and China Radio International, all actively tout China's "*Hepin Fazhan*" (peaceful development)[10] and desire to build a "*Hexie Shijie*" (harmonious world).[11]

Chinese leaders from Deng Xiaoping, through Jiang Zemin and Hu Jintao to current president Xi Jinping have all tried hard on many different occasions to present a positive image for China. Most recently President Xi Jinping, who is believed to be the least active leader to adhere to the *Taoguang Yanghui* principle, has also reiterated on different international occasions that China is a peaceful country with no intention to bully other nations. For example, during his speech at the celebrations marking the 50th anniversary of bilateral ties between China and France in Paris on March 27, 2014, he specifically quoted Napoleon's famous remark on China as a sleeping lion. He emphasized that although this lion has awakened, "It is a peaceful, lovely and civilized lion."[12] The undertone of this remark is that even China is a powerful country, but there is no need to fear it since it is friendly. This is also a counterargument against the "China threat" theory.

All Xi's messages on other international occasions can be summarized in the following: upholding the authority and status of the United Nations, committing to the climate change accord, maintaining free trade, and creating a world community with a shared future for humanity (Bosu 2018). He wants the world to know that China has the resolve to shoulder greater responsibilities in the global economic and political system with the growth of China's capabilities, hopefully presenting a good image to the world.[13]

Xi's predecessor President Hu Jintao did the same, too. For example, President Hu used his 2009 New Year address to express that China "sincerely hope(s) all countries support and help each other and work together to promote peace, stability and prosperity and bring peace and happiness to people across the world" (China Daily 2009a). Chinese Foreign Minister

Yang Jiechi, in an interview before the 60th anniversary of the PRC in 2009, avowed that his country wanted to build a harmonious world of lasting peace and common prosperity (China Daily 2009b). In China's 2010 National Defense White Paper, Beijing reiterated that "China unswervingly takes the road of peaceful development . . . China will never seek hegemony, nor will it adopt the approach of military expansion now or in the future, no matter how its economy develops" (Information Office of the State Council (SCIO) 2010).

To supplement its rhetoric, the CCP regime makes substantial efforts to turn these policy declarations into actual actions. Such doings can be roughly divided into two categories that complement each other. One is *Qingjinlai* (inviting to come in) and the other is *Zouchuqu* (walking out).[14] The first one means that China will open its door to the outside world and welcome people from abroad to China to see, experience, understand, and hopefully even to support what is going on in the country. The second one implies China will take the initiative and be proactive in presenting itself to the world using media outlets and other means.

Soft Power Development Strategies

These guiding principles have led the CCP regime to undertake a series of measures to bring foreign nationals into China to directly observe it. The hugely successful 2008 Beijing Olympic Games, the 2010 Shanghai World Expo and China's new bid to hosting 2022 Winter Olympic Games epitomize the more grandiose measures. On the one hand, the Chinese government desires to showcase the country's great achievements. On the other hand, Beijing wants to show its people how popular it is in the international community, and hence boost its domestic prestige.

In terms of cultural exchanges, Beijing has intensified its efforts to encourage students from other countries, especially those from the participating countries of OBOR project, to come to China to observe and learn. For example, the *Hanban* (Confucius Institute Headquarters) sponsors tours from international academic institutions for students and faculties to see and appreciate China. By 2017, there were a total of 489,200 foreign students who were studying at Chinese universities. China has become the largest destination of foreign students in Asia. Over the past few years, there was a double-digit increase. All governments of China at different levels, from the city to province to national, set up various scholarships as an encouragement (Ministry of Education of PRC 2017; Sohu News 2009). All these efforts show the determination of Chinese government to deepen China's level of integration into the international community.

China also took the lead to create the *Boao* Forum for Asia in 2008. This is the Asian version of the World Economic Forum held annually in Davos,

Switzerland. It stands now as a nonprofit organization with a fixed address in *Boao*, Hainan province, a congenial tropical setting that China uses to host high-level forums for government and business leaders as well as academia in Asia (and other continents) to discuss the most pressing issues in this region and the world at large. As it has high international stature, it is also one of China's strategies to extend its influences in the world.

Compared to the *Qingjinlai* strategy, the *Zouchuqu* strategy is more sophisticated in composition, more influential in results, and more challenging in realization. In recent years, the measures associated with the latter strategy are especially conspicuous, accentuated by China's all-round offensives that target both developing and developed, as well as neighbouring and distant, countries. Included in the *Zouchuqu* strategy are efforts by Chinese leaders to appear at all important summit meetings such as the United Nations Climate Change Conference in Paris and G20 gatherings, where they can introduce and tout China's "peaceful development" policy and benevolent intentions.

China also has intensified the use of its own media as a direct means for charm offensives and promoting the country. In May 2011, China's official *Xinhua* News Agency moved its North American bureau to Times Square, becoming a neighbor of such international media giants as Thomson Reuters and Conde Nast. China also launched its global English language TV Service—CNC World—on July 1, 2010, broadcasting English news programs 24 hours a day and covering breaking news and major political, economic, and cultural news around the globe.[15] Both moves are expected by the CCP regime to provide China a bigger voice and convey the Chinese perspective on world events by competing for audiences with other influential news media such as CNN, BBC, and Al Jazeera (Troianovski 2010).

In addition, the CCP regime makes use of Western media directly. To illustrate, it ran a six-week advertising campaign in the United States, European, and Asian media at the end of 2009 to boost the reputation of Chinese goods overseas. In early 2011, it paid handsomely to show a promotional video about China, which featured Chinese celebrities like basketball star Yao Ming and pianist Lang Lang, on six oversized screens in Times Square. Recently, in the middle of tension between the United States and China over trade in 2018, the Beijing regime also tried to reach into the U.S. heartland by publishing an advertising supplement in Iowa's largest newspaper, the *Des Moines Register* on September 23, highlighting the impact of Trump's tariff on the state's soybean farmers and President Xi's long-term connection and friendship with the state (Niquette and Jacobs 2018). Even before this, China was also buying inserts in the U.S. newspapers, including the *New York Times* and the *Washington Post* fairly often. Although the feedback received has been mixed, these endeavors manifest Beijing's strong determination to actively promote a positive image of China.

In diplomacy, the CCP regime has become quite skillful and tactical in dealing with other great powers. On sensitive issues such as Iranian and North Korean nuclear proliferation, Beijing insists on finding the solution within the framework of the United Nations, strongly opposing unilateral actions by any single country. Beijing's support for the United Nations represents an effort to convince developing countries that China will still stand with them, even if it is stronger. As a result, the CCP regime has consistently won the support of many developing countries on vital issues such as Taiwan and Tibet. However, when situations vis-à-vis Iran or North Korea worsened, China has sided with the international community as well as the West several times, agreeing to impose targeted sanctions. China has not only participated in but also supported expanded United Nations peacekeeping activities, showing itself a responsible permanent member of the United Nations Security Council. These acts help China build an image as a "responsible stakeholder."[16] They also help China to maintain a good working relationship with other great powers.

In the economic sphere, China votes in the United Nations agencies in ways to benefit developing countries. Moreover, it provides generous loans and investments with "no strings attached" to developing countries. Lastly, it frequently reduces tariffs and forgives debts to gain soft power (Liang 2011). Such measures help with the development of these countries and provide them an alternative source of financial loans and political support to restrictive World Bank conditions. In return, these countries help Beijing realize its political aims through the United Nations system and continue to supply it with raw material and energy. In dealing with developed countries, especially in the West, Beijing has also used specifically tailored policies such as making huge purchases at critical times in order to remind politicians and people in the West of the benefits of maintaining a good relationship with China (Kastner 2010; Paulson 2008; Munro 1994).

In the area of culture, China is also gaining momentum in expanding its influences from its traditional area of influence of Southeast Asia to other regions of the world. Driven by economic as well as political motives, the CCP regime encourages the export of Chinese movies, TV programs, published works and art troupes. As a result, more and more Chinese movies can be watched in Western theaters and some of them have won significant popularity, such as Zhang Yimou's *Hero* and Ang Lee's *Crouching Tiger, Hidden Dragon*. Chinese *Kungfu* has become the catchword for the younger generation males of all races and nations in the world. The Confucius Institute, aimed at promoting Chinese language and culture, continues to flourish. By December 31, 2017, *Hanban* has created 525 Confucius Institutes and 1,113 Confucius Classrooms in more than 146 countries and regions,[17] compared to only 282 Confucius Institutes and 272 Confucius Classrooms in mid-2010 (Shambaugh 2010).

This evidence supports the thesis that the CCP regime has not slowed its charm offensive even during a period when its hard power has been undergoing explosive growth. It is equally likely that its popularity at home will be high when the Beijing regime is viewed positively in the world. Therefore, it makes great sense for Beijing to continue with the endeavor.

Reevaluation of China's Prior Rationales for Soft Power Tapping

In the new decade, the two logics that initially drove the CCP regime to focus on using soft power remain. A comparison between the international and domestic environment in the 1990s and 2010s shows that the larger international context has not changed significantly. In fact, one might argue that China's border areas, particularly along its eastern and southeastern coast, have started to become more complicated since 2009. Almost all of China's neighboring countries that have territorial disputes with China have started to take concrete steps to strengthen their ties with the United States, attempting to introduce outside forces into the region to counterbalance growing Chinese power. Japan, South Korea, and Vietnam are the representative members of this group.

This changing situation seems to be the result of two interactive events: first, China's own dramatic growth in hard power has raised levels of anxiety, even fear, in its immediate neighborhood and with the distant greater power, the United States; and second, Beijing's more assertive stance and increased activities on some old disputes with its neighbors have prompted a response from these countries. These include its claim of the South China Sea as part of its "core interests" in March 2010 and its subsequent island building and expansion spree in 2014, the militarization of several South China Sea islands contrary to earlier assertions that it would not do so, expansion of its Air Defense Identification Zone, and repeated sailing of its coast guard ships into the 12 nautical mile range of the Diaoyu/Senkaku Islands. Facing the anxiety and worries of its neighbors and possible deterioration of external environment, it is therefore imperative for the CCP regime to continue its good neighborhood policy, reassuring all that it will stay on its "peaceful development" course regardless of its future power levels.[18]

From the perspective of domestic needs, China's original rationale for garnering global soft power remains valid because a good reputation abroad directly benefits domestic politics. China's acceptance by the international community is an important way for the CCP regime to confirm its legitimacy and righteousness to the Chinese people. On the other hand, improved domestic governance such as more respect for human rights and a stronger place for rule of law can also demonstrate to the outside world that the Chinese government is an effective and benign ruler that treats its own people fairly. As observed by Nye and Wang (2009), "In international politics, the resources that produce soft power arise in large part from the values an organization or country expresses in its culture, in the examples it sets by its internal practices and policies, and in the way it handles its relations with others." This observation accurately describes the correlation between domestic and international politics with regard to soft power; it fits China's case exactly. In short, the domestic and international circumstances in the 1990s that prompted Beijing to start exploiting soft power tools remain largely unchanged.

IMPLICATIONS FOR CHINA AND THE WORLD IN THE FUTURE

Having examined China's rise in hard and soft power over the past few decades, one more question remains. If Beijing has succeeded in utilizing its ever growing hard and soft power for maintaining its legitimacy and monopoly on political power, what do these imply for China, the CCP and the outside world?

From the perspective of political leadership, the Party's prime directive is to perpetuate its rule. For this purpose, the CCP is expected to continue down the path it has taken in the past decades. "If it ain't broke, don't fix it." From the perspective of China, the continuous rise is definitely good for it. Some countries friendly to China, such as Pakistan, Cambodia and some African countries, would welcome it. Some countries would remain neutral, such as Russia and most Latin American countries. Yet, most Western countries would look at China's rise with an ambivalent attitude, sometimes with suspicion. As China's neighbor that has an unresolved historical relationship with China, Japan views China very warily and many times anxiously.

As the current hegemon, the United States is the most concerned country in the world. Due to the narrowing gap in hard power, the United States' anxiety about a rising China that might soon challenge its global dominance has reached an unprecedented level. Since Trump's presidency, he has adopted a wide range of policies trying to slow China's pace even though he has been reiterating that China's Xi is his good friend. Some of China's domestic propaganda, clearly exaggerated to glorify the Party's rule, also fuels U.S. anti-China sentiment. Having an export-driven economy, with the United States being such an important market for Chinese commodities, sources of technology and capital as well as the popular destination of Chinese students, the gradual closing of the American door to China is a serious matter. The future legitimacy of the CCP has much to do with its hard power expansion. If the deteriorating economic relationship between the United States and China impacts the Chinese economy severely and even causes a serious recession and large-scale unemployment, it could cause a ruling crisis for the CCP. However, if Beijing were able to handle this crisis successfully and tide it over skillfully, the CCP's position and base of support would barely be affected.

Nevertheless, Beijing's charm offensive is also facing a new Trump variable. The new U.S. president is one who behaves differently and more erratically than any of his predecessors. He is reshaping U.S. domestic and international policies in a way that never occurred before. Under him, the United States is no longer considered a leader, much less a *status quo* power. Instead Washington behaves more and more like a revisionist power, as exemplified by dramatic changes in U.S. foreign policy, such as withdrawing from various international agreements, treaties, and organizations.

Trump has also changed his policy toward China with regard to security issues. The United States' "freedom of navigation" in the South China Sea and more challenging acts of sailing within the 12 nautical mile range of China's occupied islands will strengthen rather than weaken Beijing's position domestically. It gives the Beijing regime new opportunities to be seen as the defender of China with the United States as the invader. Only in an unthinkable conflict situation, if China were defeated completely, would it trigger a ruling crisis for the CCP.

Due to China's continuous growth as a model of development for developing countries and Beijing's strong intention to conduct a "smile policy," the CCP regime is able to find sympathizers, collaborators and supporters in the international community. Trump's bold alienation of its allies on economic and security issues and his withdrawal from various international organizations and treaties give the Beijing regime an opportunity to build and present a contrasting image of a responsible great power. Indeed, many countries have started to look to Beijing as the new defender of the current economic and trade system with the United States as the defector. Trump's policies gave the CCP regime and unexpected boost to expand its soft power.

Obviously, the CCP regime has won the war on this other front of hard and soft power expansion and utilization. With strong hard and soft power in capable hands, the CCP rule will be sustainable through the foreseeable future. Predicting the collapse of the Beijing regime, against this background, is both near-sighted and premature.

NOTES

1. For definition of the term and its original discussions, see a series of works by Joseph Nye (1990, 2004, 2005).

2. See the article "China's Military Spending." *China File*, March 6, 2018, http://www.chinafile.com/conversation/chinas-military-spending.

3. It was formerly referred to as the BRICS Development Bank.

4. For details of the case, see "South China Sea: Philippines v. China." *The Diplomat*, July 27, 2015. https://thediplomat.com/2015/07/south-china-sea-philippines-v-china/.

5. For a detailed study and report on Chinese navy and its operations, please see O'Rourke (2018).

6. For the full text of China's White Paper in English, visit: http://www.xinhuanet.com/english/2018-01/26/c_136926498_2.htm.

7. For more details, see Cain (2017).

8. Box Office Mojo. 2018. "All Time Box Office." https://www.boxofficemojo.com/alltime/world/?pagenum=2&p=.htm; *The Numbers*. 2018. "All Time Worldwide Box Office (Rank 101–200)." https://www.the-numbers.com/box-office-records/worldwide/all-movies/cumulative/all-time/101.

9. For a detailed discussion of the translation and manipulation of this term, please see "Tao Guan Yang Hui—What Is the Best Translation?" by Bin Sun, accessed July 22, 2010, http://sun-bin.blogspot.com/2010/06/tao-guan-yang-hui-what-is-best.html.

10. "Peaceful Development" is a term that was used to replace the controversial "Peaceful Rise" originally proposed by Zheng Bijian, former vice president of China's Central Party School in 2003. Since the word "rise" could fuel perceptions that China is a threat to the established order, it was later replaced by "development." However, both were used to describe China's foreign policy approach in the early 21st century.

11. "*Hexie Shijie*" (Harmonious World) was a concept proposed by the Chinese President Hu Jintao in his address to the delegates during the 2005 World Summit and 60th General Assembly of the United Nations in New York on September 15, 2005. Hu enunciated that China's foreign policy goal was to build a harmonious society where multilateralism, mutually beneficial cooperation and the spirit of inclusiveness should be upheld in realizing common security and prosperity. Since then, this concept has been reiterated by Chinese leaders and on various occasions.

12. See the article "*Xi Jinping Zai Bali Fabiao Yanjiang: Zhongguo Zhetou Shizi Yijing Xingle* (Speech of President Xi Jinping at the 50th Anniversary Celebration for the Establishment of Sino-French Diplomatic Relationship—This Lion Is Awaken)." *News China*, March 28, 2014. http://news.china.com.cn/2014-03/28/content_31927442.htm.

13. See the article "Chinese President Xi Jinping Delivers 2018 New Year Speech." *China Plus*, December 31, 2017. http://chinaplus.cri.cn/news/china/9/20171231/72084.html.

14. Theoretical discussions of these strategies could be found in various articles, such as "*2007 Zhongguo Zai Yalizhong Wenjian Jueqi* (China Rises Steadily under Pressure)" by Zheng, Yongnian, *Cankao Xiaoxi (Reference News)*, December 27, 2007. It is also available at the website of the Institute of Political Science, Chinese Academy of Social Sciences, accessed July 20, 2010, http://chinaps.cass.cn/readcontent.asp?id=8237; "*Zhongguo Shiyue Waijiao Zhangxian Ruanshili* (China's October Diplomacy: a Display of Soft Power)." *Zhongguo Tese Net*, October 10, 2010, http://www.tese.me/html/shijieshijiao/waijiaozhongguo/20091023/38131.html.

15. See the article "Xinhua Launches CNC World English Channel." *Xinhuanet*, July 15, 2010. http://news.xinhuanet.com/english2010/china/2010-07/01/c_13378575.htm.

16. "Responsible Stakeholder" was a term first used by the former U.S. Deputy Secretary of State Robert Zoellick in a speech on U.S.-China relations in New York in September 2005. Since then, it has been quoted and used widely to refer to U.S. expectation for China's role in the world.

17. Data are from the website of *Hanban*. http://www.hanban.edu.cn/confuciousinstitutes/node_10961.htm, accessed November 1, 2018.

18. See the article "Hu Says China Firmly Committed to Peaceful Development." *People Daily Online*, June 11, 2007. http://english.peopledaily.com.cn/200706/11/eng20070611_382823.html.

Chapter Nine

International Political Crisis and the CCP's New Opportunities

From the 1990s through the early 21st century, the newly democratized as well as established democracies around the world suffered a series of crises and setbacks. These events have tainted the glory and stained the reputation of democratization and democracy. What contrasted with democracies in this scenario was the dramatic economic progress and social prosperity achieved in China under the one-party communist rule. This situation opened up new opportunities of resurrection for the once unpromising CCP.

In the former communist countries in Eastern Europe and Russia, the transition to democracy did not bring about the prosperity and good life that were once promised. In the Middle Eastern countries where the forced toppling of dictatorships occurred, the establishment of democracies generally brought about disruption of the established social order, chaos, and even civil war. In more mature democracies in the developing as well as the developed world, the inherent weaknesses of democracy have been revealed, providing abundant ammunition for doubters and detractors of democracy. The CCP seized this opportunity to defame Western democracy and emphasize its arguments for its own continued monopoly on political power. Furthermore, the West's stereotypical attitudes toward some sensitive issues for the Chinese masses, such as those related to Taiwan and Tibet, alienated many Chinese and deepened their mistrust of the West. This mistrust in the West would soon turn into trust in their own government. Provided this external background, the CCP regime worked hard to market at home the correctness and benefits of its rule. As a result, this idea gained widespread acceptance, strengthening the CCP's legitimacy in Chinese society.

THEORETICAL SUPPORT FOR LINK BETWEEN DOMESTIC AND INTERNATIONAL POLITICS

In the past, there was extensive research focusing on the internal-external conflict nexus, especially theoretical and empirical research centering on diversionary theory (e.g., Zhang 2002). But most of that research focused on unidirectional impact—domestic politics upon international politics. Few studies explored the reverse impact: the effects of the international political environment—the contextual factor that impacts political support at the domestic level. In the era of globalization, with a very high degree of interdependence between states, the global political, financial, economic, and security environment has become increasingly relevant to the domestic public. Therefore, it is important to study how the international context affects how the public evaluates domestic government performance and the amount of political trust ascribed to it.

Gourevitch (1978), examining the link between international and domestic politics, calls for more research on the effects of international relations on domestic political outcomes. He suggests that two powerful explanatory variables at the international level account for the characteristics of domestic regimes: "the distribution of power among states, or the international state system; and the distribution of economic activity and wealth, or the international economy" (Gourevitch 1978, 882–883). One notable example comes from Gerschenkron's famous hypothesis that the world economic context in which late developers industrialize is more advanced, competitive, and complex than that of early developers. Higher entry costs force a late developer to form strong central coordinating state apparatus as it attempts to catch up with early industrializers (Gerschenkron 1962). Thus, the international political economic structure affects domestic political structures for late developers.

While there is a growing interest in public opinion research from an international angle, this topic is still widely neglected. Studies of political trust or satisfaction with government have been largely restricted to domestic issues, such as economic performance, cultural background, and political system, etc. Extant research on the influence of the international political environment on domestic attitudes toward government has been mainly attributed to "rally 'round the flag" effects, that is, political trust increases in times of external threat. International conflict literature implies that international crises mobilize public political support toward their state institutions, evoke high levels of patriotism and nationalism, and enforce cohesion and conformity throughout the nation (Hutchison and Gibler 2007; Mueller 1973). Another strand of literature focuses on the effect of terrorist threats on domestic political support. The studies note that there was an increase in public trust and a decline in cynicism after the World Trade Center attack on

September11, 2001 (Chanley 2002; Hetherington and Suhay 2011). Scholars also find that international terrorist threats fostered more radical and conservative positions among citizens (Gadarian 2010; Nacos, Block-Elkon, and Shapiro 2007; Hetherington and Suhay 2011).

Reilly (2016) conducted a survey experiment in which Chinese university students, who were exposed to a situation designed to increase feelings of international threats, were significantly more likely to prefer "pure materialists" ideas such as "maintaining order in the nation" to "post-materialist" values like "protecting freedom of speech." Therefore, he deduces that perception of an external threat (in this case, a hostile international environment) may incite Chinese citizens' authoritarian and nationalistic sentiments and attitudes "at the expense of more democratically favorable value orientations" (Reilly 2016, 571).

While studies of this rally effect emphasize the critical role that external threats play in bolstering domestic political support and patriotism, most theories of state functions and state building point to an alternative conclusion. Scholars maintain that states derive their legitimacy from their capacity to fulfill fundamental functions: to provide domestic order and material well-being to its citizenry and to protect territorial integrity from outside threats (Weber 1994; Tilly 1993; North 1982). Therefore, failure by the state to perform any of its primary functions or obligations would undermine its legitimacy and generate pessimistic or critical attitudes toward government. For example, Hutchison (2011) assesses the relationship between external threats and political trust using cross-sectional, multilevel models. The results suggest that feelings of being threatened territorially undercut African citizens' political trust toward their governments, because they perceived the governments had little capability or power to protect territorial integrity. These studies corroborate the "rally 'round the flag" attitude of the Chinese masses toward their government when relations between China and Western countries deteriorate.

The domestic effect of another type of national threat, international economic and financial crises, has also been examined. Roth, Nowak-Lehmann D., and Otter (2011) show that the 2008 financial crisis has had significant effects on domestic political trust in national institutions. But the effects involved two steps. First, in the direct aftermath of the financial crisis in 2008, the immense decline in the real economy galvanized the national political support temporarily. But these positive effects disappeared when analyzing the entire crisis period, indicating that as the crisis prolonged, pessimistic feelings of ineffective and impotent governments prevailed. Kroknes, Jakobsen, and Gronning (2015) also report similar loss of public confidence in 25 European countries due to the severe domestic economic impacts of the 2008 financial crisis.

Most studies based on the theories of state function and state building find a negative relationship between external threats and domestic political support in situations of perceived government failure. However, the same logic of the academic theory of state could apply to the opposite scenario, where the state assertively and successfully confronts and deters external threats. Thus, in this case, we should expect to see a positive effect of external threats on domestic trust.

Very few research has explored the effects of foreign media on domestic political attitude formation. The extant scholarly works mainly focus on American foreign policy and domestic public opinions. Hayes and Guardino (2011, 832) challenge the conventional wisdom that "Foreign discourse reported in domestic mass media is irrelevant for public opinion formation." Their empirical study suggests that foreign media coverage played an important role in shaping American citizens' attitudes toward the foreign policy decision making regarding the 2003 Iraq War. Brody (1994) argues that rising criticisms of domestic administration policy by foreign elites could conversely lead to increased government approval and public backlash. This was exactly what happened when the Western media collectively bombarded the Chinese government before the 2008 Olympic Games, ironically raising support of the Chinese masses for their government.

These studies of the link between domestic and international politics, though most *per se* are not directly related to China, provide a theoretical as well as an empirical foundation to examine the triangular relationship among the Chinese government, the Chinese masses, and foreign media and governments.

The international political and economic crises in the 1990s and in the new century have aroused Chinese nationalism and patriotism and helped the CCP rebuild a reputation that was severely damaged by the suppression of the student movement in 1989. All these external crises ironically furnished the CCP much needed justification for its rule. The Party took advantage of the external situations, launched offensives against Western-style democracy and successfully made the CCP's legitimacy even more rational and acceptable domestically.

BAD POLITICAL EXAMPLES—THE FAILURE OF NEWLY DEMOCRATIZED COUNTRIES

Disappointing Cases of Democratization in the Former Communist Countries

In the early 1990s, failures of the international communist movement led to the birth of a series of democratic regimes in Eastern Europe and Russia. Optimism and expectations for the benefits of democratization were so high that Fukuyama (1992) makes his famous conclusion about "the end of history." He states that only liberal democracy and free market economy had satisfactorily provided all the necessities for happiness.

However, reality has been much more complicated than expected: democracy has not brought the prosperity and benefits once promised and anticipated. On the contrary, these countries slid into various misfortunes. The Soviet Union collapsed and disintegrated. The flagship country, Russia, suffered incessantly from various mishaps. Most of its satellite states joined the prior enemy camp NATO. The Russian economic, financial, military, and political conditions deteriorated quickly toward bankruptcy. The life expectancy for the average Russian dropped quickly for a decade and still has not recovered to its level before the disintegration of the Soviet Union. The same happened with several other former Soviet republics such as Lithuania and Belarus (Tomiuc 2013).

Ukraine failed even worse. In the former Soviet Union, Ukraine was the second largest and the most economically and technologically advanced of all Soviet republics. What came with democratization was a political divide in the country leading to a split between the pro-Russian and the pro-Western regions. This political divide tore the country apart, almost leading to open civil war. The independence of the Crimean Peninsula and its subsequent reintegration into Russia has delivered a heavy blow to the sovereignty and territorial integrity of the country. Under these circumstances, the economic and technologic foundation of the previously advanced Ukraine eroded quickly, and the country began to suffer from various maladies, all closely linked to its political transition.

The deteriorating situations of these countries and people's disappointment with their political and economic changes are consistently supported by the surveys conducted by the Pew Research Center over the past decades. In a survey conducted in nine former communist countries from East Germany to Ukraine, people's enthusiasm for democracy declined in most of the countries; in some, support for either democracy or capitalism has diminished very sharply (Pew Research Center 2009). In another report on Lithuania, Ukraine and Russia released in 2011, it is shown that approval of change to both democracy and capitalism from 1991 to 2011 has dropped markedly from over 50–70 percent to the range of 30–40 percent (Pew Research Center 2011). An observer could easily draw the conclusion that after 20 years' experience with democratization, it is difficult to demonstrate that the political transition in these countries is a positive thing. Beside these examples, few other former satellite states of the Soviet Union have been performing satisfactorily; both Yugoslavia and Czechoslovakia have disintegrated under democracy, and Ukraine may yet join that group.

The Tragic Cases of Democratization in Chaos

If those communist countries completed their transformation into democracy out of willingness and mostly peacefully and orderly, then the countries in the Middle East represent the opposite. Earlier in Iraq, Saddam Hussein was toppled and arrested following the U.S. invasion in 2003, then sentenced to death in 2006. Over a decade later, a stable democracy and peaceful society have not yet to be established in the country. Since 2011, the wave of democratization and protest that started in Tunisia spread rapidly to five other countries: Libya, Egypt, Yemen, Syria and Bahrain. In these countries either the authoritarian regime was toppled or major uprisings with social violence occurred. Everything happened in the name of "the people wanting to bring down the regime," which symbolized their struggle for democracy. Even though most of these authoritarian regimes were overturned, it is questionable whether true democracy was ever realized. To a great extent, these are all forced democratizations in which the previous dictators were removed by outside forces or by internal forces with assistance from the outside, particularly the United States.

In Libya, the political strongman Muammar Gaddafi, who had controlled the politics of the country for four decades, was expelled, captured, and put to death in 2011. In Egypt, political chaos followed the Egyptian Revolution of 2011 when Hosni Mubarak stepped down after 18 days of demonstrations, replaced first by a Muslim extremist then by another former military officer. In the same year following the Arab Spring protests, the political situation in Syria went from bad to worse centering on the future position of President Bashar al-Assad. Soon the country was turned into a battle ground influenced heavily by two outside powers Russia and the United States, and the civil war has persisted until even today. After the overthrow of most of these countries' previous leaders, a superficial rule by the people was established. But in reality, most of these countries are becoming failed states, where different political forces are competing to control the country in a lawless fashion. Ironically the situations seem even worse than when dictators were in power; open conflicts and violence have become daily events. No benefits of democratization have been harvested; crime, murder, corruption, and conflicts have become rampant.

In short, democracy's advance in the Middle East has stalled. The Bush administration's strategic effort to install democracy in Iraq led the country into chaos and more conflicts. The 2011 Arab Spring uprisings failed to usher in real democratic systems or economic prosperity to the Middle East; instead, the democratic movement left Egypt, Libya, Syria, and Yemen with crippled new governments, floundering economies, and prolonged instability.

A New Justification for the CCP's Monopoly on Political Power

Even though the above examples occurred elsewhere, they have useful implications for the CCP regime; they present contrasting examples that help underline the benefits of one-party rule in China. Both groups are very relevant: the first group was either the "big brother" or "little brothers" of communist China while the second group was all developing countries, as Beijing still claims itself to be.

The failures of former communist countries and the Middle Eastern states are routinely quoted as arguments against Western-style democracy. Based on these situations, the CCP regime makes great efforts to convince its people of the dangers and dismal consequences of Western-style democratization (Hu 2018, Han 2005). A common agreement seems to be accepted in the polity that Western-style democracy is not for China, at least at this stage, as the official Party stance corroborates. Thus, when Liu Xiaobo was arrested and sentenced to an 11-year imprisonment by the CCP regime, it caused only very few ripples inside China. Far fewer Chinese had sympathy for him than they had with earlier democracy advocates, such as Wei Jingsheng, when they were jailed by Beijing in the 1980s.

These reactions clearly indicate the decline of public support for Western-style democracy and highlight the greatest obstacle for democratization in China. It is barely possible to challenge the CCP rule in China at present using the rationale of Western democracy, which does not have a positive connotation in the context of China's current political and economic atmosphere. Nor will it change in an optimistic direction in the near future. It is an undeniable fact that the historical failures of democratization in so many countries in the world give the CCP's authoritarian rule extended time for its legitimacy in China and abroad.

DEFECTIVE ECONOMIC AND SOCIAL EXAMPLES — IMPASSE IN THE ESTABLISHED DEMOCRACIES

The Best Scenery Is in the East — The Savior in the 2008 Financial Crisis

Two thousand eight was destined to be a special year, not only for China but also for the world. That year, China successfully hosted the Games of the XXIX Olympiad, marking its remarkable eagerness and efforts to be seen as a major player in the international community. The CCP regime invested so heavily into this game without considering the cost that it dwarfed not only previous Olympic Games but also potentially has overshadowed the Games elsewhere in the decades to come.

This successful international event presented a splendid picture, demonstrating the full potential of a unique "Comcapitalist" country in its full grandeur and glory in the post–Cold War era. In contrast with China was the concurrent gloomy scene of the Western capitalist world led by the United States into the worst financial crisis in nearly 80 years (Amadeo 2018). Like the Great Depression of the 1930s, this global crisis quickly devolved into economic stagnation that had affected almost every Western country. Credit froze, trade stumbled, banks disappeared, businesses went bankrupt, and the unemployment rate soared. The crisis hurt the world economy severely and countries in over half of the world suffered and slid into recession, while China, whose government took swift measures of infrastructure investment to alleviate the problem, emerged unscathed.

In the years following 2008, China played the role of a locomotive in helping the world economy to recover. Driven by remarkably effective government policies, China not only survived the crisis, but its economy continued to thrive. The country's grand investment in infrastructure drove the demand for many different commodities from around the world and supported the economies of quite a number of countries, developing and developed alike.[1] Its contribution to the growth of the world economy exceeded that of the United States which was initially heavily bogged down in the recession.

The stark contrast in performance during the crisis between China and most of the Western world broke the hitherto rosy impression of the Western democracies' capitalistic monopoly on economic progress and reminded the Chinese public that economic prosperity is not necessarily dependent on regime type.

Further Disillusionment—Malfunctions in Other Democracies

In addition to the widespread failures of the newly democratized countries, established democracies have not seemed to fare better. As the second decade approached, scandals and bad news dominated headlines in established liberal democratic states from every corner of the world, including both economically developed and developing countries.

Western democracy has too often become associated with debts, partisan competition, dysfunction, political impasse, economic slowdown and corruption. Fires and gun shots on the streets of Paris, debt issues in Greece and Spain, immigrant crimes in Germany, and the UK's erratic domestic strife over Brexit issues and conflicts with the EU have become recurrent features of Western democracy.

In Latin America, debts, drugs, refugees, gun violence, organized crimes and misuse of law enforcement have added more to the grim situations in established democracies. In the democratic countries of Africa, the same problems exist. South Africa's practice of democracy was not enforced; under Jacob Zuma's ANC, it quickly slid from sub-Saharan Africa's shining star into a country known for crimes, AIDs, a poor economy, and other hallmarks of failed states. Most importantly, the democratic mechanisms in these countries have generally not been able to find remedies for such problems, which led to widespread discontent. As shown in a new Pew Research Center survey, public views about "the performance of democratic systems are decidedly negative in many nations. Across 27 countries polled, a median of 51 percent are dissatisfied with how democracy is working in their country; just 45 percent are satisfied" (Wike, Silver and Castillo 2019). As for solving political, financial, economic and social issues more efficiently and effectively, it seems true that the one-party authoritarian China has been doing far better than these democracies. These situations have strengthened the impression in Chinese society that democracy is too inept and too corrupt to work. To some extent it can be argued that the straw that has broken the arguments of China's democracy advocators came nearly simultaneously from democracies themselves.

Embarrassment of American Democracy — The Trump Election and Repercussions

In the world, the United States throughout the 20th century was usually regarded as the flagship for as well as a model of democracy. Unfortunately, the reputation of American democracy and the image of democracy in general were badly hurt by the electoral process and the results of the extremely intense and controversial presidential election in 2016. This election was special in many respects. The most significant was the unexpected rise of a very unlikely candidate, Donald Trump, who defeated all other Republican candidates by denigrating and demeaning them. Then he defeated his final opponent, the Democratic candidate Hilary Clinton, by using her naiveté with regards to Internet communications and security protocols as a surprise weapon against her. As a presidential candidate, expected by the American public to project a positive image, Trump did not live up to expectations. He made numerous bold but controversial remarks about a variety of sensitive issues in the country: race, immigration, and gender. He was accused of inciting violence against protestors at his rallies and faced allegations of sexual misconduct. Thanks to modern media, especially the social media nowadays, the entire process of this election was relayed to every corner on the planet. Details about the candidates, their families, inappropriate remarks, misbehaviors, and especially their rumors and scandals, can today be known by the entire world instantly.

The cost of the campaigns, supporting interest groups, and especially the scandals about Trump surprised the Chinese. Most people began to realize that democracy in America is not as rosy as it had seemed, and it is actually the game of the rich: a plutocracy and a game of manipulation. They have been similarly amazed that a person like Trump, with so many personality, moral and even psychological issues, could be elected as president.

The 2016 presidential election and the post-election conflict and political impasse in the United States, especially the unprecedented month-long shut-down of the federal government beginning at the end of 2018, did not im-press the Chinese public positively. Instead, the political conflict and chaos in American politics severely discredited the American political system and any intellectual support for democracy in China. By thus directly disillusion-ing China's democracy advocates ironically, the United States, the most ardent proponent of democracy, has made the CCP single-party argument far stronger.

A Second New Justification for the CCP's Monopoly on Power

Problems intrinsic to mature democracies that emerged in the 2008 financial crisis have given the CCP regime new ammunition to criticize the democratic system *per se* and advocate its own authoritarian system. While attacking Western-style democracy, the CCP does not hesitate to advance its main argument and thesis—the serious problems in Western democracies and their inability to handle and solve their own problems within their own political frameworks has apparently disqualified them from criticizing China.

Beijing also makes use of domestic propaganda, boasting about its actual achievements in economic and social progress. It repeatedly emphasizes that every country has its special historical, political, social, economic, and cultu-ral conditions and that China is no exception. Based on hard facts, the current political and economic system under the CCP suits China the best, because the country's current achievements under its leadership is not only unprece-dented in China's history, but outstanding compared to those of any other country. The message is straightforward: the CCP leadership is the best for China, and no change is needed for a system that has been proven to perform well. Any changes without the CCP could only lead China into the abyss. The justification is generally accepted by the Chinese public, from the lower social class to the elites.

THE WEST'S UNEXPECTED HELP TO THE CCP—"RALLY 'ROUND THE FLAG" OF THE PARTY

The Emergence of Distrust in Western Media and Western Governments

As the authors of *China Can Say No* confessed, they were part of the generation in China that trusted Western media unconditionally at first but gradually began to change their perceptions of Western journalism (Song et al. 1996). China's media in the early years primarily blasted propaganda. That was why the younger generation in the 1980s was so eager to listen to the Voice of America (VOA), BBC, and Radio Australia. Indeed, Western media helped the young Chinese in the 1980s open their eyes and see an outside world that was unveiled for them after a generation from the civil war to the end of the Cultural Revolution. Even when listening to Western broadcast was an infraction that would incur punishment, college students in that era bravely tuned in secretly, eager for "truth" from the other world. It was no exaggeration that the Chinese youth once trusted the West much more than their own government and its media.

This is no longer the case; the turning point happened first during the 1989 student protests. It was a time when all people, students as well as people in other professions, were anxiously looking to the West to inform them about what was going on in the streets of Beijing. Unfortunately, the major Western media such as VOA and BBC relayed some stories which were later found to be false, such as the death of Deng Xiaoping during the movement. Uncovered fake news caused initial damage to the reputation of Western media. The CCP regime seized this opportunity to defame Western media and condemned it for harboring a covert mission of "peaceful evolution" with the intent to deliberately cause chaos in China as they did in other countries. The roles of Western governments in openly or secretly assisting student movement leaders to escape from China were interpreted by the CCP regime as deliberately violating China's sovereignty and interfering in China's internal affairs. Although most people sympathized with the student leaders, the CCP successfully focused public attention on the roles of foreign media and governments during the movement. The trust in Western media and governments declined, and doubts started to rise.

If Chinese trust in and positive attitude toward Western media started to change after the 1989 student movement, a downward process followed. The public attitude moved from doubt to apathy to suspicion, with Chinese media leading a counterattack. The honeymoon between the Chinese elites and Western media not only drew to a conclusion, but a kind of hostility started to develop in the new century when China bashing became a fad for much of Western media before China hosted its first Olympic Games in 2008.

The Olympics Syndrome and Deepening Public Sentiment against China Bashing

The 2008 Olympic Games in Beijing was a hallmark event marking a dramatic change of Chinese public attitude toward the West. Despite the controversy within China about the cost of hosting this expensive athletic event, the prevalent public attitude toward it was supportive, for several reasons. The first was the inner eagerness of the Chinese masses to see their country integrated into the international community. The second was the public's desire to show the hospitality, progress and achievements of China to the outside world. The third was inherent Chinese pride and patriotism, which saw hosting the games as a symbol of China's rise. Putting these together, along with promotional advertising in the media, the seminal and famous international sporting event became infused with emotional significance and personal implications of national and cultural pride for most citizens. Anything that sabotaged it, especially if from the outside world, would have hurt Chinese public sentiment and would have been viewed negatively. Indeed, activities contrary to such feelings did start to materialize outside of China when the event was around the corner.

The earliest sign of Western media incompatibility with Chinese expectations occurred months before the Games, when the Western media started to bombard China intensively with various negative reports, ranging from China's role in the tragedies of the Darfur region in Sudan to extensive concurrent human rights violations in Tibet. Such reports, when publicized in China, frustrated and alienated many. Why and how were the Chinese hospitality and kindness viewed so negatively in the West? Opinion reports on negative events during such an occasion might be normal in the West; however, the public in China perceived foreign media coverage on China differently. One reason was that it obviously conflicted with an aspect of Chinese culture that forbids the mention of unhappy things during a happy occasion. Violation of that would be considered unfriendly, rude, and even malevolent.

The other reason was related to what was being reported and other happenings at this time. Critical foreign media reports–some of which included errors like mislabeled photos—evoked a fierce reaction in China. When identified errors were repeated without apologies from Western media, anger and doubts about their intentions mounted. More and more people in China began to accept the idea that the Western media outlets were unfairly and deliberately biased against China. China's public mood started to blaze against Western countries when footage showing the disruption of torch relaying began to appear in domestic media. One, showing some protesters on the street of Paris trying to seize the torch from a handicapped young female Chinese athlete in a wheelchair while French policemen present did not seem to intervene responsibly, triggered widespread Chinese indignation.

Large-scale public protests against the Western media coverage started to increase notably after various Western organizations launched attacks on China with regard to its actions against human rights and Tibetan issues, etc. A seemingly athletic event now began to take on more and more political meaning. Western media reporting during and after the Olympic Games radically changed Chinese attitudes and opinion toward the West, with many Chinese thinking the West was hostile to China's attempt to join the international community and did not want to accept China's friendliness and openness by hosting the Olympic Games.

Unfortunately, the way Western media dealt with a number of terrorist attacks in China in 2009, 2013, and 2014 became the straw that broke the back of positive Chinese perspectives about Western media and even Western governments. If the Western media's probity was first questioned after the 1989 events and more suspected and doubted because of perceived biased criticism of China in the eyes of the Chinese, criticism during a putatively apolitical event such as the 2008 Olympics, followed by selective exaggerated and patently biased reports on Chinese issues, backfired. Among these, biased coverage of terrorist attacks in Urumqi, Kunming and Beijing was especially offensive to the Chinese masses. Those who had axed and stabbed innocent civilians on the street or passengers in a railroad station or who had run over pedestrians with cars, exactly the kinds of acts terrorists did in the West and elsewhere, were being described in the Western media as an "oppressed minority group" or even "freedom fighters." Hardly any Western media or government openly expressed condolences to the Chinese people or condemned the terrorists. On the contrary, they blamed the Chinese government, suggesting that its policies toward the minority groups or directed migration of the Han people to the minority regions were the causes of the violence.

Such perceived as undoubtedly double standards on terrorism angered the Chinese government to such an extent that the Foreign Ministry openly expelled a vocal French journalist, Ursula Gauthier, despite protests (Rauhala 2015). These biased reports hurt the feelings of the ordinary Chinese to such an extent that some young people spontaneously took up the job of counterattacking Western media. For example, angry Chinese students organized a large-scale anti-CNN movement, including launching a popular website called "*anti-CNN.com*" to accuse Western media of hopeless bias toward their country. This website attracted a lot of young people who held grudges against Western media reporting China. The unfavorable and negative news coverage and critical editorial opinions reminded the Chinese masses of the historic humiliation of China at the hands of Western powers during the colonial era.

The intellectuals and other social elites are increasingly convinced that Western media and Western governments were not as previously perceived—free, open, fair, unbiased, and friendly. Instead they began to be viewed as unfriendly, biased, stereotypical, narrow-minded and untrustworthy. For example, in a survey of more than 3,000 Chinese Internet users on their perceptions of bias and trustworthiness of both domestic and foreign media outlets, Truex (2016, 21) finds that the vast majority of Chinese deemed foreign media outlets the least trustworthy. This study clearly shows the attitude of the Chinese public toward Western media, an attitude the CCP has found useful for manipulation.

Blazing Nationalism and New Incentives for Rallying around the Party

In the early period of economic reform, Chinese foreign policy closely adhered to Deng Xiaoping's dictum *"Taoguang Yanghui"* (Keep a low profile and bide one's time) so that China could avoid major conflicts with the West and the neighbors and devote its resources and energy to economic development. But along with the rapid economic advancement, this "low profile" foreign policy doctrine became problematic. An example in China was waves of spontaneous anti-Japanese movements from 2012 to 2015 because of Japan's nationalization of the Diaoyu/Senkaku Islands. These spontaneous movements also showed people's rising dissatisfaction with the government for its weak and unassertive responses. Xi, after taking office in 2012, never mentioned Deng's "low profile" dictum. Rather, he called for *"Fenfa You-wei"* (striving for achievement) to realize the "Chinese dream" and to rejuvenate China as a prosperous and strong world power. The improved international status and rising national pride of China have evoked passions, especially patriotism and nationalism, and resulted in a new general attitude toward Western countries. Following the change in attitude toward Western media, views of Western governments in the new century also took a drastic turn when certain international events that involve China were exposed to the public. Those sporadic events, in particular those that involve such sensitive territorial issues as Taiwan, Hong Kong, Tibet, Diaoyu/Senkaku Islands, and the South China Sea, have stoked Chinese nationalism across the country.

The memories of being victimized by Western and Japanese imperialism in modern history rapidly became a driving force that reshaped the people's attitude toward the CCP. In accordance with the Party propaganda slogan that "There is no new China without the CCP," increasingly more people have started to agree with and accept the Party's stand.

In addition, China's conflicts with the United States over other issues also make people believe that the country needs strong central leadership in order to stand up to the pressure of other countries. If the Chinese ship *Yinhe* was stopped by the U.S. navy for a forced check was a relatively distant event,[2] then the following events are fresh in the memories: the bombing of the

Chinese embassy in Belgrade in May 1999, the military planes' collision in South China Sea in 2001 (Zeng 2017), the rejection of China's application to join the International Space Station in 2010, the frequent American "freedom of navigation" assertions in sailing warships close to Chinese-occupied islands in the past few years, and most recently Trump's trade war on China starting in 2018.

To confront a more powerful and purportedly aggressive United States and its allies, the Chinese increasingly accept the Party thesis that only a strong central government can counter such hostile forces abroad. The improved international status and rising national pride have also evoked passions of patriotism and resulted in more positive attitudes toward the CCP regime. Any attempt to weaken the leadership of the Party is often seen as sabotaging the country's upward path. An unexpected "rally 'round the flag" effect caused by external threats has started to intensify and gain momentum quickly in the past decade.

A Third New Justification for the CCP's Monopoly on Power

In addition to the aforementioned two justifications, the Party found a third justification for its monopoly on political power—the necessity of a powerful central government in order to confront a perceived hostile Western alliance led by the United States, and protect China's national interests.

Chinese intellectuals have always had ambivalent feelings toward the West. For them, the West is the source of new technology, knowledge, and ideology; and it is the place from which China has a lot to learn. However, the West is also the victimizer of China who brought tremendous harm and miseries to the country over the past century. In the reform era, China has benefited greatly from its interactions with the West; on the other hand, China is frequently hurt by their policies. Many Chinese think that the West has not changed much since the colonial era. Western countries are still aggressive, war-like, meddling and hypocritical, often using the pretext of promoting democracy and human rights to invade and harm other nations. The existence of this kind of ambivalent feelings gives the CCP regime abundant room to maneuver for its needs. What happened in Iraq, Yugoslavia, and Syria, for example, are usually interpreted as the result of those countries' weaknesses, which lured Western countries to interfere. The U.S. ban on a Chinese telecommunication giant along with its allies and Canada's arrest of its CFO Meng Wanzhou at the request of the United States are cited as evidence of Western countries' joint attempts to sniper China's high-tech company and contain China's growth.

No matter whether the external environment is hostile to China, Beijing is successfully making the people believe so, using both propaganda and actual examples. Such a "rally 'round the flag" effect tremendously benefits the

Party's continuous monopoly of power. The successes in its efforts have marginalized most critics and suppressed challenges to its rule.

SUCCESS OF LEGITIMACY BATTLE
WITH COMBINED STRATEGY

Denouncing Democratization and Stressing Its Weaknesses

Using the former communist countries and Middle Eastern states as examples, the CCP has utilized real cases to show its people that Western-style democratization is not only unbeneficial but even detrimental to the country.[3] Even though these could be some special examples, the CCP has highlighted their relevance successfully: the contrasts between China's political system and political legacy and those of the former communist countries, and between China's status as a developing country and that of the Middle Eastern states. To date, as China is performing far better economically than almost all those countries, the Party has gained needed evidence supporting its thesis.

The CCP has also demonstrated that even mature democracies, such as the United States and Western European countries, have their problems, which are sometimes very serious. Their system had caused not only economic crisis but also political divide and government dysfunction. Furthermore, a democracy could be very inefficient in handling many problems in society, such as terrorist attacks, financial crises and uncontrollable immigrants. The financial crisis in 2008 and China's becoming the locomotive for world economy have furnished the CCP extra material for self-praise. Therefore, the Party claims that China's political and economic systems are the most appropriate for China; hence, there is no need to change a system that is proven to function well.

In a survey conducted by the Chinese Academy of Social Sciences with 1,750 random samples across four different regions in China, 55 percent of the respondents considered democracy as a good thing while over 40 percent of the same respondents believed that the answer should be contingent on whether democracy is appropriate for China's current conditions.[4] According to the College Students Attitude Survey with over 1,100 Chinese college students in 2015, only 12 percent of the respondents were willing to support democratization unconditionally. Another 30 percent would support democratization only if it would bring economic growth. And 38 percent of the respondents expressed no interest in democratization if the process is unpredictable and costly.[5] This result is informative in that these college students belong to an elite educated group that is also most likely to influence the mainstream of Chinese society in the future. If this group is not keen in democratizing their country, it can be expected that any democratization of China would occur only slowly.

Beijing's "West Scare" Strategy

Paralleling the "China threat" theory prevalent in Western countries, the CCP regime adopts a "West Scare" strategy—emphasizing and sometimes exaggerating the threat from Western countries. This strategy similarly works since it is not difficult to find various issues where Chinese and Western interests diverge. The CCP, with domestic media, adopts abundant cases where the West executes policies that conflict with China or may harm China's interests or its argument.

The CCP regime always emphasizes that the West never abandons its "peaceful evolution" policy and is constantly ready to overthrow the governments it dislikes, citing the Velvet Revolution in Eastern Europe and the Jasmine Revolution in the Middle East. It also warns that democratization could lead to the disintegration of China, as happened to the Soviet Union, Yugoslavia, Czechoslovakia and Ukraine.[6] A fragmented China would thus become a victim again as happened after the Opium Wars in the mid-19th century. It also hints that the Umbrella Revolution in Hong Kong and the Sunflower Revolution in Taiwan had support of the hidden hands of Western governments which do not want to see a unified and prosperous China.

The Party contends that the West does not really care about democracy in China. Even if China became a democracy, the West would not halt its containment of China, as happened with the Soviet Union. Even though Russia has become a quasi-democracy, NATO never stops its expansion toward the East, squeezing Russia's strategic space. And the West has been tightening sanctions on Russia repeatedly.

The "West Scare" strategy seems to function well. It is widely believed in Chinese society that Taiwan, South China Sea, etc. are all issues employed by the United States to restrain and weaken China. A powerful China is not what they want to see. Therefore, it is naive to expect the West to accept China as an equal partner even if it became a democracy. Because of these, logically, to the public writ large only a centralized political leadership can guarantee China's sovereignty, progress and prosperity. Everyone would suffer if the Party's leadership were terminated.

The Chaos Syndrome from History

By 1949 when the PRC was founded, China had gone through domestic chaos and foreign invasions for a full century during which people suffered immeasurably. From the First Opium War in 1839 to PRC's founding in 1949, the country had suffered from various horrendous human and natural disasters. Almost all major Western countries were involved in the invasions and exploitation of China during the colonial era. Most Chinese believed that those historical tragedies happened because the country was fragmented and lacked a powerful government able to mobilize the resources of a vast country against foreign invasions. The fragmentation gave the foreign powers, in particular Japan, the opportunity to invade and hurt China. Thus, China needs a powerful political and military force able to unify the entire country and create an environment for peace and stability. It can also centralize all its resources to defend and develop the country.

Because of this logic and such interpretations of Chinese history, Chinese intellectuals as well as the masses are wary of the loss of a powerful political center. Additionally, unlike Westerners, the Chinese have always had a special penchant for a strong central government with the "Mandate of Heaven" that is able to bring and maintain peace.

In the first 30 years of the PRC, the country went through another round of chaos due to the Party's wrong policies. The Chinese people, especially the older generations who have lived through and kept especially vivid and bitter memories of those chaotic years, pre-1949 as well as post 1949, are especially allergic to potential chaos. The stability and relative security gained since the reform and opening up at the end of the 1970s is most precious for them and must be guarded at all cost. Most Chinese accept that their country is now on the right track of development and revival. They would oppose any major change to the current system that could incur another round of chaos.

So, when Beijing used heavy hands to quench the student movements in 1989 using the slogan of "*Fandui Dongluan*" (opposing chaos) and "*Weihu Shehui Zhixu*" (safeguarding social order), it encountered much less resistance and backlash from Chinese society than anticipated in the West. Similarly, in the later years when Beijing used an iron fist to crush pro-democracy and anti-CCP forces that might have jeopardized social stability and Party rule, it employed the same tactic of "*Weiwen*" (maintaining stability). Responses from the public were usually positive if not openly supportive. Most people agree that taking measures to maintain peace and development is necessary and is deemed to be much more important than advancing democracy.

The Combined Strategy Works

In conclusion, all these events that had happened outside China objectively gave the CCP strong as well as convincing excuses and means through media control to rationalize its monopoly on political power. By denouncing Western-style democracy and emphasizing its weaknesses at the right time, by adopting the "West Scare" strategy in an appropriate context and by inciting the domestic chaos anxiety complex, the CCP has successfully used a combined strategy highlighting and supporting its relevance, importance and indispensability to China's security, stability and progress.

Indeed, the international environment over the past one to two decades has given the CCP unprecedented and often perfect opportunities to advance its agenda and fan up nationalism to manipulate public mood and opinions. Polls cited above indicate that the Party has achieved most of its goals in convincing the Chinese public about its legitimacy. Various public opinion polls in China show consistent popularity of and support for the Party; some of this popularity can now even be found in Taiwan.[7]

In a worst case scenario, the CCP can always revert to the tried, true, and well established political strategy for dealing with a crisis: diversionary policy. By being able to divert domestic problems to seemingly international crises, as many other countries have successfully done before, the CCP is secure politically.[8] The CCP regime has a good number of highly sensitive issues that can be manipulated easily as needed: Taiwan, the South China Sea, Diaoyu/Senkaku Islands, the border dispute with India, etc. All these issues are highly relevant to nationalist sentiments. Unless the CCP were to lose in a major military conflict, barely anything can shake its ruling foundation at present. In an international crisis, real or contrived, the CCP would present itself as the only defender of China's national security, only guarantor of domestic order and economic development and even as the Messiah of the country's future prosperity and prestige.

NOTES

1. See the article "China's Development Brings Opportunity to the World." English Edition of *QiuShi* 10, no 37, 2018. http://english.qstheory.cn/2018-12/21/c_1123801049.htm.

2. The *Yinhe* incident was a conflictual event between the United States and China over a Chinese container ship *Yinhe* on July 23, 1993. The United States government made a false claim that the China-based regular container ship was carrying chemical weapon materials to Iran. The *Yinhe* was forced to stop by the U.S. Navy in the international waters of the Indian Ocean for a month. After the Chinese government agreed to an inspection by the U.S. Navy, it turned out that there were no chemical weapon materials at all, and the Chinese ship was proven innocent. The United States signed a final inspection report on September 4 that confirmed this result, but it refused to apologize "because the United States had acted in good faith on intelligence."

3. See the article "*Xifang Mouxie Guojia Qiangxing Tuixiao de 'Minzhuhua' Anhan Naxie Weixian* (What Hidden Dangers Exist in the Forced Democratization by Certain Western Countries)?" *Guancha*, June 21, 2011. https://www.guancha.cn/indexnews/2011_06_21_58096.shtml.

4. The data are from the website of *The Atlantic*. Accessed on December 29, 2017. https://www.theatlantic.com/china/archive/2013/07/young-chinese-people-may-just-not-be-that-into-western-style-democracy/277885/.

5. See the appendix for more details about the survey.

6. See the article "*Yidan Zhongguo 'Minzhuhua': Zhongguo Shouxian Shiqu de Jiangshi baifenzhi 70 de Guotu* (Once Democratized, China Will Lose Seventy Percent of Its Territory)." *Xilu East Military*, January 26, 2010. http://junshi.xilu.com/2010/0126/news_334_62041.html.

7. For example, a number of intellectuals from Taiwan, including professors as well as graduate students who teach or study at the universities on the mainland, openly declare that they want to join the CCP. They did so even at the cost of losing their welfare packages in

Taiwan and facing other prosecutions after going back. See "The Strange Case of Tom Wang, the Taiwanese Who Wants to Be a CCP Member." *Taiwan Sentinel*, October 31, 2017, https://sentinel.tw/the-strange-case-of-tom-wang-the-taiwanese-who-wants-to-be-a-ccp-member/ and "Taiwan to Strip Citizenship of Beijing Devotees." *Asia Times*, March 14, 2019, https://www.asiatimes.com/2019/03/article/taiwan-to-strip-citizenship-of-beijing-devotees/.

8. For an empirical study of how democratic countries divert domestic crises, see Zhang (2002).

Chapter Ten

Conclusion

In China studies literature, many prior works overemphasize the legitimacy issue of the CCP regime from Western perspectives and experiences based on the One-Person One-Vote Rule. Thus, when this criterion is applied to the study of the politics of communist China, a prejudged framework forms and leads many scholars to question the CCP regime's "legitimacy" and longevity; they subsequently conclude, often hastily and stereotypically, that communist China is doomed to collapse. The tremendous difficulties and problems of the CCP in running a country with a population exceeding 1.4 billion facilely expedite this conclusion.

While we do not deny the rational argument and bountiful evidence presented in such research, many works neglect or underrate a number of important factors that may help solve the puzzle faced by most China observers: why communist China isn't collapsing despite waves of prophets of doom. To understand and explore incisively the CCP rule and state-society dynamics in China over the past decades, it is important to transcend the current conceptual framework calibrated primarily based on Western values and democratic criteria. Our contributions in this work lie in filling in gaps in prior works and enriching those under-examined areas of China studies by contriving a new framework, one that is based on China's peculiar political history and culture but that has also instilled necessary Western ingredients.

MISUSE OF "DEMOCRACY" AND PECULIARITIES OF CHINA'S POLITICAL CULTURE

The first and maybe the most misleading issue in prior studies is the adoption of "democracy" as the universally applicable rule to measure political viability in China, almost completely neglecting the impact of China's millennia-long political culture and history upon China's political reality. Without factoring in and understanding the peculiarities of China's unique culture and history, it is very difficult, if not impossible, to logically explain the unprecedented economic achievements and social progress in China that have been realized since the reform and how this single-party authoritarian regime has gained long-standing support from its people.

External observers need to be aware that Western and Chinese political cultures diverge in significant ways. The foremost is their assumption about human nature. The West, as represented by Thomas Hobbes, assumes that the nature of human is self-centered. Without government, men will be in a constant state of war on each other. This mindset necessitates the making of laws to restrain the inner devils. Logically a government staffed by humans must also be treated as such, making laws to control its power. The social contract theory developed by Jean-Jacques Rousseau and John Locke implies an antagonistic relationship between the ruler and the ruled in the West—a government must be checked and constrained by the governed so as to be legitimate; and this end should be realized through democratic means of free and fair election.

In Chinese culture, it is widely believed that humans are good in nature at the beginning, but gradually get corrupted by society. Therefore, it is important to select those who remain uncorrupt and virtuous to run the government on behalf of all for the common good. Because of genuine trust in governance by virtuous people, the Chinese tend to emphasize self-cultivation and self-improvement of the rulers. It is worth noting that, in China, its ruling elites and intellectuals usually have possessed a strong sense of mission and responsibility throughout most of its history. In modern times, this sense of mission and responsibility, reflected as devotion to the revival of a weak China in a competitive world as well as pride and loyalty to one's homeland, has exerted its impact upon generations of contemporary Chinese leaders from Sun Yat-Sen to Mao Zedong in the revolutionary years, and from Deng Xiaoping to Xi Jinping in the reform era. It has forged a powerful intrinsic driving force among the Chinese political, economic and social elites in running this country. In addition, deeply rooted cultural collectivism favors a versatile and capable government that is able to take care of the entire population like members in a family. This Chinese concept of state-society relations is best represented by the Chinese terminology for state "*guojia*," which literally means "*country-family*." The Chinese masses have always had high expectations that the government should take care of its people in all aspects. Thus, when Western demonstrators protest against government interfering too much in their lives, conversely Chinese protestors complain that the government is not doing enough for theirs.

Furthermore, while Western political culture since the 18th century emphasizes the *process* of building a legitimate government through democratic election, the Chinese political culture prizes the *outcome* of governance. This precludes any preoccupation with adopting "democracy" as the basis of judging a government's legitimacy. In the Chinese context, so long as the ruler is able to bring perceived benefits to the people, it is considered a legitimate government regardless of the *process* of its establishment and the nature of its ruling. The state-society relation in China bears the imprint of this unique and pragmatic view of legitimacy.

Neglecting cultural influence also prevents scholars from understanding the underlying momentum of the CCP's restless efforts in reform and governance improvement. One key element in China's political culture that is like a Damocles Sword above all its rulers, including the CCP, originated in the "Mandate of Heaven." This mandate concept defines a fundamental contractual relationship between the ruler and the ruled in China: the ruler is supposed to be virtuous and lenient and to provide the ruled care, stability, prosperity and protection in exchange for loyalty, submissiveness, obedience and respect from the ruled. Each of the parties must properly carry out their respective duties and obligations, the missions of Heaven. If the ruled does not perform his functions, he deserves punishment. Conversely, if the ruler fails to play his role as expected, the ruled have legitimate reasons to overthrow the ruler. A new government can always legitimize its overthrowing the previous regime using this widely accepted principle as "*Titian Xingdao*" (carry out the Mandate of the Heaven). The perpetual and profound existence of this logic in Chinese culture gives a strong sense of insecurity to the current ruler—the CCP.

Even though the Party-state controls most propaganda mechanisms in the country and can always utilize them to give self-praise and claim whatever achievements the country has made, it has to similarly absorb all blames and accusations of the wrongdoings if things go wrong, such as widely reported pollution, faulty vaccines and poison milk incidents. In such a one-party system (even though China has eight other "democratic parties" in name), the CCP does not have any excuse to blame others as so often happens in a multiparty system. Though the central authority in China does manage to take advantage of the division within levels of governments to divert part of the discontent and anger to the localities, eventually the Party has to take ultimate responsibility. Thus, the sense of insecurity/urgency as a single dominant ruling party largely accounts for the relatively benevolent governance of the potentially iron-fisted CCP. In return, this benevolence, though with flaws, helps the CCP gain popular endorsement from the ruled.

INTERNATIONAL ENVIRONMENT AS A POWERFUL VARIABLE

While most scholars in China studies often analyze the CCP regime as a non-democratic entity, few pay attention to the political effects of two other characteristics of the regime that have primarily shaped its interactions with the West. The first is that China is a country that still holds the banner of Communism, at least officially, which belongs to a rival ideology. The second is that it is still categorized as a developing country.

China's identity as a communist party-ruled country often makes itself look like an outcast to Western countries in many ways. So there is a quite long list of incompatibilities between China and Western countries. In the process of China's growth, it has not been rare to see concerted efforts of Western media and governments to demonize China and limit its expansion. The most striking efforts happened during the 2008 Olympic Games. And the most recent of such endeavors is their coordinated action against China's most rapidly rising telecommunication giant Huawei.

China's identity as both a developing country and a late developer further expands the gap between China and the West in ways of thinking and conduct. China's modern history as a victim of Western colonialism and imperialism makes its people leery of and sensitive toward Western policies on China. Perceived double standards of the West on issues such as terrorism increase Chinese distrust in Western countries and strengthen trust in their own government. Moreover, facing an international system already dominated by the West in market, capital, technology, and rules, it is very difficult for late developers to compete with advanced countries in an open international market place. Industries of late developer countries usually need state support in order to grow, and the state needs the growth of its economy to become stronger. Therefore, an interdependent relationship normally develops. The growth of China's private businesses and the middle class follows this pattern. Therefore, as a protector of domestic market position and defender of national interests in a relatively rivalrous international political and economic environment, it is not difficult for the CCP regime to win support from its people in any conflict with foreign competitors, particularly Western countries.

In sum, such external pressure and threats paradoxically strengthened the rally 'round the Party effect. The external "help" expanded the CCP's propaganda ability to caution the Chinese masses regarding dangers coming from outside and to emphasize the necessity of a strong central authority to mobilize domestic resources to fend off such external challenges. They help raise the legitimacy of the CCP regime domestically. Factoring in this variable would provide China scholars more lucidity in studying China's rise, and contribute to the literature on diversionary theory and links between domestic and international politics.

DETERMINANTS OF REGIME COLLAPSE

Having completed studying the strategies and tactics of the CCP in perpetu-ating its rule as well as the state-society dynamics in China, we do not support doomsayers' assertions about China's collapse. Over the period of reform, there is a common thread that weaves through all the political, eco-nomic and social policies—a *people-centered* policy aiming at improving public well-being. This is considered the key priority of the CCP at all levels from the bottom up to the top in order to justify its rule.

The first two steps of Deng Xiaoping's "Three-Step" plan in doubling China's GDP from 1981 to 1990 and doubling it again in the 1990s had already been realized before the end of the last century. After Deng, all Chinese leaders from Jiang to Hu to Xi have closely adhered to the policy of economic development as the top priority of the CCP, though their respective emphases on other aspects have differed. Based on the current development trajectory, Deng's "Step Three," achieving modernization by 2050 through raising incomes to the levels of medium-size developed countries, can also be optimistically expected. In addition to raising living standards, the CCP regime has been adopting a more sophisticated and proactive ruling strategy: self-improving and self-correcting its policies for better economic and social performance, normalizing some communication channels with the mass pub-lic in order to probe and assess public opinion and sentiment, allowing the growth and expansion of certain social groups to provide extensive and often more efficient social services, and being relatively responsive and tolerant to grievances and complaints to ease social tensions, etc. Such benevolent and aspiring governance has been widely recognized by the Chinese public, evi-denced by high political support rates from various surveys and polling.

From a comparative perspective, the 1990s reforms in other former com-munist countries were almost all *process-oriented*. They tried to solve the issue of government legitimacy using the Western concept of democracy—voting and electing. It was believed then that so long as the process of creating a representative government is right, good governance results could be anticipated. However, the reality has been much more complicated and gloomy than previously expected.

Using only democratic criteria to judge the CCP's rule, the regime's legitimacy can be said to have a weak foundation. However, looking at it through the lens of Chinese political theory and traditional culture as well as external context, its legitimacy appears solid with little chance of collapse. The ruling results of the CCP in the past four decades have been remarkably good, better than any other regime has achieved in the same period. Then it is pointless for changing a regime that is proven to work well already. Even though the CCP regime's legitimacy is questionable from the *process-orient-ed* legitimacy perspective of the West, the regime is still likely to last so long as it continues what it has been doing. Its rule is more prone to collapse only if it deviates from its *people-centered* principles. In this argument of governance by process or results, to date, flexible pragmatism has overruled inflexible standards in China.

However, this argument does not exclude a looming danger the CCP regime is facing—Xi's increasingly radical policies, such as his reemphasis on political studies and indoctrination, power concentration, and tightening social control, etc., much like a return to Mao's time. These policies have given rise to wider complaints both inside the Party and in larger society. In the long term, if this trend is not halted, the CCP's long cherished *people-centered* policy might wither. Chinese society might evolve into another round of chaos and incur people's dissatisfaction with the CCP rule. Since Xi has terminated term limits for the presidency, he leaves an unpredictable future for the Party and the country.

Above all, the West needs to understand that the CCP regime is the product of a different political culture and an extended model of rule built on China's millennia-long history and culture. Studying or examining China using a purely Western lens and framework implies neglecting or nullifying all the age-condensed forces and their effects upon China's historical course, thus producing biased or unreliable results that consequently provide wrong policy suggestions for politicians, businessmen and other policy-makers. This is detrimental to understanding an increasingly influential country and making constructive policies to engage it. For China's part, it needs to interact with the West more actively and explain more proactively about its unique history, culture, and politics so as to increase the West's understanding of it.

For the authors, we hope our studies of China, its ruling party and social actors will provide new perspectives on this authoritarian regime and accurately communicate to our readers the new and internal intricacies of China's politics as well as the effects of international context on the CCP. We also hope that this work will enhance the under-studied aspects of China's politics such as its *outcome-oriented* political culture and will enrich the political theories of studying authoritarian regimes of the world.

Appendix

Global Survey of College Students' Knowledge of International Affairs and Attitude toward Great Power Politics and Good Governance is an anonymous survey project initiated and conducted by Wanfa Zhang, Sugu Narayanan, and Feng Sun in 2015 to 2018. The researchers surveyed over 1,180 random students at over 25 universities in China, including Beijing University, Tsinghua University, and Shanghai University. Details about the project can be found at: https://research.fit.edu/politics-research.

Part of the Questionnaires:

1. Democracy is good, but it might come with a high price, such as racial tension and conflict, civil war, even national disintegration. Which of the following situations will you choose?

   a. I will take whatever consequences so long as democracy can be achieved.
   b. I will support democracy if it comes with economic growth.
   c. I will support democracy if it does not take more than 3–5 years.
   d. I will support democracy if it does not take more than 10 years.
   e. I will not support it if the result is unpredictable or the price is high.

2. The following indicators are considered very important factors for a good government. Please rank their importance in your eyes. (people can vote their government officially, political stability and no violence

in society, government effectiveness in implementing policies, rule of law in the society, control of corruption, etc.)

3. In your opinion, what is the most important function of a government? Answer: "A government that is able to. . . ."

    a. raise the standard of living for its people.
    b. raise the international status of its country in the world.
    c. build a large and powerful army for its country.
    d. bring democracy and rule of law
    e. ensure freedom of religion.

4. If China becomes the Number 1 country in the world and enjoys a preponderance of power, how should China interact with Japan?

    a. Leave behind historical burdens and develop a friendly relationship with Japan
    b. Develop a normal state-to-state relationship with Japan
    c. Develop a normal state-to-state relationship with Japan but keep certain distance
    d. Develop a state-to-state relationship but needs to cause discomfort for Japan like it does to China
    e. Use war to revenge Japan for its invasion of China in history

References

Acemoglu, Daron. 2014. "Does Democracy Boost Economic Growth." *World Economic Forum,* May 20, 2014. https://www.weforum.org/agenda/2014/05/democracy-boost-economic-growth/.

Acemoglu, Daron, and J. A. Robinson. 2000. "Why Did the West Extend the Franchise? Democracy, Inequality and Growth in Historical Perspective." *Quarterly Journal of Economics* 115, no. 4: 1167–99.

———. 2005. *Economic Origins of Dictatorship and Democracy.* New York: Cambridge University Press.

Albert, E., and Beina Xu. 2018. "The Chinese Communist Party." *Council on Foreign Relations*, March 14, 2018. https://www.cfr.org/backgrounder/chinese-communist-party.

Allison, Graham. 2017a. "What Xi Jinping Wants." *The Atlantic*, May 31, 2017.

———. 2017b. *Destined for War: Can America and China Escape Thucydides Trap?* Boston: Houghton Mifflin Harcourt.

Almeida, Heitor, and Daniel Ferreira. 2002. "Democracy and the Variability of Economic Performance." *Economics and Politics* 14, no. 3 (November): 225–57.

Almond, G. A., and S. Verba. 1963. *The Civic Culture: Political Attitudes and Democracy in Five Nations*. Princeton, NJ: Princeton University Press.

Amadeo, Kimberly. 2018. "The 2008 Financial Crisis: The Causes and Costs of the Worst Crisis since the Great Depression." *The Balance*, November 7, 2018. https://www.thebalance.com/2008-financial-crisis-3305679.

An, Baijie. 2013. "Xi Jinping Vows 'Power within Cage of Regulations'." *China Daily*, January 23, 2013. http://www.chinadaily.com.cn/china/2013-01/23/content_16157933.htm?utm_source=twitterfeed&utm_medium=twitter.

An, Baijie, and Cao Yin. 2013. "Judicial Move Aims at Online Rumor." *China Daily,* September 10, 2013. http://www.chinadaily.com.cn/china/2013-09/10/content_16955947_2.htm.

Arnove, A., P. Binns, P. Binns, C. Harman, and A. Shawki. 2003. *Russia from Workers' State to State Capitalism*. Chicago: Haymarket Books.

Baker, Benjamin David. 2016. "Sino-Norwegian Relations, 5 Years after Liu Xiaobo's Nobel Peace Prize." *The Diplomat*, January 4, 2016.

Barro, Robert Joseph. 1996. *Getting It Right: Markets and Choices in a Free Society*. Cambridge, MA: MIT Press.

Baum, R. 1992. "Political Stability in Post-Deng China: Problems and Prospects." *Asian Survey* 32, no. 6 (June): 491–505.

BBC. 2015. "Yemen Crisis: China Evacuates Citizens and Foreigners from Aden." April 3, 2015. https://www.bbc.com/news/world-middle-east-32173811.

Beja, Jean-Philippe. 2006. "The Changing Aspects of Civil Society in China." *Social Research* 73, no. 1 (Spring): 53–74.

Bell, Daniel A. 2006. "China's Leaders Rediscover Confucianism." *International Herald Tribune*, September 14, 2006.

———. 2010. *China's New Confucianism: Politics and Everyday Life in a Changing Society.* Princeton, NJ: Princeton University Press.

———. 2015. *The China Model: Political Meritocracy and the Limits of Democracy.* Princeton, NJ: Princeton University Press.

Bellin, Eva. 2000. "Contingent Democrats Industrialists, Labor, and Democratization in Late-Developing Countries." *World Politics* 52 (January): 175–205.

———. 2004. "The Robustness of Authoritarianism in the Middle East: Exceptionalism in Comparative Perspective." *Comparative Politics* 36, no. 2 (January): 139–57.

Bergere, Marie-Claire. 1989. *The Golden Age of the Chinese Bourgeoisie 1911–1937.* Translated by Janet Lloyd. New York: Cambridge University Press.

Berkley, S., J. Bobadilla, R. Hecht, K. Hill, D. T. Jamison, C. J. L. Murray, P. Musgrove, H. Saxenian, and J. Tan. 1993. *World Development Report 1993: Investing in Health.* Washington, DC: World Bank Group.

Bermeo, Nancy. 1997. "Myths of Modernization: Confrontation and Conflict during Democratic Transition." *Comparative Politics* 29, no. 3: 305–22.

Bernstein, Thomas, and Xiaobo Lu. 2009. *Taxation without Representation in Contemporary Rural China.* New York: Cambridge University Press.

Biddulph, Sarah. 2015. *The Stability Imperative Human Rights and Law in China.* Vancouver, Toronto: UBC Press.

Billioud, Sebastien. 2007. "Confucianism, 'Cultural Tradition' and Official Discourse in China at the Start of the New Century." *China Perspective* no. 3: 53–68.

Billioud, Sébastien, and Joël Thoraval. 2015. *The Sage and the People the Confucian Revival in China.* Oxford: Oxford University Press.

Bo, Zhiyue. 2007. *China's Elite Politics: Political Transition and Power Balancing.* Singapore: World Scientific Publishing Company.

———. 2010. *China's Elite Politics: Governance and Democratization.* New Jersey: World Scientific Publishing Company.

Bol, Peter K. 2018. "Why Do Intellectuals Matter to Chinese Politics?" In *The China Questions: Critical Insights into A Rising Power*, edited by Jennifer Rudolph and Michael Szonyi, 244–51. Cambridge, MA: Harvard University Press.

Bosu, Rabi Sankar. 2018. "Xi's New Year Speech Signals China's Role in Global Governance." *China Plus,* January 2, 2018. http://chinaplus.cri.cn/opinion/opedblog/23/20180102/72615.html.

Brody, Richard A. 1994. "Crisis, War and Public Opinion." In *Taken by Storm: Media, Public Opinion, and U.S. Foreign Policy in the Gulf War,* edited by W. L. Bennett and D. L. Paletz, 210–30. Chicago: University of Chicago Press.

Buckley, Chris. 2018a. "As China's Woes Mount, Xi Jinping Faces Rare Rebuke at Home." *New York Times*, August 1, 2018. LexisNexis Academic.

———. 2018b. "Marching across China, Army Veterans Join Ranks of Protesters." *New York Times*, June 25, 2018. LexisNexis Academic.

Bueno de Mesquita, Bruce, A. Smith, R. M. Siverson, and J. D. Morrow. 2003. *The Logic of Political Survival.* Cambridge, MA: MIT Press.

Burnett, John. 2015. "China Is Beating the U.S. in Africa—China Is in the Lead When It Comes to Investment and Influence on the African Continent." *US News*, March 24, 2015. https://www.usnews.com/opinion/economic-intelligence/2015/03/24/china-beating-us-in-race-to-invest-in-africa.

Burkhart, Ross E., and Michael S. Lewis-Beck. 1994. "Comparative Democracy: The Economic Development Thesis." *The American Political Science Review* 88, no. 4: 903–10.

Cabestan, Jean-Pierre. 2005. "The Many Facets of Chinese Nationalism." *China Perspectives* no. 59. https://journals.openedition.org/chinaperspectives/2793.

Cai, Peter. 2015. "How China Can Avoid the Middle-Income Trap." *The Australian Business Review*, April 28, 2015. https://www.theaustralian.com.au/business/business-spectator/how-china-can-avoid-the-middle-income-trap/news-story/6ccc1e2695b4d48250a2c9aa9eea532d.

Cai, Youngshun. 2006. *State and Lai-off Workers in Reform China: The Silence and Collective Action of the Retrenched.* London: Routledge.

Cain, Rob. 2017. "China's 'Wolf Warrior 2' Becomes 2nd Film in History to Reach $800M in a Single Territory." *Forbes*, August 27, 2017.

Cao, Tian Yu. 2005. *The Chinese Model of Modern Development.* London: Routledge.

Chan, A. 1993. "Confucianism and Deng's China." In *Modernization of the Chinese Past*, edited by M. Lee and A. D. Syrokomla-Stefanowska, 16–24. Sydney: Wild Peony Press.

Chan, K. 2010. "Civil Society and Social Capital in China." In *International Encyclopedia of Civil Society*, edited by H. K. Anheier and S. Toepler, 242–47. New York: Springer.

Chan, V. C., J. Backstrom, and T. D. Mason. 2014. "Patterns of Protest in the People's Republic of China: A Provincial Level Analysis." *Asian Affairs: An American Review* 41: 91–107.

Chang, Gordon G. 2001. *The Coming Collapse of China.* New York: Random House.

Chang, Xiaojun. 2017. "Chinese Private Enterprise Overseas Investment Index 2017." *iFeng Finance*, December 19, 2017. http://finance.ifeng.com/a/20171219/15877704_0.shtml.

Chanley, Virginia A. 2002. "Trust in Government in the Aftermath of 9/11: Determinants and Consequences." *Political Psychology* 23, no. 3 (September): 469–83.

Chen, Feng, and Yi Kang. 2016. "Disorganized Popular Contention and Local Institutional Building in China: A Case Study in Guangdong." *Journal of Contemporary China* 25, no. 100: 596–612.

Chen, Jidong, Jennifer Pan, and Yiqing Xu. 2016. "Sources of Authoritarian Responsiveness: A Field Experiment in China." *American Journal of Political Science* 60, no. 2: 383–400.

Chen, Jie, and Chunlong Lu. 2011. "Democratization and the Middle Class in China: The Middle Class's Attitudes toward Democracy." *Political Research Quarterly* 64, no. 3: 705–19.

Chen, Xi. 2011. *Social Protest and Contentious Authoritarianism in China.* New York: Cambridge University Press.

Chen, Yu. 2018. "*Zhongguo Shouge Nanji Yongjiu Jichang Jijiang Kaijian, Nandu Buyayu Jianshe Kaochazhan* (China Will Build Its First Permanent Airfield in Antarctica)." *Xinhuanet*, October 29, 2018. http://www.xinhuanet.com/politics/2018-10/29/c_1123625571.htm.

Chen, Zhihua. 2014. *Lishi Weiwu Zhuyi yu E'guoshi Yanjiu (Historical Materialism and the Study of Russian History).* Beijing: China Social Science Press.

Cheng, J. Y. S. 2012 "Challenges for Hu-Wen and Their Successors: Consolidating the 'Beijing Consensus' Model." In *China: A New Stage of Development for an Emerging Superpower*, edited by J. Y. S. Cheng, 1–48. Hong Kong: City University of Hong Kong Press.

China Daily. 2009a. "President Calls for Peace and Prosperity." *China Daily,* January 1, 2009. http://www.chinadaily.com.cn/cndy/2009-01/01/content_7358502.htm.

———. 2009b. "Chinese FM Pledges to Help Build Peace, Prosperity." *China Daily*, August 24, 2009. http://www.chinadaily.com.cn/china/2009-8/24/content_8609998.htm.

China Today. 2014. "China Commemorates Confucius with High-Profile Ceremony." *China Today,* September 25, 2014. http://www.chinatoday.com.cn/english/news/2014-09/25/content_641732.htm.

Choi, Eun K. 2012. "Patronage and Performance: Factors in the Political Mobility of Provincial Leaders in Post-Deng China." *China Quarterly* no. 212: 965–81.

Chung, Yousun. 2015. "Pushing the Envelope for Representation and Participation: The Case of Homeowner Activism in Beijing." *Journal of Contemporary China* 24, no. 91: 1–20.

Clarke, S., C. Lee, and Q. Li. 2004. "Collective Consultation and Industrial Relations in China." *British Journal of Industrial Relations* 42, no. 2 (June): 235–54.

CLB. 2000–2017. "*Zhongguo Gongren Yundong Guancha Baogao* (The Annual Report on Chinese Workers' Movement)." August 13, 2018. https://clb.org.hk/section/old-chinese-site.

———. 2005. "*Gonghui Zhujian Yundong Yu Fazhan Nongmingong Huiyuan* (Trade Union Movement and Recruitment of Migrant Workers)." September 21, 2005.

————. 2016. "Strikes and Protests by China's Workers Soar to Record Heights in 2015." July 1, 2016. https://clb.org.hk/en/content/strikes-and-protests-china%E2%80%99s-workers-soar-record-heights-2015.

CNNIC. 2018. "The 41st China Statistical Report on Internet Development." January 2018. http://www.cnnic.cn/hlwfzyj/hlwxzbg/hlwtjbg/201803/P020180305409870339136.pdf.

Cody, Edward. 2006. "In Face of Rural Unrests, China Rolls Out Reforms." *Washington Post*, January 28, 2006. LexisNexis Academic.

Cohen, David. 2012a. "China's Factional Politics" *The Diplomat*, December 8, 2012.

————. 2012b. "What Wukan Really Meant." *The Diplomat*, January 1, 2012.

Cook, Linda J. 1993. *The Soviet Social Contract and Why It Failed: Welfare Policy and Workers' Politics from Brezhnev to Yeltsin.* Cambridge, MA: Harvard University Press.

Cook, Linda J., and Martin K. Dimitrov. 2017. "The Social Contract Revisited: Evidence from Communist and State Capitalist Economies." *Europe Asia Studies* 69, no. 1 (January): 8–26.

Corne, Peter, and Johnny Browaeys. 2017. "China Cleans up Its Act on Environmental Enforcement." *The Diplomat*, December 9, 2017.

Dahl, Robert A. 1971. *Polyarchy: Participation and Opposition.* New Haven, CT: Yale University Press.

Dai, Jianzhong. 2002. "*Zhongguo Siying Qiye he Siying Qiyezhu* (Chinese Private Enterprises and Entrepreneurs)." *Aisixiang*, December 27, 2002. http://www.aisixiang.com/data/2329.html.

Delury, John. 2008. "'Harmonious' in China." *Policy Review, Hoover Institution* 148 (March).

Deng, Jinting, and P. Liu. 2017. "Consultative Authoritarianism: The Drafting of China's Internet Security Law and E-Commerce Law." *Journal of Contemporary China* 26, no. 107: 679–95.

Denyer, Simon. 2013. "In China, Communist Party Takes Unprecedented Step: It Is Listening." *Washington Post*, August 2, 2013. LexisNexis Academic.

Diamond, Larry. 2013. "Chinese Communism and the 70-Year Itch." *The Atlantic*, October 29, 2013.

Dib, H. H., Xilong Pan, and H. Zhang. 2008. "Evaluation of The New Rural Cooperative Medical System in China: Is It Working or Not?" *International Journal of Equity Health* 7, no. 17.

Dickson, Bruce J. 2003. *Red Capitalists in China: The Party, Private Entrepreneurs, and Prospects for Political Change*. New York: Cambridge University Press.

————. 2007. "Integrating Wealth and Power in China: The Communist Party's Embrace of the Private Sector." *The China Quarterly* no. 192 (December): 827–54.

————. 2008. *Wealth into Power: The Communist Party's Embrace of China's Private Sector.* Cambridge: Cambridge University Press.

————. 2016. *The Dictator's Dilemma: The Chinese Communist Strategy for Survival.* New York: Oxford University Press.

Dotson, John. 2011. "The Confucian Revival in the Propaganda Narratives of the Chinese Government." *US-China Economic and Security Review Commission*, Staff Research Report.

Downs, Erica S. 2007. "The Fact and Fiction of Sino-African Energy Relations." *China Security* 3, no. 3 (Summer): 42–86.

Durkee, Jack. 2018. "Should We Worry about China's Ambitions in the North Pole?" *Newsweek*, February 7, 2018. https://www.newsweek.com/should-we-worry-about-chinas-ambitions-north-pole-800754.

Ebeling, Richard M. 1999. "Friedrich A. Hayek: A Centenary Appreciation." *The Freeman* 49, no. 5 (May). Archived from the original on 2013-04-15.

Economy, Elizabeth. 2012. "China's Land Grab Epidemic Is Causing More Wukan-Style Protests." *The Atlantic*, February 8, 2012.

Edin, Maria. 2003. "State Capacity and Local Agent Control in China: CPP Cadre Management from a Township Perspective." *The China Quarterly* no. 173 (March): 35–52.

Ergenc, Ceren. 2014. "Political Efficacy through Deliberative Participation in Urban China: A Case Study on Public Hearings." *Journal of Chinese Political Science* 19, no. 2: 191–213.

Esarey, A., D. Stockmann, and J. Zhang. 2017. "Support for Propaganda: Chinese Perceptions of Public Service Advertising." *Journal of Contemporary China* 26, no. 103: 101–17.

Evans, Peter B. 1995. *Embedded Autonomy: States and Industrial Transformation*. Princeton, NJ: Princeton University Press.

Fairebank, John King. 1983. *The United States and China, 4th ed*. Cambridge, MA: Harvard University Press.

Fewsmith, Joseph. 2004. "Promoting the Scientific Development Concept." *China Leadership Monitor* no. 11. http://www.hoover.org/publications/china-leadership-monitor/article/6226.

Fisher, Max. 2012. "How China Stays Stable Despite 500 Protests Every Day." *The Atlantic*, January 5, 2012.

Fishkin, James S., Baogang He, R. C. Luskin, and Alice Siu. 2010. "Deliberative Democracy in An Unlikely Place: Deliberative Polling in China." *British Journal of Political Science* 40, no. 2 (April): 435–48.

Francois, P., F. Trebbi, and K. Xiao. 2016. "Factions in Nondemocracies: Theory and Evidence from the Chinese Communist Party." *The National Bureau of Economic Research*, Working Paper No. 22775, October 2016.

Frank, Robert. 2009. "In China, They Really Hate the Rich." TheWealthReport (blog), *The Wall Street Journal*, December 11, 2009, http://blogs.wsj.com/wealth/2009/12/11/in-china-they-really-hate-the-rich.

Frentzel-Zagorska, Janina. 1990. "Civil Society in Poland and Hungary." *Soviet Studies* 42, no. 4: 759–77.

Froissart, Chloe. 2014. "The Ambiguities between Contention and Political Participation: A Study of Civil Society Development in Authoritarian Regimes." *Journal of Civil Society* 10, no. 3: 219–22.

Fu, Diana. 2017. *Mobilizing without the Masses Control and Contention in China*. London, UK: Cambridge University Press.

Fukuyama, Francis. 1992. *The End of History and the Last Man*. New York: Free Press.

Gadarian, S. Kushner. 2010. "The Politics of Threat: How Terrorism News Shapes Foreign Policy Attitudes." *The Journal of Politics* 72, no. 2 (April): 479–83.

Gallagher, Mary E. 2002. "'Reform and Openness' Why China's Economic Reform Have Delayed Democracy." *World Politics* 54, no. 3 (April): 338–72.

———. 2017. *Authoritarian Legality in China: Law, Workers, and the State*. New York: Cambridge University Press.

Gallagher, Mary E., and Blake Miller. 2017. "Can the Chinese Government Really Control the Internet?" *Washington Post*, February 21, 2017. LexisNexis Academic.

Gandhi, Jennifer, and E. Lust-Okar, 2009. "Elections under Authoritarianism." *Annual Review of Political Science* 12, no. 1: 403–22.

Gao, Xujun, and Jie Long. 2015. "On the Petition System in China." *University of St. Thomas Law Journal* 12, no. 1 (Fall): 34–55.

Gerschenkron, Alexander. 1962. *Economic Backwardness in Historical Perspective*. Cambridge, MA: Harvard University Press.

Glassman, R. M. 1997. *The New Middle Class and Democracy in Global Perspective.* New York, St. Martin's; London: Macmillan.

Gleiss, M. S. 2016. "From Being a Problem to Having Problems: Discourse, Governmentality and Chinese Migrant Workers." *Journal of Chinese Political Science* 21, no. 1: 39–55.

Gourevitch, Peter. 1978. "The Second Image Reversed: The International Sources of Domestic Politics." *International Organization* 32, no. 4: 881–912.

Griffiths, James. 2016. "China on Strike." *CNN*, March 29, 2016. https://www.cnn.com/2016/03/28/asia/china-strike-worker-protest-trade-union/index.html.

———. 2018. "A Software Developer Just Became the Latest Victim of China's VPN Crackdown." *CNN*, October 10, 2018. https://www.cnn.com/2018/10/10/asia/china-vpn-censorship-intl/index.html.

Guan, Bing, and Y. Cai. 2015. "Interests and Political Participation in Urban China: The Case of Residents' Committee Elections." *China Review* 15, no. 1(Spring): 95–116.

Guan, Bing, Ying Xia, and Gong Cheng. 2017. "Power Structure and Media Autonomy in China: The Case of Southern Weekend." *Journal of Contemporary China* 26, no. 104: 233–48.

Gui, Y., Joseph Y. S. Cheng, and Weihong Ma. 2006. "Cultivation of Grass-Roots Democracy: A Study of Direct Election of Residents Committees in Shanghai." *China Information* 20, no. 1(March): 7–31.

Guo, Chao, and Pei Jianfei. 2017. *"Beijin Shiming Zhian Zhiyuanzhe Chao 85wan* (Public Security Volunteers registered with Real Name in Beijing has exceeded 850,000)." *Beijing News*, July 12, 2017. http://www.bjnews.com.cn/feature/2017/07/12/450097.html.

Guo, E. 2018. "Liu Xia Talks about Liu Xiaobo, Thanks Supporters for Their Concern at New York Human Rights Event." *SCMP*, September 27, 2018.

Guo, Taihui. 2014. "Rights in Action: The Impact of Chinese Migrant Workers' Resistances on Citizenship Rights." *Journal of Chinese Political Science* 19, no. 4: 421–34.

Guo, Zhonghua, and Ying Xia. 2016. "Introduction." *Journal of Chinese Political Science* 21: 413–15.

Halper, Stefan. 2010. *The Beijing Consensus: How China's Authoritarian Model Will Dominate the Twenty-First Century.* New York: Basic Books.

Han, Jun. 2016. "The Emergence of Social Corporatism in China: Nonprofit Organizations, Private Foundations, and the State." *China Review* 16, no. 2 (June): 27–53.

Han, Ruizhen. 2005. *"Weixian De Mingzhu—Meiguo Quanqiu Mingzhu Zhanlue He Dazhongdong* (Dangerous Democracy: Global Democratization Strategy of the U.S. and the Big Middle East)." *Journal of Urumqi Vocational University* 14, no. 2 (June): 52–56.

Harlan, Chico, and William Wan. 2010. "Japan to Release Chinese Boat Captain." *Washington Post*, September 24, 2010. LexisNexis Academic.

Harwell, Drew. 2017. "Workers Endured Long Hours, Low Pay at Chinese Factory Used by Ivanka Trump's Clothing-Maker." *Washington Post*, April 25, 2017. LexisNexis Academic.

Hayek, F. A. 2007, *The Road to Serfdom: Text and Documents*. Chicago: University of Chicago Press.

Hayes, Danny, and Matt Guardina. 2011. "The Influence of Foreign Voices on U.S. Public Opinion." *American Journal of Political Science* 55, no. 4: 831–51.

He, Baogang. 2014. "From Village Election to Village Deliberation in Rural China: Case Study of a Deliberative Democracy Experiment." *Journal of Chinese Political Science* 19, no. 2: 133–50.

He, Zhengshen. 2014. *"Xi Jinping Weihe Zunzhong Kongzi* (Why Does Xi Jinping Show Respect for Confucius)?" *Shanghai Observer*, September 25, 2014. https://www.jfdaily.com/news/detail?id=1801.

Heberer, Thomas, and C. Gobel. 2011. *The Politics of Community Building in Urban China.* Abingdon, Oxon: Routledge.

Heilmann, Sebastian. 2008. "Policy Experimentation in China's Economic Rise." *Studies in Comparative International Development* 43, no. 1 (March): 1–26.

Helgeson, J. 2016. "American Labor and Working Class History, 1900–1945." In *Oxford Research Encyclopedia of American History*, edited by Butler J. Oxford: Oxford University Press. http://oxfordre.com/americanhistory/page/about.

Herbst, Jeffrey. 2001. "Political Liberalization in Africa after Ten Years." *Comparative Politics* 33, no. 3: 357–75.

Hernandez, Javier. 2017. "Xi Jinping Vows No Poverty in China by 2020. That Could Be Hard." *New York Times*, October 31, 2017.

Hetherington, M. J., and E. Suhay. 2011. "Authoritarianism, Threat, and Americans' Support for the War on Terror." *American Journal of Political Science* 55, no. 3 (July): 546–60.

Heurlin, Christopher. 2016. *Responsive Authoritarianism in China: Land, Protests, and Policy Making*. New York: Cambridge University Press.

Ho, Wing-Chung. 2012. "The Rise of the Bureaucratic Bourgeoisie and Factional Politics in China." *Journal of Contemporary Asia* 42, no. 3 (August): 514–21.

Hong, Zhengkuan. 2017. "'*Lianghuiwang' Beijiezhi* (Influential Blogger 'Lianghuiwang' was Fired by the Employer)." *New York Times Chinese edition*, August 10, 2017. https://cn.nytimes.com/opinion/20170810/china-punished-professors/.

Howell, Jude A. 2012. "Civil Society, Corporatism and Capitalism in China." *Journal of Comparative Asian Development* 11, no. 2: 271–97.

Hsu, Philip, Yu-Shan Wu, and Suisheng Zhao. 2011. *In Search of China's Development Model: Beyond the Beijing Consensus.* London: Routledge.

Hu, Muren. 2018. "*Fouren Douzheng de Shiming: Jiang Gongchandang Shehui Mingzhuhua Shi Weixian de* (Invalidating the Mission of Struggles: It Is Dangerous to Social-Democratize the Communist Party)." *CWZG,* January 24, 2018. http://www.cwzg.cn/politics/201801/40771.html

Huang, D., Y. Huang, X. Zhao, and Z. Liu. 2017. "How Do Differences in Land Ownership Types in China Affect Land Development? A Case from Beijing." *Sustainability* 9, no. 123: 1–18.

Huang, Haifeng. 2015a. "International Knowledge and Domestic Evaluations in a Changing Society: The Case of China." *American Political Science Review* 109, no. 3: 613–34.

———. 2015b. "Propaganda as Signaling." *Comparative Politics* 47, no. 4: 419–37.

Huang, Jing. 2000. *Factionalism in Chinese Communist Politics.* Cambridge: Cambridge University Press.

Huang, Yasheng. 1995. "Administrative Monitoring in China." *The China Quarterly* no. 143 (September): 828–43.

———. 2008. *Capitalism with Chinese Characteristics: Entrepreneurship and the State.* Cambridge, MA: Cambridge University Press.

Huang, Yanzhong, and Dali L. Yang. 2002. "Bureaucratic Capacity and State-Society Relations in China." *Journal of Chinese Political Science* 7, no. 1–2: 19–46.

Huang, Yiping. 2016. "Can China Escape the Middle-income Trap?" *China Economic Journal* 9, no. 1: 17–33.

Huntington, S. 1968. *Political Order of Changing Society.* New Haven, CT: Yale University Press.

———. 1993. "The Clash of Civilization?" *Foreign Affairs* 72, no. 3 (Summer): 22–49.

Hurst, William. 2009. *The Chinese Worker after Socialism.* New York: Cambridge University Press.

Hurst, William, M. Liu, Y. Liu, and R. Tao. 2014. "Reassessing Collective Petitioning in Rural China." *Comparative Politics* 46, no. 4 (July): 459–78.

Hutchison, Marc L. 2011. "Territorial Threat and the Decline of Political Trust in Africa: A Multilevel Analysis." *Polity* 43, no. 1 (October): 432–61.

Hutchison, Marc L., and Douglas M. Gibler. 2007 "Political Tolerance and Territorial Threat: A Cross-National Study." *The Journal of Politics* 69, no. 1 (February): 128–42.

IMF. 2016. "IMF Launches New SDR Basket Including Chinese Renminbi, Determines New Currency Amounts." September 30, 2016. Press Release NO. 16/440.

Inglehart, R., C. Haerpfer, A. Moreno, C. Welzel, K. Kizilova, J. Diez-Medrano, M. Lagos, P. Norris, E. Ponarin, and B. Puranen ed. 2014. *World Values Survey: Round Six (2012)-Country-Pooled Datafile* Version: www.worldvaluessurvey.org/WVSDocumentationWV6.jsp. Madrid: JD Systems Institute.

Jacques, Martin. 2009. *When China Rules the World: The End of the Western World and the Birth of a New Global Order.* New York: The Penguin Press.

Jeffreys, E. 2016. "Political Celebrities and Elite Politics in Contemporary China." *China Information* 30, no. 1.

Jiang, Qing. 2016. *A Confucian Constitution Order: How China's Ancient Past Can Shape Its Political Future.* Princeton, NJ: Princeton University Press.

Johnson, Ian. 2017. "Guiyang Journal: Forget Marx and Mao, Chinese City Honors Once-Banned Confucian." *New York Times,* October 18, 2017. LexisNexis Academic.

Joshi, Madhav, and D. Mason. 2008. "Between Democracy and Revolution: Peasant Support for Insurgency versus Democracy in Nepal." *Journal of Peace Research* 45, no. 6: 765–82.

Kang, David C. 2002. *Crony Capitalism: Corruption and Development in South Korea and the Philippines.* Cambridge, UK: Cambridge University Press.

———. 2010. *China Rising: Peace, Power, and Order in East Asia.* New York: Columbia University Press.

Kastner, Scott L. 2010. "Buying Influence? Assessing the Political Effects of China's International Economic Ties." Paper presented at International Studies Association Annual Meeting, New York, NY, February 17, 2010.

Keegan, Matthew. 2018. "Dongguan in the Spotlight: Hi-tech Comeback for 'Factory of the World'?" *The Guardian*, February 16, 2018.

Kennedy, J. James. 2007. "From the Tax-for-Free Reform to the Abolition of Agricultural Taxes: The Impact on Township Governments in North-West China." *The China Quarterly* no. 189 (March): 43–59.

Kennedy, John J., Scott Rozelle, and Yaojiang Shi. 2004. "Elected Leaders and Collective Land: Farmers' Evaluation of Village Leaders' Performance in Rural China." *Journal of Chinese Political Science* 9, no. 1 (March): 1–22.

Kennedy, S. 2008. *The Business of Lobbying in China*. Cambridge, MA: Harvard University Press.

Kharas, Homi. 2017. "The Unprecedented Expansion of the Global Middle Class an Update." *Brookings Institution*, February 28, 2017. https://www.brookings.edu/research/the-unprecedented-expansion-of-the-global-middle-class-2/.

King, G., Jennifer Pan, and M. E. Roberts. 2013. "How Censorship in China Allows Government Criticism but Silences Collective Expression." *American Political Science Review* 107, no. 2 (May): 1–18.

Kornreich, Yoel, Ilan Vertinsky, and Pitman B. Potter. 2012. "Consultation and Deliberation in China: The Making of China's Health-Care Reform." *The China Journal* no. 68 (July): 176–203.

Korolev, A. 2017. "De-ideologized Mass Line, Regime Responsiveness, and State-Society Relations." *China Review* 17, no. 2: 7–36.

Koty, A. C. 2018. "Export Tax Rebates in China Increase for 397 Products." *China Briefing*, September 17, 2018. http://www.china-briefing.com/news/export-tax-rebates-china-increase-397-products/.

Kroknes, Veronica F., Tor G. Jakobsen, and Lisa-Marie Gronning. 2015. "Economic Performance and Political Trust: The Impact of the Financial Crisis on European Citizens." *European Societies* 17, no. 5: 700–23.

Kuhn, R. L. 2009. *How China's Leaders Think: The Inside Story of China's Reform and What This Means for the Future*. Singapore: John Wiley & Sons (Asia) Pte Ltd.

Kurlantzick, Joshua. 2007. *Charm Offensive: How China's Soft Power Is Transforming the World*. New Haven, CT: Yale University Press.

Lam, Willy Wo-Lap. 1999. *The Era of Jiang Zemin*. Singapore: Prentice Hall.

———. 2017. "The Irresistible Rise of the 'Xi Family Army'." *The Jamestown Foundation*, October 20, 2017. https://jamestown.org/program/irresistible-rise-xi-family-army/.

———. 2018. "Xi's Grip Loosens amid Trade War Policy Paralysis." *The Jamestown Foundation*, August 1, 2018. https://jamestown.org/program/xis-grip-on-authority-loosens-amid-trade-war-policy-paralysis/.

Lampton, David M. 2008. *The Three Faces of Chinese Power: Might, Money, and Minds*. Berkeley: University of California Press.

Lee, Ann. 2017. *Will China's Economy Collapse?* Malden, MA: Polity.

Lee, C. Kwan, and Eli Friedman. 2009. "China Since Tiananmen: The Labor Movement." *Journal of Democracy* 20, no. 3: 21–24.

Lee, Charlotte P. 2015. *Training the Party: Party Adaptation and Elite Training in Reform-Era China*. Cambridge, UK: University of Cambridge Press.

Leeb, Stephen. 2013. "Paul Krugman Is as Wrong about China as He Was about Singapore." *Forbes*, July 23, 2013.

Lei, Xuchuan, and Jie Lu. 2017. "Revisiting Political Wariness in China's Public Opinion Surveys: Experimental Evidence on Responses to Politically Sensitive Questions." *Journal of Contemporary China* 26, no. 104: 213–32.

Leonard, Mark. 2008. *What Does China Think?* New York: Public Affairs.

Levin, Dan, and Sue-Lin Wong. 2013. "Beijing's Retirees Keep Eye out for Trouble during Party Congress." *New York Times*, March 15, 2013. LexisNexis Academic.

Lewis-Beck, Michael S., Wenfang Tang, and Nicholas F. Martini. 2014. "A Chinese Popularity Function: Sources of Government Support." *Political Research Quarterly* 67, no. 1: 16–25.

Li, A. Jiajia. 2017. "Beijing's Cruel Eviction of Its Migrant Workers Is a Stain on China's Urbanization Drive." *SCMP*, November 29, 2017.

Li, Cheng. ed. 2010. *China's Emerging Middle Class: Beyond Economic Transformation.* Washington, DC: Brookings Institution Press.

———. 2013. "Rule of the Princelings." *Brookings*, February 10, 2013. https://www.brookings.edu/articles/rule-of-the-princelings/

———. 2014a. "Xi Jinping's Inner Circle (Part 1: The Shaanxi Gang)." *China Leadership Monitor, Hoover Institution* no. 43 (Spring): 1–21.

———. 2014b. "Xi Jinping's Inner Circle (Part 3: Political Protégés from the Provinces)." *China Leadership Monitor, Hoover Institution* no. 45 (Fall): 1–18.

———. 2016. *Chinese Politics in the Xi Jinping Era: Reassessing Collective Leadership.* Washington DC: Brookings Institution Press.

———. 2017. "The Paradoxical Outcome of China's 19th Party Congress." *Brookings, Hoover Institution*, October 26, 2017. https://www.brookings.edu/blog/order-from-chaos/2017/10/26/the-paradoxical-outcome-of-chinas-19th-party-congress/

———. 2018. "How China's Middle Class Views the Trade War." *Foreign Affairs*, September 10, 2018.

Li, Chengrui. 2006. "*Guanyu Woguo Muqian Gongsi Jingji Bizhong de Chubu Cesuan* (Initial Calculation of the Proportion between Public and Private Economies in China)." *Tan Suo* (Probe) no. 4. http://mall.cnki.net/magazine/article/SUTA200604045.htm.

Li, Gang. 2014. "*Xi Jinping: Lai Qufu Wei Biaoming Zhongyang Zhongshi Chuantong Wenhua* (Xi Jinping: I Come to Qufu to Show the Central Government's Concerns for Traditional Culture)." *Qilu Evening* News (Qilu Wanbao), November 10, 2014. http://www.qlwb.com.cn/2014/1110/247470.shtml.

Li, Jing. 2012. "Wang Yang, the Party Chief Who Transformed Guangdong." *SCMP*, October 26, 2012.

Li, Xiaoping. 2002. 'Focus' and the Changes in the Chinese Television Industry." *Journal of Contemporary China* 11, no. 30: 17–34.

Li, Zifei, and Jin Li. 2004. "*Quxiao Zhian Lianfangdui* (China Will Abolish Community Security Team)." *Sina News Center*, September 21, 2004. http://news.sina.com.cn/c/2004-09-21/15043730041s.shtml

Lian, Yizheng. 2018. "Could There Be Another Chinese Revolution?" *New York Times*, September 7, 2018.

Liang, Jane. 2017. "The Enduring Challenges for Collective Lobbying: The Case of China's Elite Universities." *The China Journal* no. 78: 81–99.

Liang, Shuming. 1921. *Dongxi Wenhua Jiqi Zhexue (Eastern and Western Cultures and Their Philosophies).* Shanghai: Shanghai Commercial Press.

Liang, Wei. 2011. "The Too 'Hard' Sources of China's Soft Power in Africa: Is Economic Power Sufficient?" Paper presented at the 42nd Association of Chinese Political Studies Annual Meeting, London, UK, June 19, 2011.

Lin, Leo. 2015. "China's Imploding Pressure Cooker: Xinfang Petitions." *The Diplomat*, July 16, 2015. https://thediplomat.com/2015/07/chinas-imploding-pressure-cooker-xinfang-petitions/.

Lin, W. 2009. "*Liangqichao zhi 'Guomin Yundong' yu Lingba Xianzhang zhi Gongmin Yundong* (08 Charter and Citizen Movement)." *Democracy China*, December 7, 2009. http://minzhuzhongguo.org/MainArtShow.aspx?AID=12471.

Lin, X. 2017. "*Yixian Chengshi Wailai Renkou Jiexi* (An Analysis of Migrants in the First Tier Cities)." *YiCai*, November 27, 2017. https://www.yicai.com/news/5377967.html.

Lipset, S. M. 1959. "Some Social Requisites of Democracy: Economic Development and Political Legitimacy." *American Political Science Review* 53, no. 1: 69–105.

Liu, F. 2010. "*Shenzhen Fabu Quanguo Shoufen Xinshengdai Nongmingong Diaocha* (Shenzhen Issued First Report on New Generation of Migrant Workers)." *China Youth Daily*, July 15, 2010. http://zqb.cyol.com/content/2010-07/15/content_3325601.htm.

Liu, I. Jay, and Chris Ip. 2013. "Analysis: China's Next Inner Circle." *Reuters*, March 3, 2013.

Liu, Jian, and Xiaoyan Wang. 2015. "Expansion and Differentiation in Chinese Higher Education." *International Higher Education* no. 60: 7–8.

Liu, Yu, and Dingding Chen. 2012. "Why China Will Democratize." *Washington Quarterly* 35, no. 1: 41–63.

Long, Y. Q. 2012. "*Baifenzhi 40 Dangwai Siying Qiyezhu Yuanyi Jiaru Gongchandang* (40 percent of Private Entrepreneurs Who Are Not Party Members Want to Join the Party)." *Southern Metropolis Daily*, December 20, 2012. http://news.sina.com.cn/c/2012-12-20/042025852029.shtml.

Lorentzen, Peter. 2013. "Regularized Rioting: Permitting Public Protest in an Authoritarian Regime." *Quarterly Journal of Political Science* 8: 127–58.

———. 2014. "China's Strategic Censorship." *American Journal of Political Science* 58, no. 2 (April): 402–14.

Lu, Chunlong. 2015. "Urban Chinese Support for the Chinese Dream: Empirical Findings from Seventeen Cities." *Journal of Chinese Political Science* 20, no. 2: 143–61.

Lu, Hanlong. 2010. "The Chinese Middle Class and *Xiaokang* Society." In *China's Emerging Middle Class*, edited by Cheng Li, 104–34. Washington, DC: The Brookings Institution.

Lu, Mai, and Mingliang Feng. 2008. "Reforming the Welfare System in the People's Republic of China." *Asian Development Review* 25, no. 1: 58–80.

Luebbert, Gregory M. 1987. "Social Foundations of Political Order in Interwar Europe." *World Politics* 39, no. 4 (July): 449–78.

Lum, Thomas G. 2000. *Problems of Democratization in China*. New York: Garland Publishing.

———. 2009. "China's Assistance and Government-Sponsored Investment Activities." *Congressional Research Service Report R40940*, November 25, 2009.

Ma, Alexandra. 2018. "China Has Started Ranking Citizens with a Creepy 'Social Credit' System." *Business Insider*, October 29, 2018. https://www.businessinsider.com/china-social-credit-system-punishments-and-rewards-explained-2018-4.

Ma, Tianjie. 2008. "Environmental Mass Incidents in Rural China: Examining Large-Scale Unrest in Dongyang, Zhejiang." *China Environment Series, Woodrow Wilson International Center for Scholars* 2008/2009: 33–56.

MacKinnon, Rebecca. 2011. "China's 'Networked Authoritarianism'." *Journal of Democracy* 22, no. 2 (April): 32–46.

Mai, Jun. 2017. "Why A Xi Jinping Protégé Came under Fire in Beijing over Mass Eviction of Migrant Workers." *SCMP*, December 22, 2017.

Manion, Melanie. 1996. "The Electoral Connection in the Chinese Countryside." *American Political Science Review* 90, no. 4: 736–48.

———. 2015. *Information for Autocrats: Representation in Chinese Local Congresses*. New York, NY: Cambridge University Press.

Mann, James. 2007. *The China Fantasy: Why Capitalism Will Not Bring Democracy to China*. New York: Penguin Books.

Margolis, Eric. 2011. "The North Pacific Is No Longer an American Lake." *Huff Post*, January 11, 2011, Updated May 25, 2011. https://www.huffpost.com/entry/the-north-pacific-is-no-l_b_806885.

Martina, Michael. 2016. "China's Xi Calls for Universities' Allegiance to the Communist Party." *Reuters,* December 8, 2016. https://www.reuters.com/article/us-china-education-idUSKBN13Y0B5.

Marx, Karl, F. Engels, and P. Gasper. 2005. "Preface." In *The Communist Manifesto: A Road Map to History's Important Political Document*, edited by Phil Gasper, 39–57. Chicago: Haymarket Books.

Maslow, A. H. 1943. "A Theory of Human Motivation." *Psychological Review* 50, no. 4: 370–96.

Matsuzawa, Setsuko. 2012. "Citizen Environmental Activism in China: Legitimacy, Alliances, and Rights-Based Discourses." *Asian Network Exchange* 19, no. 2 (Spring): 81–91.

Marshall, T. H. 1950. *Citizenship and Social Class*. Cambridge: Cambridge University Press.

McNally, Christopher A. 2008. *China's Emergent Political Economy: Capitalism in the Dragon's Lair*. London: Routledge.

Meisels, A. Greer. 2013. "Lessons Learned in China from the Collapse of the Soviet Union." *Policy Paper Series, China Studies Center, the University of Sydney,* Paper 3, January. https://sydney.edu.au/china_studies_centre/images/content/ccpublications/policy_paper _series/2013/Lessons-learned-in-China-from-the-collapse-of-the-Soviet-Union.shtml.pdf.

Melvin, Sheila. 2007. "Modern Gloss on China's Golden Age." *New York Times,* September 3, 2007. LexisNexis Academic.

Meng, A. 2014. "Beijing Still Struggles to Make Voice Heard through *Sina Weibo.*" *SCMP,* March 3, 2014.

Miao, Ying. 2016."The Paradox of the Middle Class Attitudes in China: Democracy, Social Stability and Reform." *Journal of Current Chinese Affairs* 45, no. 1: 169–90.

Miller, Alice L. 2015. "The Trouble with Factions." *China Leadership Monitor* no. 46: 1–12.

Ministry of Education of PRC. 2017. "*2016 Niandu Woguo Laihua Liuxuesheng Qingkuang Tongji* (Statistics of International Students in China in 2016)." March 1, 2017. http://www.moe.gov.cn/jyb_xwfb/xw_fbh/moe_2069/xwfbh_2017n/xwfb_170301/170301_sjtj/201703/t20170301_297677.html.

Minzner, Carl. 2009. "China's Citizen Complaint System: Prospects for Accountability." *Congressional Executive Commission on China Roundtables working paper,* December 4, 2009. https://www.cecc.gov/events/roundtables/chinas-citizen-complaint-system-prospects-for-accountability.

———. 2018. *End of an Era: How China's Authoritarian Revival Is Undermining Its Rise.* New York: Oxford University Press.

Mitchell, T. 2017. "Wealth of China's Richest 200 Lawmakers Tops $500bn." *Financial Times,* March 2, 2017.

Mitchell, Ann, and Larry Diamond. 2018. "China's Surveillance State Should Scare Everyone." *The Atlantic,* February 2, 2018.

Moore, B. 1966. *Social Origins of Dictatorship and Democracy.* Boston, MA: Beacon Press.

Moraze, Charles. 1968. *The Triumph of the Middle Classes.* Garden City, NY: Anchor Books.

Morley, James W. ed. 1999. *Driven by Growth: Political Change in the Asia-Pacific Region.* Armonk, NY: M.E. Sharpe.

Mueller, John E. 1973. *War, Presidents and Public Opinion.* New York: Wiley.

Munro, Ross H. 1994. "Giving Taipei a Place at the Table." *Foreign Affairs* 73, no. 6: 109–24.

Nacos, Brigitte. L., Y. Block-Elkon, and R. Y. Shapiro. 2007. "Post 9/11 Terrorism Threats, News Coverage, and Public Perceptions in the United States." *International Journal of Conflict and Violence* 1, no. 2: 105–26.

Nagai, Oki. 2018. "China Dials Down Xi's Personality Cult as Criticism Mounts." *NIKKEI Asian Review,* July 24, 2018. https://asia.nikkei.com/Politics/China-dials-down-Xi-s-personality-cult-as-criticism-mounts.

Nathan, Andrew J. 2003. "Authoritarian Resilience." *Journal of Democracy* 14, no. 1: 6–17.

———. 2016. "The Puzzle of the Chinese Middle Class." *Journal of Democracy* 27, no. 2: 5–19.

Nathan, Andrew, and Bruce Gilley. 2002. *China's New Rulers: The Secret Files.* New York: New York Review of Books.

NBS. 2009–2017. "*Nongmingong Jiance Diaocha Baogao* (Annual National Survey Report on Migrant Workers)." http://www.stats.gov.cn/tjsj/zxfb/201804/t20180427_1596389.html.

Neureiter, Michael. 2013. "Organization Labor and Democratization in Southeast Asia." *Asian Survey* 53, no. 6 (November/December): 1063–86.

Niquette, Mark, and Jennifer Jacobs. 2018. "China Looks to Influence Iowa in Trade War over Trump Tariffs." *Bloomberg,* September 23, 2018. https://www.bloombergquint.com/business/china-looks-to-influence-iowa-in-trade-war-over-trump-tariffs.

North, Douglass. 1982. *Structure and Change in Economic History.* New York: W.W. Norton.

O'Brien, Kevin J. 2013. "Rightful Resistance Revisited." *Journal of Peasant Studies* 40, no. 6: 1051–62.

O'Brien Kevin J., and Lianjiang Li. 2006. *Rightful Resistance in Rural China.* New York: Cambridge University Press.

Odgaard, Ole. 1992. "Entrepreneurs and Elite Formation in Rural China." *The Australian Journal of Chinese Affairs* no. 28: 89–108.

Ong, L. H., and D. Han. 2019. "What Drives People to Protest in an Authoritarian Country? Resources and Rewards vs. Risks of Protests in Urban and Rural China." *Political Studies* 67, no. 1: 224–48.

Owen, David A. 2015. "The Impact of Economic Development on Political Interest across Social Classes in China" *Journal of Chinese Political Science* 20, no. 2: 185–202.

Nye, Joseph S. 1990. *Bound to Lead: The Changing Nature of American Power.* New York: Basic Books.

———. 2004. *Soft Power: The Means to Success in World Politics.* New York: Public Affairs.

———. 2005. "The Rise of China's Soft Power." *Wall Street Journal*, December 29, 2005.

Nye, Joseph S., and Jisi Wang. 2009. "Hard Decisions on Soft Power Opportunities and Difficulties for Chinese Soft Power." *Harvard International Review*, Summer. https://www.hks.harvard.edu/publications/hard-decisions-soft-power-opportunities-and-difficulties-chinese-soft-power.

O'Rourke, Ronald. 2018. "China Naval Modernization: Implications for U.S. Navy Capabilities—Background and Issues for Congress." *Congressional Research Service Report*, August 1, 2018. https://fas.org/sgp/crs/row/RL33153.pdf.

Pan, Jennifer, and Kaiping Chen. 2018. "Concealing Corruption: How Chinese Officials Distort Upward Reporting of Online Grievances." *American Political Science Review* 112, no. 3 (August): 602–20.

Panda, Ankit. 2015. "China Evacuates Foreign Nationals from Yemen." *The Diplomat*, April 6, 2015.

Park, Cheol H. 2001. "Factional Dynamics in Japan's LDP since Political Reform Continuity and Change." *Asian Survey* 41, no. 3 (May/June): 428–61.

Paulson, Henry M. 2008. "A Strategic Economic Engagement: Strengthening U.S.-Chinese Ties." *Foreign Affairs* 87, no. 5: 59–77.

Peerenboom, Randall. 2007. *China Modernizes: Threat to the West or Model for the Rest.* Oxford: Oxford University Press.

Pei, Minxin. 1994. *From Reform to Revolution: The Demise of Communism in China and the Soviet Union.* Cambridge, MA: Harvard University Press.

———. 2006. *China's Trapped Transition: The Limits of Developmental Autocracy.* Cambridge, MA: Cambridge University Press.

———. 2016. *China's Crony Capitalism: The Dynamics of Regime Decay.* Cambridge, MA: Harvard University Press.

———. 2017. "China's Return to Strongman Rule." *Foreign Affairs*, November 1, 2017.

Perkowski, Jack. 2012. "China's Economy Is Slowing, But . . ." *Forbes*, June 5, 2012.

Perry, Elizabeth. 2001. "Challenging the Mandate of Heaven." *Critical Asian Studies* 33, no. 2: 163–80.

———. 2009. "A New Rights Consciousness?" *Journal of Democracy* 20, no. 1: 17–20

———. 2018. "Is the Chinese Communist Regime Legitimate?" In *the China Questions: Critical Insights into a Rising Power*, edited by Michael Szonyi and Jennifer Rudolph, 11–17. Cambridge, MA: Harvard University Press.

Pew Research Center. 2009. "End of Communism Cheered but Now with More Reservations." November 2, 2009. https://www.pewglobal.org/2009/11/02/end-of-communism-cheered-but-now-with-more-reservations/.

———. 2011. "Confidence in Democracy and Capitalism Wanes in Former Soviet Union." December 5, 2011. http://www.pewglobal.org/2011/12/05/confidence-in-democracy-and-capitalism-wanes-in-former-soviet-union/.

———. 2014a. "Crime and Corruption Top Problems in Emerging and Developing Countries." November 6, 2014. http://www.pewglobal.org/2014/11/06/crime-and-corruption-top-problems-in-emerging-and-developing-countries/.

———. 2014b. "Where People Say Giving Bribes Gets You Ahead in Life." October 23, 2014. http://www.pewresearch.org/fact-tank/2014/10/23/where-people-say-giving-bribes-gets-you-ahead-in-life/.

———. 2015. "Chinese Happy with Economic Situation." September 28, 2015. http://www.pewglobal.org/2015/09/24/corruption-pollution-inequality-are-top-concerns-in-china/china-report-10/.

Pomfret, John. 2002. "Chinese Oil Country Simmers as Workers Protest Cost-Cutting." *Washington Post*, March 17, 2002. LexisNexis Academic.

Pop-Eleches, Grigore, and Joshua Tucker. 2017. *Communism's Shadow: Historical Legacies and Contemporary Political Attitudes.* Princeton, NJ: Princeton University Press.

Przeworski, Adam, and Fernando Limongi. 1997. "Modernization: Theories and Facts." *World Politics* 49, no. 2: 155–83.

Puett, Michael. 2018. "Who Is Confucius in Today's China?" In *The China Questions: Critical Insights into a Rising Power*, edited by Jennifer Rudolph and Michael Szonyi, 231–36. Cambridge, MA: Harvard University Press.

Pye, Lucian W. 1992. *Spirit of Chinese Politics.* Cambridge: Harvard University Press.

Qiang, Xiao. 2011. "The Battle for The Chinese Internet." *Journal of Democracy* 22, no. 2 (April): 47–61.

Qin, Bei, David Stromberg, and Yanhui Wu. 2017. "Why Does China Allow Freer Social Media? Protests versus Surveillance and Propaganda." *Journal of Economic Perspective* 31, no. 1: 117–40.

Raiklin, Ernest. 1989. *After Gorbachev? A Mechanism for the Transformation of Totalitarian State Capitalism into Authoritarian Mixed Capitalism.* Washington, D.C.: The Council for Social and Economic Studies Inc.

Ramo, J. Cooper. 2004. *The Beijing Consensus.* London: Foreign Policy Centre.

Rauhala, Emily. 2015. "China Expels French Journalist for Terrorism Coverage." *Washington Post*, December 26, 2015. LexisNexis Academic.

Read, Benjamin L. 2000. "Revitalizing the State's Urban 'Nerve Tip'." *The China Quarterly* no. 163 (September): 806–20.

Reilly, Jonathan J. 2016. "No Postmaterialists in Foxholes: Postmaterialist Values, Nationalism, and National Threat in the People's Republic of China." *Political Psychology* 37, no. 4: 565–72.

Reynolds, James. 2009. "Communists Turn to Confucius." *BBC*, March 20, 2009. http://www.bbc.co.uk/blogs/thereporters/jamesreynolds/2009/03/communists_turn_to_confucius.html.

Rocca, Jean-Louis. 2017. *The Making of the Chinese Middle Class.* New York: Palgrave Macmillan.

Roth, Felix, Felicitas Nowak-Lehmann D., and Thomas Otter. 2011. "Has the Financial Crisis Shattered Citizens' Trust in National and European Governmental Institutions? Evidence from the EU Member States, 1999–2010." *CEPS Working Document* No. 343 (June).

Roy, J. Stapleton, and Charles Kraus. 2016. "The Communist Domino That Would Not Fall: China's Resilience at the End of the Cold War." *The Wilson Quarterly*, Fall 2016.

Rozental, Alek A. 1956. "The Enclosure Movement in France." *The American Journal of Economics and Sociology* 16, no. 1(October): 55–71.

Ruan, Lotus Yang. 2015. "The Chinese Communist Party and Legitimacy—What Is the Chinese Communist Party's Official Discourse on Legitimacy?" *The Diplomat,* September 30, 2015.

Rueschemeyer, D., E. H. Stephens, and J. D. Stephens. 1992. *Capitalist Development and Democracy.* Chicago: University Chicago Press.

Schneider, Florian, and Yih-Jye Hwang. 2014. "The Sichuan Earthquake and the Heavenly Mandate: Legitimizing Chinese Rule through Disaster Discourse." *Journal of Contemporary China* 23, no. 88: 636–56.

Schubert, Gunter, and Anna L. Ahlers. 2012. *Participation and Empowerment at the Grassroots: Chinese Village Elections in Perspective.* Lanham, MD: Lexington Books.

Schubert, G., and T. Heberer. 2017. "Private Entrepreneurs as a 'Strategic Group' in the Chinese Polity." *The China Review* 17, no. 2 (June): 95–122.

Schwarcz, Vera. 1991. "No Solace from Lethe: History, Memory and Cultural Identity in Twentieth Century China." In *The Living Tree: The Changing Meaning of Being Chinese Today,* edited by Tu Wei Ming, 64–88. Stanford, CA: Stanford University Press.

SCIO. 2010. "China's National Defense in 2010." March 31, 2011. http://www.china.org.cn/government/whitepaper/node_7114675.htm.

SCMP. 2014a. "'Petroleum Gang' Star Held Wide Sway." *SCMP*, December 7, 2014.

————. 2014b. "Two More Senior Chinese Officials from the 'Shanxi Gang' Expelled after Graft Probe." *SCMP*, December 22, 2014.

Seales, R. 2017. "The Country Where 70 Percent of Millennials Are Homeowners." *BBC*, April 6, 2017. https://www.bbc.com/news/world-39512599.

Shambaugh, David. 2009. *China's Communist Party: Atrophy and Adaptation*. Washington, D.C.: Woodrow Wilson Center Press.

————. 2010. "China Flexes Its Soft Power." *New York Times*, June 7, 2010.

————. 2016. *China's Future*. Cambridge, UK: Polity Press.

Shi, Jiangtao. 2012. "Former China President Jiang Zemin Played Key Role in Punishing Bo Xilai, Say Analysts." *SCMP*, October 2, 2012.

Shi, Tianjian. 1997. *Political Participation in Beijing*. Cambridge, MA: Harvard University Press.

————. 2000. "Cultural Values and Democracy in the People's Republic of China." *The China Quarterly* no. 162 (June): 540–59.

————. 2015. *The Cultural Logic of Politics in Mainland China and Taiwan*. New York: Cambridge University Press.

Shih, Victor, C. Adolph, and Mingxing Liu. 2012. "Getting Ahead in the Communist Party: Explaining the Advancement of Central Committee Members in China." *American Political Science Review* 106, no. 1 (February): 166–87.

Shira, Dezan. 2017. "China's Business Reform Agenda." *China Briefing*, November 6, 2017. http://www.china-briefing.com/news/chinas-business-reform-agenda/.

Shirk, Susan L. 2011. "Changing Media, Changing Foreign Policy." In *Changing Media, Changing China*, edited by Susan L. Shirk, 1–37. Oxford: Oxford University Press.

————. 2018. "China in Xi's 'New Era' The Return to Personalistic Rule." *Journal of Democracy* 29, no. 2 (April): 22–36.

Shu, Lei. 2018. "The Effect of the New Rural Social Pension Insurance Program on the Retirement and Labor Supply Decision in China." *The Journal of the Economic of Ageing* 12: 135–50.

Skocpol, Theda. 1985. "Bringing the State Back In: Strategies of Analysis in Current Research." In *Bringing the State Back In*, edited by Peter B. Evans, Dietrich Rueschemeyer, and Theda Skocpol, 3–37. New York: Cambridge University Press.

Smith, Helena. 2017. "Greece Blocks EU's Criticism at UN of China's Human Rights Record." *The Guardian*, June 18, 2017.

Sohu News. 2009. "*Zhongguo Mingnian Xiang Waiguo Liuxuesheng Tigong Liangwan Ming Zhengfu Jiangxuejin* (The Chinese Government Will Award 20,000 Scholarships to Foreign Students Next Year)." *Sohu News*, December 5, 2009. http://learning.sohu.com/20091205/n268698375.shtml.

Song, Qiang, Z. Zhang, B. Qiao, Q. Gu, and Z. Tang. 1996. *Zhongguo Keyi Shuobu (China Can Say No)*. Beijing: China United Press of Industry and Commerce.

Sorace, Christian. 2016. "Party Spirit Made Flesh: The Production of Legitimacy in the Aftermath of the 2008 Sichuan Earthquake." *The China Journal* no. 76 (July): 41–62.

Stapleton, Katherine. 2017. "China Now Produces Twice as Many Graduates a Year as the US." *World Economic Forum*, April 13, 2017.

Steinberg, David A., and Victor C. Shih. 2012. "Interest Group Influence in Authoritarian States: The Political Determinants of Chinese Exchange Rate Policy." *Comparative Political Studies* 45, no. 11: 1405–34.

Steinhardt, H. Christoph, and Fengshi Wu. 2016. "In the Name of the Public: Environmental Protest and the Changing Landscape of Popular Contention in China." *The China Journal* no. 75 (January): 61–82.

Stephens, Evelyne Huber. 1989. "Capitalist Development and Democracy in South America." *Politics & Society* 17, no. 3: 281–352.

Stockmann, Daniela. 2013. *Media Commercialization and Authoritarian Rule in China*. New York: Cambridge University Press.

Strand, David. 1993. *Rickshaw Beijing: City People and Politics in the 1920s*. Berkeley: University of California Press.

Su, Fubing, Ran Tao, Xin Sun and Mingxing Liu. 2011. "Clans, Electoral Procedures and Voter Turnout: Evidence from Villages' Committee Elections in Transitional China." *Political Studies* 59, no. 2: 432–57.

Subramaniam, Surain. 2000. "The Asian Values Debate: Implications for the Spread of Liberal Democracy." *Asian Affairs: An American Review* 27, no. 1: 19–35.

Sun, F. 2013. "The Medium Is the Message: Political Effects of Internet Penetration in China." *Journal of US-China Public Administration* 10, no. 2 (February): 136–45.

Sun, Xin. 2014. "Autocrats' Dilemma: The Dual Impacts of Village Elections on Public Opinion in China." *The China Journal* no. 71 (January): 109–31.

Sundqvist, Gustav. 2016. "Marxism Still Matters: the Chinese Communist Party's Description of Foreign Democracies as an Ideological Strategy." *Studia Orientalia Electronica* 4: 89–107. http://ojs.tsv.fi/index.php/StOrE.

Sutter, Robert G. 2009. *Chinese Foreign Relations: Power and Policy since the Cold War.* Lanham, MD: Rowman & Littlefield Publishers.

Tang, Wenfang. 2016. *Populist Authoritarianism: Chinese Political Culture and Regime Sustainability.* New York, NY: Oxford University Press.

Tang, Wenfang, Michael S. Lewis-Beck, and Nicholas F. Martini. 2013. "Government for the People in China?" *The Diplomat,* June 17, 2013.

Tarrow, S. 1995. "Cycles of Collective Action." In *Repertoires and Cycles of Collective Action,* edited by M. Traugott, 89–116. Durham, NC: Duke University Press.

Teets, Jessica C. 2013. "Let Many Civil Societies Bloom: The Rise of Consultative Authoritarianism in China." *The China Quarterly* no. 213 (March): 19–38.

———. 2014. *Civil Society under Authoritarianism: The China Model.* New York: Cambridge University Press.

The BRICS Post. 2016. "IMF Reforms: China, India, Brazil, Russia Get Greater Say." January 28, 2016. http://thebricspost.com/imf-reforms-china-india-brazil-russia-get-greater-say/#.W9V0c3szYdU.

The Economist. 2007. "Confucius Makes a Comeback." May 17, 2007. http://www.economist.com/node/9202957.

———. 2013. "Xi Jinping's Vision: Chasing the Chinese Dream." May 4, 2013. http://www.economist.com/news/briefing/21577063-chinas-new-leader-has-been-quick-consoli date-his-power-what-does-he-now-want-his.

———. 2015. "The Critical Masses." April 11, 2015. https://www.economist.com/china/2015/04/11/the-critical-masses.

———. 2018. "A Chinese Writer Calls for Private Companies to Fade Away." October 6, 2018. https://www.economist.com/china/2018/10/06/a-chinese-writer-calls-for-private-compa
nies-to-fade-away.

Therborn, Goran. 1977. "The Rule of Capital and The Rise of Democracy." *New Left Review* I/103 (May-June): 3–41.

Thompson, E. P. 1963. *The Making of the English Working Class.* New York: Pantheon.

Thompson, William R. 1996. "Democracy and Peace: Putting the Cart before the Horse?" *International Organization* 50: 141–74.

Tilly, Charles. 1993. *Coercion, Capital and European States: AD 990–1992.* Hoboken, NJ: Wiley.

Tilly, Chris. 2013. "Trade Unions, Inequality, and Democracy in the US and Mexico." *Rethinking Development and Inequality* 2: 68–83.

Tomba, Luigi. 2014. *The Government Next Door: Neighborhood Politics in Urban China.* Ithaca, NY: Cornell University Press.

Tomiuc, Eugen. 2013. "Low Life Expectancy Continues to Plague Former Soviet Countries." *Radio Free Europe/Radio Liberty,* April 2, 2013. https://www.rferl.org/a/life-expectancy-cis-report/24946030.html.

Tong, Yanqi. 2011. "Morality, Benevolence, and Responsibility: Regime Legitimacy in China from Past to the Present." *Journal of Chinese Political Science* 16, no. 2: 141–59.

Tong, Yanqi, and Shaohua Lei. 2010. "Large Scale Mass Incidents in China." *East Asian Policy* 2, no. 2 (April/June): 23–33.

———. 2014. *Social Protest in Contemporary China, 2003–2010*. London: Routledge.

Troianovski, A. 2010. "China Agency Nears Times Square." *Wall Street Journal,* June 30, 2010.

Tse, Chun Wing. 2016. "Urban Residents' Prejudice and Integration of Rural Migrants into Urban China." *Journal of Contemporary China* 25, no. 100: 579–95.

Truex, Rory. 2016. "Bias and Trust in Authoritarian Media." *SSRN*, June 30, 2016. https://ssrn.com/abstract=2802841 or http://dx.doi.org/10.2139/ssrn.2802841.

———. 2017. "Consultative Authoritarianism and Its Limits." *Comparative Political Studies* 50, no. 3: 329–61.

Unger, Jonathan. 2002. *The Nature of Chinese Politics: From Mao to Jiang*. Armonk, NY: M. E. Sharpe.

Wang, Kevin. 2015. "Yemen Evacuation a Strategic Step forward for China." *The Diplomat*, April 10, 2015.

Wang, P. 2018. "The First Self-Govern Village in China." *Beijing News*, May 7, 2018. http://www.bjnews.com.cn/feature/2018/05/07/485946.html.

Wang, Yanlai. 2016. *China's Economic Development and Democratization*. New York: Routledge.

Warren, K. F. 2001. *In Defense of Public Opinion Polling*. Boulder, CO: Westview Press.

Weber, Max. 1946. "Characteristics of Bureaucracy." In *From Max Weber: Essays in Sociology*, edited by H. H. Gerth and C. W. Mills, 196–97. New York: Oxford University Press.

———. 1984. "Legitimacy, Politics and the State." In *Legitimacy and the State*, edited by William Connolly, 32–62. Oxford: Basil Blackwell.

———. 1994. "The Profession and Vocation of Politics." In *Political Writings*, edited by Peter Lassman and Ronald Speirs, 309–69. Cambridge: Cambridge University Press.

Welsh, William A. ed. 1981. *Survey Research and Public Attitudes in Eastern Europe and the Soviet Union.* New York: Pergamon Press.

Wen, Xiaoyi, and K. Lin. 2015. "Restructuring China's State Corporatist Industrial Relations System: The Wenling Experience." *Journal of Contemporary China* 24, no. 94: 665–83.

Whyte, Martin K. 2015. "China's Dormant and Active Social Volcanoes." *The China Journal* no. 75: 9–37.

Wike, Richard, Laura Silver, and Alexandra Castillo. 2019. "Many across the Globe Are Dissatisfied with How Democracy Is Working." Pew Research Center, April 29, 2019. https://www.pewglobal.org/2019/04/29/many-across-the-globe-are-dissatisfied-with-how-democracy-is-working/.

Wintrobe, R. 1998. *The Political Economy of Dictatorship*. Cambridge, UK: Cambridge University Press.

Wong, Edward. 2008. "Factories Shut, China Workers Are Suffering." *New York Times*, November 13, 2008.

World Bank. 2018. "The World Bank in China Overview." Last updated: September 26, 2018. https://www.worldbank.org/en/country/china/overview.

Wright, Teresa. 2008. "State-Society Relations in Reform-Era China." *Comparative Politics* 40, no. 3 (April): 353–74.

———. 2010. *Accepting Authoritarianism: State-Society Relations in China's Reform Era.* Stanford, CA: Stanford University Press.

———. 2015. *Party and State in Post-Mao China*. Cambridge: Polity.

Xia, Ying, and Bing Guan. 2014. "The Politics of Citizenship Formation: Homeowners' Collective Action in Urban Beijing." *Journal of Chinese Political Science* 19, no. 4: 405–19.

Xiao, Kezhou, and Brantly Womack. 2014. "Distortion and Credibility within China's Internal Information System." *Journal of Contemporary China* 23, no. 88: 680–97.

Yan, Sophia. 2018. "Deng Xiaoping's Son Urges China to 'Know Its Place' in Counterpoint to Xi's Expansionist Foreign Policy." *The Telegraph*, October 30, 2018.

Yang, Ray Ou. 2015. "Political Process and Widespread Protests in China: The 2010 Labor Protest." *Journal of Contemporary China* 24, no. 91: 21–42.

Yang, Zi. 2018. "The Militarization of China's People's Armed Police." *Asia Times*, March 25, 2018. http://www.atimes.com/article/militarization-chinas-peoples-armed-police/.

Yang, Hongxing, and Dingxin Zhao. 2015. "Performance Legitimacy, State Autonomy and China's Economic Miracle." *Journal of Contemporary China* 24, no. 91: 64–82.

Yao, Kevin. 2018. "China Pledges to Allow More Foreign Investment in Financial Sector by Year-End." *Reuters*, April 10, 2018.

Yao, Kevin, and Dominique Patton. 2019. "China Pledges to Expand Financial Market Opening as U.S. Trade Delegation Arrives." *Reuter*, March 27, 2019.

Yao, Yuan, and R. Han. 2016. "Challenging, but Not Trouble-Making: Cultural Elites in China's Urban Heritage Preservation." *Journal of Contemporary China* 25, no. 98: 292–306.

Yardley, Jim. 2005. "Rural Chinese Riot as Police Try to Halt Pollution Protest." *New York Times*, April 14, 2005.

Yeung, Henry Wai-Chung. 2003. *Chinese Capitalism in a Global Era: Towards Hybrid Capitalism.* London: Routledge.

Yu, Guangyuan. 2005. "Accomplishments and Problems: A Review of China's Reform in the Past Twenty-Three Years." In *The Chinese Model of Modern Development*, edited by Tian Yu Cao, 23–54. London: Routledge.

Yu, Jianxing, K. Yashima, and Y. Shen. 2014. "Autonomy or Privilege? Lobbying Intensity of Local Business Association in China." *Journal of Chinese Political Science* 19, no. 3: 315–33.

Yu, S. 2010. "*Xinnongchun Hezou Yiliao Fazhan Yanjiu Baogao* (Report on the New Rural Cooperative Medical Care)." *Iolaw.org.cn*, 2010. http://iolaw.org.cn/showNews.asp?id=22842.

Yu, Yongding, 2010. "China's Response to the Global Financial Crisis." *East Asia Forum,* January 24, 2010. https://www.eastasiaforum.org/2010/01/24/chinas-response-to-the-global-financial-crisis/.

Zang, Xiaowei, and Nabo Chen. 2015. "How Do Rural Elites Reproduce Privileges in Post-1978 China? Local Corporatism, Informal Bargaining and Opportunistic Parasitism." *Journal of Contemporary China* 24, no. 94: 628–43.

Zeng, Jinghan. 2013. "What Matters Most in Selecting Top Chinese Leaders? A Qualitative Comparative Analysis." *Journal of Political Science* 18: 223–39.

Zeng, Menglong. 2017. "'*Zhongguo Keyi Shuobu' He Gengda de Minzu Zhuyi Langchao—Changxiaoshu rang Wo'men Kandaole Shenmeyang de Zhongguo* ('China Can Say NO' and a Bigger Nationalism Wave—What Can We See from a Best Seller Book)" *QDaily*, April 28, 2017. http://www.qdaily.com/articles/40262.html.

Zenz, Adrian. 2018. "China's Domestic Security Spending: An Analysis of Available Data." *China Brief* 18, no. 4 (March): 5–11.

Zhan, Shaohua. 2017. "Hukou Reform and Land Politics in China: Rise of a Tripartite Alliance." *The China Journal* no. 78 (July): 25–49.

Zhan, X., and S. Y. Tang. 2016. "Understanding the Implications of Government Ties for Nonprofit Operations." *Public Administrative Review* 76: 569–600.

Zhang, C. D. 2017. "Reexamining the Electoral Connection in Authoritarian China: The Local People's Congress and Its Private Entrepreneur Deputies." *China Review* 17, no. 1: 1–27.

Zhang, H.Y. 2012. *ZhongGuo Siying Qiyezhu 20Nian (Chinese Private Enterprise Owners—A 20-Year Review).* Beijing: Institute of Sociology, Chinese Academy of Social Sciences.

Zhang, Shu, and Elias Glenn. 2018. "Beijing Struggles to Defuse Anger over China's P2P Lending Crisis." *Reuters*, August 12, 2018.

Zhang, Wanfa. 2002. "How Domestic Factors Affect Conflict Behavior of Democratic Countries—A Path Analysis (1885–1983)." MA Thesis, The University of Mississippi, 2002.

———. 2007. "Tapping Soft Power: Managing China's 'Peaceful Rise' and the Implications for the World." In *New Dimensions of Chinese Foreign Policy*, edited by Sujian Guo, 109–31. Lexington, KY: Lexington Press.

———. 2012. "Has Beijing Started to Bare Its Teeth? China's Soft Power Tapping Revisited." *Asian Perspective* 36, no. 4 (October-December): 615–39.

Zhao, W. 2018. "*Geti Gongshanghu he Siying Qiye Zhan Shichang Zhuti de baifenzhi 94* (Individual Businesses and Private Enterprises Account for 94 percent of the Market)." *Xinhuanet*, January 22, 2018. http://www.xinhuanet.com/2018-01/22/c_1122297394.htm.

Zheng, Shiping. 1997. *Party vs. State in Post-1949 China: The Institutional Dilemma*. Cambridge: Cambridge University Press.

Zheng, Yongnian. 1994. "Development and Democracy: Are They Compatible in China?" *Political Science Quarterly* 109, no. 2: 235–59.

Zhong, Yang. 2013. *Political Culture and Participation in Rural China.* London: Routledge.

Zhu, L. 2018. "China Lists Top 100 Outstanding Private Entrepreneurs." *China Daily*, October 25. http://www.chinadaily.com.cn/a/201810/25/WS5bd169f7a310eff303284882.html.

Zhu, Xufeng. 2016. "In the Name of 'Citizens': Civic Activism and Policy Entrepreneurship of Chinese Public Intellectuals in the Hu-Wen Era." *Journal of Contemporary China* 25, no. 101: 745–59.

Index

About the Authors

Feng Sun earned her PhD from the University of Alabama in 2009 and is now an associate professor in the Department of Political Science at Troy University. She has published several peer-reviewed journal articles and book entries. Her research interests include contemporary Chinese politics, international political economy, comparative politics, and quantitative research methods.

Wanfa Zhang is an associate professor of Political Science at Florida Institute of Technology. He was previously a lecturer at China Foreign Affairs University. He is also the author of book chapters, journal articles, and book reviews published in the referred academic journals or books in the United States and other countries. His research interests cover great power politics, contemporary Chinese politics and diplomacy, quantitative study of international conflict, and security issues in the Asia-Pacific region. Zhang received his PhD from the University of Alabama in 2009.

www.ingramcontent.com/pod-product-compliance
Lightning Source LLC
Chambersburg PA
CBHW050413280326
41932CB00013BA/1846